MULTIPLE-CHOICE AND FREE-RESPONSE QUESTIONS IN PREPARATION FOR THE AP ENGLISH LITERATURE AND COMPOSITION EXAMINATION

(SEVENTH EDITION)

By

DR. RICHARD VOGEL

D&S MARKETING SYSTEMS, INC.
1205 38th Street Brooklyn, NY 11218

w w w . d s m a r k e t i n g . c o m

ISBN #0-9787199-0-5

PREFACE

The 7th edition of *Multiple Choice & Free-Response Questions in Preparation for the AP English Literature and Composition Examination* was not completed without a measure of heartache. All books exact a physical and psychological toll, and trolling endlessly through literature for potential poems and passages, developing question sets that run aground before yielding the necessary number of questions, trying to reconcile the delicate balance of gender, ethnicity, and period with the constrictive parameters of passage and exam length, and grinding through the typing, revising, editing and typesetting stages of the book is a grueling and enervating process.

This edition, however, exacted an emotional toll as well with the death in April 2005 of my co-author, Charles Winans. "Charlie," as he was affectionately known to all, was my senior English teacher in Brooklyn Preparatory High School, but his influence extended far beyond my days in the classroom. It was Charlie who persuaded me to take a turn on the stage (as Dick Deadeye in *H.M.S. Pinafore*) and who later directed me in more substantive fare as Creon in *Antigone* and Thomas á Becket in *Murder in the Cathedral*. It was Charlie who first took me to Europe, a six-country barnstorming tour with two other students that took us from Athens to Sligo. It was Charlie who first introduced me to community service through his Toy Drive that annually distributed gifts and a measure of holiday cheer to convalescent children in at least six New York hospitals. And it was Charlie who confirmed my desire to teach, who mentored me through my fledgling days in the profession, and who saw me through my graduate and doctoral studies. Writing the book with him was always a delight—long afternoons and dinners spent discussing what has always been the chief love of our lives, arguing passionately over textual ambiguities, uncovering new subtext and influences, and discovering new authors and overlooked passages. For the first time writing the book became predominantly *work*, and I found I had to fight to prevent it from becoming drudgery. Though the last years of Charlie's life were marred by the annoying impediments of age and illness and, as a result, his contribution to this book was limited, I think he would be as proud of it as I am of my nearly forty-year association with him—forever teacher, mentor, friend, and colleague.

There are others to acknowledge here as well: David Lederman, my publisher, for continuing to sponsor my AP English endeavors; Rachel and Tammi, for their invaluable assistance negotiating permissions and typesetting the book; Mary and Pamela Chesser for question evaluation and proofreading; my many AP colleagues from across the country whose acumen and repartee at the June AP English Reading continue to inspire me; and the members of my last four Croton-Harmon AP English classes who graciously contributed sample essays to this edition. To all, I express my gratitude for a job well done.

All communications concerning this book should be addressed to:

D&S Marketing Systems, Inc.
1205 38th Street
Brooklyn, NY 11218
www.dsmarketing.com

MULTIPLE-CHOICE AND FREE-RESPONSE QUESTIONS as A Resource for Students and Teachers of Advanced Placement English Literature

This book has been designed to help students prepare for the Advanced Placement Exam in English Literature and Composition. It is not filled with definitions of literary terms nor saccharine advice on how to 'psych' students up for the examination. Rather, its passages are selected and its questions designed with the singular purpose of developing in students the habits of mind that good readers possess, that they actively employ while reading, and that they use to structure and develop their written responses to the text. Not being the examination itself, it is designed more for instruction than assessment, though it may certainly be used to measure student progress throughout the school year.

As a teacher in a relatively small public school, I have for the last twenty years enjoyed luxuries of class size and budget with which other teachers are not always blessed. I have not had to battle inordinately large enrollment, rigid forty-minute class schedules, students who take the class but not the test, censorship, or any of the other privations and problems that teachers regularly convey to me at AP English workshops. Even so, the continued success our AP English students is due less to our size than to our program, part of which involves the use of this text.

Though the book is divided into sample "exams," there is no pressing need to use it in this manner. I generally try to do one or two random selections of poetry and prose per eight-day cycle for the duration of the school year, incorporating multiple-choice and free-response practice as a regular part of my AP syllabus. Though our block-schedule gives me the opportunity to administer an entire sample examination in one class period, I seldom do, preferring to use the extra class time to discuss with students the stylistic or thematic aspects of the passage that they found interesting. Inasmuch as the book is intended to supplement, not replace, the actual AP exam, I use it to build the confidence and knowledge base of my AP English students so that they will find the exam to be more of a sequence of interesting challenges than an oppressive, three-hour literary gauntlet. Discussion of the passages and debate over the merit of a particular answer are encouraged as healthy and necessary steps toward developing higher-level thought. As we get deeper into the academic year, I gradually shift from this book to the released AP English Literature exams, administering one per month, February through May. Though exam preparation never takes precedence over our core reading list, I believe that if you do not sufficiently expose students to the modes of AP questioning, you cannot expect them to answer such questions with success.

I have always maintained that teaching is really little more than a dialogue, a reciprocation of insights and ideas, an establishment of a position or a reevaluation of one. The greatest teachers throughout time have always been able to inspire such engagement, and the best AP English classrooms are forums for such exchange. If this book helps to foster insightful discussion about literature in your classroom, I believe it will have achieved its goal.

TABLE OF CONTENTS

Sample Examination I...1

Student Guide to Sample Examination I..17

Sample Examination II...73

Student Guide to Sample Examination II..90

Sample Examination III..148

Sample Examination IV..165

Sample Examination V..180

Sample Examination VI..194

Sample Examination I

Section I

Questions 1-12. Refer to the following poem.

The Thief

Thou robst my days of business and delights,
    Of sleep thou robst my nights;
    Ah, lovely thief, what wilt thou do?
    What, rob me of heaven too?
(5)   Thou even my prayers dost steal from me;
    And I with wild idolatry
Begin, to God, and end them all to thee.

Is it a sin to love, that it should thus
    Like an ill conscience torture us?
(10)   Whate'er I do, where'er I go
    (None guiltless e'er was haunted so),
    Still, still methinks thy face I view,
    And still thy shape does me pursue,
As if, not you me, but I had murdered you.

(15)   From books I strive some remedy to take,
    But thy name all the letters make;
    Whate'er 'tis writ, I find that there,
    Like points and commas everywhere.
    Me blest for this let no man hold;
(20)   For I, as Midas did of old,
Perish by turning everything to gold.

What do I seek, alas, or why do I
    Attempt in vain from thee to fly?
    For, making thee my deity,
(25)   I gave thee then ubiquity.
    My pains resemble hell in this:
    The divine presence there too is,
But to torment men, not to give them bliss.

—Abraham Cowley

1. The "thief" in the poem is the speaker's

(A) death
(B) age
(C) conscience
(D) beloved
(E) anxiety

2. According to the speaker, the "thief" in the poem does all of the following EXCEPT

(A) disrupt his concentration
(B) deprive him of rest
(C) jeopardize his salvation
(D) plague his conscience
(E) make him ponder suicide

1

3. The primary dilemma confronting the speaker is his

   (A) considerable loss of income
   (B) deleterious attraction to his beloved
   (C) precipitous decline in health
   (D) easy distraction from his studies
   (E) misdirected faith

4. The speaker questions all of the following EXCEPT

   (A) the thief's designs on his soul
   (B) the thief's mental cruelty
   (C) his own level of culpability
   (D) his attempts to find a solution in books
   (E) the wisdom of his attempted flight

5. In the second stanza, the speaker emphasizes the extent of his torment through all of the following EXCEPT

   (A) simile
   (B) repetition
   (C) parenthetical comment
   (D) irony
   (E) metonymy

6. Lines 10-14 and 15-18 are primarily intended to bring out what aspect of the thief's nature?

   (A) her omnipresence
   (B) her stealth
   (C) her ruthlessness
   (D) her illiteracy
   (E) her desperation

7. The speaker's allusion to Midas (lines 20-21) emphasizes his own

   (A) material obsession
   (B) intolerable hubris
   (C) myopic foolhardiness
   (D) advancing age
   (E) unwarranted optimism

8. The word "ubiquity," as it is used in line 25, is BEST interpreted as

   (A) omnipotence
   (B) adulation
   (C) guerdon
   (D) fealty
   (E) satisfaction

9. In which of the following lines does the speaker offer the strongest admonition to the reader?

   (A) line 5
   (B) lines 8-9
   (C) line 19
   (D) lines 22-23
   (E) line 26

10. All of the following may be considered highly ironic EXCEPT

    (A) the initial direction of the speaker's prayers and the ultimate recipient of these appeals
    (B) the speaker's obsession with his beloved and his sense of being pursued.
    (C) the deification of the speaker's beloved and the hellish torment he claims to be experiencing
    (D) the willing submission of the speaker to his beloved and the emotional dominion she exacts
    (E) the title of the poem and the alleged actions of the speaker's beloved

11. Which of the following is NOT characteristic of the poet's style?

    (A) the use of a central conceit to develop the poem's theme
    (B) irregular lines of predominantly iambic rhythm
    (C) rhetorical questions that reflect the speaker's acute frustration
    (D) highly imagistic descriptions of suffering
    (E) religious diction

12. The tone of the poem is BEST classified as

    (A) nostalgic
    (B) exasperated
    (C) reverential
    (D) vindictive
    (E) defiant

Questions 13-24. Refer to the following passage.

August, the month that bears fruit, closed around the shop and Pete and Fritzie left for Minnesota to escape the heat. A month running, Fleur had won thirty dollars
(5) and only Pete's presence had kept Lily at bay. But Pete was gone now, and one payday, with the heat so bad no one could move but Fleur, the men sat and played and waited while she finished work. The cards
(10) sweat, limp in their fingers, the table was slick with grease, and even the walls were warm to the touch. The air was motionless.
      Fleur was in the next room boiling heads. Her green dress, drenched, wrapped
(15) her like a transparent sheet. A skin of lakeweed. Black snarls of veining clung to her arms. Her braids were loose, half unraveled, tied behind her neck in a thick loop. She stood in steam, turning skulls
(20) through a vat with a wooden paddle. When scraps boiled to the surface, she bent with a round tin sieve and scooped them out. She'd filled two dishpans.
      "Ain't that enough now?" called
(25) Lily. "We're waiting." The stump of a dog trembled in his lap, alive with rage. It never smelled me or noticed me above Fleur's smoky skin. The air was heavy in the corner, and pressed Russell and me down.
(30) Fleur sat with the men.
      "Now what do you say?" Lily asked the dog. It barked. That was the signal for the real game to start.
      "Let's up the ante," said Lily, who
(35) had been stalking this night for weeks. He had a roll of money in his pocket. Fleur had five bills in her dress. Each man had saved his full pay that the bank officer had drawn from the Kozkas' account.
(40) "Ante a dollar then," said Fleur, and pitched hers in. She lost, but they let her scrape along, a cent at a time. And then she won some. She played unevenly, as if chance were all she had. She reeled them
(45) in. The game went on. The dog was stiff now, poised on Lily's knees, a ball of vicious muscle with its yellow eyes slit in concentration. It gave advice, seemed to sniff the lay of Fleur's cards, twitched and
(50) nudged. Fleur was up, then down, saved by a scratch. Tor dealt seven cards, three down. The pot grew, round by round, until it held all the money. Nobody folded. Then

it all rode on one last card and they went
(55) silent. Fleur picked hers up and drew a long breath. The heat lowered like a bell. Her card shook, but she stayed in.
      Lily smiled and took the dog's head tenderly between his palms.
(60) "Say Fatso," he said, crooning the words. "You reckon that girl's bluffing?"
      The dog whined and Lily laughed. "Me too," he said. "Let's show." He tossed his bills and coins into the pot and then they
(65) turned their cards over.
      Lily looked once, looked again, then he squeezed the dog like a fist of dough and slammed it on the table.
      Fleur threw out her arms and swept
(70) the money close, grinning that same wolf grin that she'd used on me, the grin that had them. She jammed the bills inside her dress, scooped the coins in waxed white paper that she tied with string.
(75) "Another round," said Lily, his voice choked with burrs. But Fleur opened her mouth and yawned, then walked out back to gather slops for the big hog that was waiting in the stockpen to be killed [. . . .].

13. The atmosphere in the room in which the card game is played is BEST described as

    (A) claustrophobic
    (B) bellicose
    (C) sultry
    (D) frenzied
    (E) lascivious

14. The events that take place are seemingly recounted by

    (A) Lily
    (B) Fleur
    (C) Tor
    (D) an unidentified youth
    (E) an omniscient narrator

15. The oppressive heat causes all of the following EXCEPT

    (A) the playing cards to become slick
    (B) the air to become stagnant
    (C) Fleur's dress to become diaphanous
    (D) Lily to become impatient
    (E) the other players to become irritable

16. The narrator implies which of the following about Fleur?

    (A) That she has cheated the other players.
    (B) That she is reluctant to give them an opportunity to recoup their losses.
    (C) That she has only experienced "beginner's luck."
    (D) That she lures the men into a more risky wager.
    (E) That she is being victimized by more experienced card sharks.

17. Lines such as "Let's up the ante" (line 34) and "Let's show" (line 63) are likely intended to convey Lily's

    (A) growing annoyance at Fleur's procrastination in the kitchen
    (B) brash confidence that he will win back his losses
    (C) reckless disregard for money
    (D) desperate need to win a big hand
    (E) impatient desire to bring the game to an end

18. The author mirrors Lily's changing fortunes and attitude through which of the following?

    I. The demeanor and body language of his dog.
    II. The changing size of the pot on the table.
    III. The facial expressions of the other card players.

    (A) I only
    (B) III only
    (C) I and II
    (D) II and III
    (E) I, II and III

19. The narrator likely describes Lily's voice as "choked with burrs" (line 76) to illustrate his

    (A) dehydration
    (B) stuttering
    (C) moroseness
    (D) resignation
    (E) ire

20. Which of the following pairs of words captures the impression of Fleur that the author MOST wishes to convey to the reader?

    (A) sensual and seductive
    (B) dutiful and hardworking
    (C) cunning and conniving
    (D) outcast and exploited
    (E) selfish and avaricious

21. The author draws an ironic and incongruous connection between the two principal characters in the episode through which of the following?

    (A) their attire
    (B) their names
    (C) their expressions
    (D) their thought
    (E) their dialogue

22. The passage subtly intimates which of the following?

    I. That after collecting her winnings Fleur will resign from her arduous job.
    II. That the "real game" (line 33) does not necessarily involve card-playing.
    III. That, as a result of her winning, Fleur may be a victim of violence.

    (A) I only
    (B) III only
    (C) I and II
    (D) II and III
    (E) I, II and III

23. Which of the following demonstrates the literary device known as synaesthesia?

    (A) "the table was slick with grease [. . .]." (lines 10-11)
    (B) "A skin of lakeweed." (lines 15-16)
    (C) "The air was heavy in the corner, and pressed Russell and me down." (lines 28-29)
    (D) "a ball of vicious muscle, with its yellow eyes slit in concentration." (lines 46-48)
    (E) "The heat lowered like a bell." (line 56)

24. Which of the following is NOT characteristic of the author's style?

    (A) predominantly simple sentences whose brevity augments the episode's tension
    (B) the delineation of the dog as an integral character
    (C) descriptions of physical actions that reflect the antithetical emotions of Lily and Fleur
    (D) a modicum of dialogue
    (E) ubiquitous symbols of imminent death

Questions 25-39. Refer to the following poem.

After The Last Practice
(Grinnell, Iowa, November 1971)

Someone said, I remember the first hard crack
Of shoulderpads on the sidelines before a game,
And the bruises that blossom on your arms
    afterward.
Someone else remembered the faint, medicinal
    smell
(5) Seeping through the locker room on Saturday
    mornings,
Getting your ankles taped while a halfback

Frets in the whirlpool about his hamstrings:
Steam on three mirrors, the nervous hiss
Of the first hot shower of the morning.
(10) We talked about the tension mounting all day
Until it became the sound of spikes clattering
Across the locker room floor, the low banter

Of the last players pulling on their jerseys,
Our middle-linebacker humming to himself
(15) And hammering a forearm against the lockers
While an assistant coach diagrammed a punt
Return for the umpteenth time on his clipboard
For two cornerbacks looking on in boredom…

Eventually, it always came down to a few words
(20) From the head coach—quiet, focused, intense—
While a huge pit opened up in your stomach
And the steady buzz of a crowd in the distance
Turned into a minor roaring in your skull
As the team exploded onto the field.

(25) The jitters never disappeared until the opening
Kickoff, the first contact, until a body
Hurtled down the field in a fury
And threw itself against your body
While everything else in the world faded
(30) Before the crunching action of a play, unfolding…

I remember how, as we talked, the flat Midwestern
Fields stretched away into nowhere and nothing,
How the dark sky clouded over like a dome
Covering a chilly afternoon in late November
(35) On the prairie, the scent of pine cones
And crisp leaves burning in the air,

The smoky glow of faces around a small fire.
Someone spoke of road trips and bridge games
In the back of a bus rolling across the plains,
(40) Wooden fence posts ticking off the miles
And miles of empty cornfields and shortgrasses,
Windmills treading their arms, as if underwater,

The first orange lights rising on the horizon—
Jesus, someone said, I never thought it would end
(45) Like this, without pads, without hitting anybody.
But then someone mentioned stepping out of bounds
And getting blindsided by a bone-wrenching tackle;
Someone else remembered writhing in a pile

Of players coming down on his twisted body.
(50) Torn ligaments. Sprained wrist. A black coin
Blooming under your left eye on Sunday morning.
After all those years of drills and double practices,
Seasons of calisthenics, weightrooms, coaches
Barking orders—missed blocks, squirming fumbles—;

(55) After all those summers of trying to perfect
A sideline pass and a button hook, a fly, a flag,
A deep post, a quick pass across the middle;
After the broken patterns and failed double teams,
The July nights sprinting up the stadium stairs
(60) And the August days banging against each other's bodies,

The slow walks home alone in the dusky light—;
After all those injury-prone autumns, not
One of us could explain why he had done it.
What use now is the language of traps
(65) And draws, of power sweeps and desperate on-side
Kicks, of screen passes, double reverses?

But still there was the memory of a sharp cut
Into the open and the pigskin spiraling
Into your hands from twenty yards away,
(70) The ecstasy of breaking loose from a tackle
And romping for daylight, for the green
Promised land of the endzone.

Someone said, I remember running into the field
And seeing my girlfriend in the stands at midfield—
(75) Everyone around her was chanting and shouting
And the adrenaline was coursing through my body;
I felt as if I would explode with happiness,
As if I would never falter, waver, or die…

Someone else recollected the endless, losing,
(80) Thirteen-hour drive home after he had bruised
A collarbone on the last play of the game,
The whole bus encased in silence, like a glass
Jar, like the night itself, clarified. Afterward,
He recalled the wild joy of his first interception…

(85)   The fire sputtered and smoldered, faded out,
         And our voices trembled in the ghostly woodsmoke
         Until it seemed as if we were partly warriors
         And partly Boy Scouts ringed around the flame,
         Holding our helmets in our arms and trying
(90)   To understand an old appetite for glory,

         Our raging, innocent, violent, American
         Boyhoods gone now, vanished forever
         Like the victories and the hard losses.
         It was late. A deep silence descended
(95)   As twilight disintegrated in the night air
         And the fire glowered down to embers and ashes,

         To red bits of nothing. But no one moved. Oh,
         We were burning, burning, burning, burning…
         And then someone began singing in the darkness.

                                        —Edward Hirsch

25. The main focus of the poem involves the

    (A) enduring legacy of athletic triumph
    (B) fleeting nature of youth and glory
    (C) inordinate cruelty of coaches
    (D) physical betrayal of the body
    (E) idyllic nature of small-town America

26. The tone of the poem is BEST labeled

    (A) melancholy
    (B) quizzical
    (C) vindictive
    (D) reflective
    (E) nostalgic

27. All of the following help to reinforce the sensory nature of the first two stanzas EXCEPT

    (A) "first hard crack / Of shoulderpads on the sidelines [. . .]" (lines 1-2)
    (B) "bruises that blossom on your arms [. . .]" (line 3)
    (C) "faint, medicinal smell / Seeping through the locker room on Saturday mornings [. . .]" (lines 4-5)
    (D) "the nervous hiss / Of the first hot shower [. . .]" (lines 8-9)
    (E) "the tension mounting all day [. . .]" (line 10)

28. The most common feeling displayed by the players *before* the contest is

    (A) belligerence
    (B) apprehension
    (C) impatience
    (D) pride
    (E) tedium

29. The sixth and seventh stanzas of the poem (lines 31-42) do which of the following?

    I. Provide a measure of local color by introducing the reader to a specific geographical setting.
    II. Imagistically reinforce the friends' enduring camaraderie.
    III. Symbolically mirror the teammates' vanishing youth.

    (A) I only
    (B) II only
    (C) I and III
    (D) II and III
    (E) I, II and III

30. Lines 44-45—"Jesus, someone said, I never thought it would end / Like this, without pads, without hitting anybody"—are primarily intended to

    (A) intimate subtly that the players' adult lives have been anticlimactic
    (B) bemoan the brevity of adolescence
    (C) divorce one individual from his former teammates
    (D) trigger the subsequent flashbacks of gridiron heroism
    (E) deny the reality of a particularly depressing loss

31. The memories presented in lines 46-61

    (A) celebrate individual character and toughness
    (B) acknowledge the temporal sacrifices demanded by sport
    (C) confirm the virtues of hard work and self-discipline
    (D) censure the dirty tactics of opponents
    (E) mask the disappointing realities of their post-adolescent lives

32. The diction and imagery in stanzas twelve and thirteen (lines 67-78) are suggestive of all of the following EXCEPT

    (A) youth and freedom
    (B) heroism and celebrity
    (C) perfection and accomplishment
    (D) transience and mortality
    (E) jubilation and romance

33. The Boy Scout-warrior dichotomy, mentioned in lines 87-88, reinforces which of the following contrasts?

    (A) corruption and innocence
    (B) youth and maturity
    (C) fear and courage
    (D) strength and weakness
    (E) responsibility and freedom

34. The speaker's comment that they were all "burning, burning, etc" (line 98) may plausibly be interpreted as which of the following?

    I. Desiring to be young again.
    II. Rapidly passing into insignificance.
    III. Becoming irate over their lost youth.

    (A) I only
    (B) III only
    (C) I and II
    (D) I and III
    (E) I, II and III

35. Which of the following contributes LEAST to the contemplative mood of the last three stanzas?

    (A) the onomatopoeic nature of the word "sputtered" (line 85)
    (B) the comparison "as if we were partly warriors / And partly Boy Scouts [. . .]" (lines 87-88)
    (C) the short declarative sentences "It was late" (line 94) and "But no one moved" (line 97)
    (D) the alliterative diction of "A deep silence descended / As twilight disintegrated [. . .]" (lines 94-95)
    (E) the fire's "glower[ing] down to embers and ashes [. . .]" (line 96)

36. In the course of the poem, the poet uses simile to depict each of the following EXCEPT

    (A) the sky's manifestation of approaching winter
    (B) the sluggish motion of the windmills
    (C) the facial bruises that were the by-product of practice
    (D) the oppressive quiet after a defeat
    (E) the ephemeral nature of adolescent sport

37. When one considers the context in which it appears, which of the following is NOT intended to contribute to the transitory nature of the teammates' adolescent athletic experiences?

    (A) "The smoky glow of faces around a small fire." (line 37)
    (B) "Jesus, someone said, I never thought it would end / Like this, without pads, without hitting anybody." (lines 44-45)
    (C) "What use now is the language of traps / And draws, of power sweeps and desperate on-side / Kicks, of screen passes, double reverses?" (lines 64-66)
    (D) "Holding our helmets in our arms and trying / To understand an old appetite for glory [. . .]" (lines 89-90)
    (E) "Oh, / We were burning, burning, burning, burning [. . .]" (lines 97-98)

38. Which of the following mirrors the diminishing significance of the individuals and their exploits on the football field?

    I. The ambiguity and inconsistency of their recollections.
    II. The poet's use of indefinite personal pronouns in lieu of names.
    III. The symbol of the sputtering and smoldering fire.

    (A) I only
    (B) II only
    (C) I and II
    (D) II and III
    (E) I, II and III

39. All of the following are stylistic traits of the poem EXCEPT

    (A) a shifting narrative perspective
    (B) the technical terminology of football
    (C) a catalog of ritualistic pre-game preparation
    (D) a contrast between youth and infirmity
    (E) free verse couched in a structured stanzaic pattern

Questions 40-51. Refer to the following passage.

For a man to write well there are required three necessaries—to read the best authors, observe the best speakers, and much exercise of his own style. In style, to
(5) consider what ought to be written, and after what manner, he must first think and excogitate his matter, then choose his words and examine the weight of either. Then take care, in placing and ranking both
(10) matter and words, that the composition be comely; and to do this with diligence and often. No matter how slow the style be at first, so it be labored and accurate; seek the best and be not glad of the forward conceits
(15) or first words that offer themselves to us, but judge of what we invent, and order what we approve. Repeat often what we have formerly written; which beside that it helps the consequence, and makes the
(20) juncture better, it quickens the heat of imagination, that often cools in the time of setting down, and gives it new strength, as if it grew lustier by the going back. As we see in the contention of leaping, they jump
(25) farthest that fetch their race largest; or, as in throwing a dart or javelin, we force back our arms to make our loose the stronger. Yet, if we have a fair gale of wind, I forbid not the steering out of our sail, so the favor
(30) of the gale deceive us not. For all that we invent doth please us in the conception of our birth, else we would never set it down. But the safest is to return to our judgment, and handle over again those things the
(35) easiness of which might make them justly suspected. So did the best writers in their beginnings; they imposed upon themselves care and industry; they did nothing rashly; they obtained first to write well, and then
(40) custom made it easy and a habit. By little and little their matter showed itself to them more plentifully; their words answered, their composition followed; and all, as in a well-ordered family, presented itself in the
(45) place. So that the sum of all is, ready writing makes not good writing, but good writing brings on ready writing. Yet, when we think we have got the faculty, it is even then good to resist it, as to give a horse a
(50) check sometimes with a bit, which doth not so much stop his course as stir his mettle. Again, whither a man's genius is best able to reach, thither it should more and more

contend, lift and dilate itself; as men of low
(55) stature raise themselves on their toes, and so oft-times get even, if not eminent. Besides, as it is fit for grown and able writers to stand of themselves, and work with their own strength, to trust and
(60) endeavor by their own faculties, so it is fit for the beginner and learner to study others and the best. For the mind and memory are more sharply exercised in comprehending another man's things than our own; and
(65) such as accustom themselves and are familiar with the best authors shall ever and anon find somewhat of them in themselves, and in the expression of their minds, even when they feel it not, be able to utter
(70) something like theirs, which hath an authority above their own. Nay, sometimes it is the reward of a man's study, the praise of quoting another man fitly; and though a man be more prone and able for one kind of
(75) writing than another, yet he must exercise all. For as in an instrument, so in style, there must be harmony and consent of parts.

40. The author's tone is BEST characterized as

    (A) highbrow
    (B) reflective
    (C) disparaging
    (D) admonitory
    (E) didactic

41. In advancing his argument the author makes use of all of the following EXCEPT

    (A) subtle sarcasm that reveals his disfavor of novice writers
    (B) mild imperatives that offer counsel to his intended audience, writers
    (C) analogous situations that buttress his point
    (D) a paradox that underscores the relation between the disciplined writer and the quality of what he produces
    (E) a collective "we" that hints at his own struggles with mastering the craft of writing

42. The allusions to jumping and javelin throwing in lines 23-27 are primarily intended to buttress the author's conviction about the importance of

    (A) pondering the choice of subject matter
    (B) repeating what one has previously written to strengthen it
    (C) practicing writing daily so as to improve one's craft
    (D) studying the form of another writer to refine one's own
    (E) trying something new and more challenging

43. Which of the following may safely be said about lines 28-30?

    I. They are an admonition against insufficiently thought out developments in the plot.
    II. They seemingly contradict the author's earlier comment that "No matter how slow the style be at first, so it be labored and accurate [. . .]." (lines 12-13).
    III. They reflect the author's concession that there may be moments when a writer must flow with his inspiration or rhythm.

    (A) I only
    (B) II only
    (C) I and III
    (D) II and III
    (E) I, II and III

44. The simile couched in lines 47-51 warns writers against becoming

    (A) hasty
    (B) overconfident
    (C) undisciplined
    (D) indolent
    (E) adamant

45. Lines 52-54, "Again, whither a man's genius is best able to reach, thither it should more and more contend [. . .]," suggest that when a writer is at the height of his creative powers he should

    (A) be content with what he has accomplished
    (B) remember the common stock from which he has risen
    (C) begin to compare himself to more accomplished literary greats
    (D) be more daring in the scope and reach of his literary endeavors
    (E) bask in his newly acquired popularity

46. The author suggests that all writers—particularly novice ones—should "accustom themselves" (line 65) to the best authors for which of the following reasons?

    I. To discover some part of themselves in a more established writer's voice or material.
    II. To expose themselves to other styles and genres of writing.
    III. To utilize these authors' works as exemplars they might imitate.

    (A) I only
    (B) II only
    (C) I and III
    (D) II and III
    (E) I, II and III

47. Which of the following does NOT paraphrase advice given by Jonson as to how best to effect good writing?

    (A) Determine both the subject of your writing and the best form in which to express it.
    (B) Take care to find the most appropriate words even if it is an extremely deliberate process.
    (C) Establish your own, unique style that has not been influenced by writers who have come before you.
    (D) Reflect upon your initial inspirations to insure that they are as good as you initially considered them.
    (E) Be humble about your accomplishments so you are not seduced by your own genius.

48. In the course of his essay, the author draws comparisons to all of the following EXCEPT

    (A) athletic competition
    (B) government
    (C) horseback riding
    (D) sailing
    (E) music

49. In light of the context in which each word is embedded, which of the following would be the LEAST suitable replacement for one of the archaisms listed below?

    (A) "ponder" for "excogitate" (line 7)
    (B) "common" for "forward" (line 14)
    (C) "release" for "loose" (line 27)
    (D) "aspired" for "obtained" (line 39)
    (E) "spontaneous" for "ready" (lines 45 and 47)

50. Ironically, a purist might find Jonson's opening sentence to be marred by which of the following?

    (A) faulty parallelism
    (B) a misnomer
    (C) a dangling participle
    (D) comma splice
    (E) misplaced modifiers

51. The passage ultimately makes what point about professional writers?

    (A) They are born, not made.
    (B) They hone their craft by degrees.
    (C) They regularly mimic the work of their peers.
    (D) They remain insecure about their abilities.
    (E) They give little thought to the relation between style and subject.

Section II
<u>Question One</u>

(Suggested time—40 minutes. This question counts as one-third of the total essay section score.)

Read the following poem carefully. Then, in a well-organized essay, indicate how the poet uses images and symbols to link the predicament of the lost boy to the domestic situation of the speaker.

The Mystery of the Caves

I don't remember the name of the story,
but the hero, a boy, was lost,
wandering a labyrinth of caverns
filling stratum by stratum with water.

(5) I was wondering what might happen:
would he float upward toward light?
Or would he somersault forever
in an underground black river?

I couldn't stop reading the book
(10) because I had to know the answer,
because my mother was leaving again—
the lid of the trunk thrown open,

blouses torn from their hangers,
the crazy shouting among rooms.
(15) The boy found it impossible to see
which passage led to safety.

One yellow finger of flame
wavered on his last match.
There was a blur of perfume,
(20) my mother breaking miniature bottles,

then my father gripping her,
but too tightly, by both arms.
The boy wasn't able to breathe.
I think he wanted me to help,

(25) but I was small, and it was late.
And my mother was sobbing now,
no longer cursing her life,
repeating my father's name

among bright islands of skirts
(30) circling the rim of the bed.
I can't recall the whole story,
what happened at the end…

Sometimes I worry that the boy
is still searching below the earth
(35) for a thin pencil of light,
that I can almost hear him

through great volumes of water,
through centuries of stone,
crying my name among blind fish,
(40) wanting so much to come home.

From *Parthenopi: New and Selected Poems* (BOA Editions, 2001). Reprinted with permission of the author.

Question Two

(Suggested time—40 minutes. This question counts as one-third of the total essay section score.)

Read the following passage carefully. Then, in a well-organized essay, discuss how the literary elements of the passage reveal the nature and predicament of both Jude and Sue. In your essay, you may wish to consider such things as diction, choice of detail, symbolism, and tone.

In the lonely room of his aunt's house Jude sat watching the cottage of the Widow Edlin as it disappeared behind the night shade. He knew that Sue was sitting within its walls equally lonely and disheartened; and again questioned his devotional model that all was for the best.

He retired to rest early, but his sleep was fitful from the sense that Sue was so near at hand. At
(5) some time near two o'clock, when he was beginning to sleep more soundly, he was aroused by a shrill squeak that had been familiar enough to him when he lived regularly at Marygreen. It was the cry of a rabbit caught in a gin. As was the little creature's habit, it did not soon repeat its cry; and probably would not do so more than once or twice; but would remain bearing its torture to the morrow, when the trapper would come back and knock it on the head.
(10) He who in his childhood had saved the lives of the earthworms now began to picture the agonies of the rabbit from its lacerated leg. If it were a 'bad catch' by the hind-leg, the animal would tug during the ensuing six hours till the iron teeth of the trap had stripped the leg-bone of its flesh, when, should a weak-springed instrument enable it to escape, it would die in the field from the mortification of the limb. If it were a 'good catch,' namely, by the fore-leg, the bone would be broken, and the limb nearly torn in
(15) two in attempts at an impossible escape.

Almost half-an-hour passed, and the rabbit repeated its cry. Jude could rest no longer till he had put it out of its pain, so dressing himself quickly he descended, and by the light of the moon went across the green in the direction of the sound. He reached the hedge bordering the widow's garden, when he stood still. The faint click of the trap as dragged about by the writhing animal guided him now, and
(20) reaching the spot he struck the rabbit on the back of the neck with the side of his palm, and it stretched itself out dead.

He was turning away when he saw a woman looking out of the open casement at a window on the ground floor of the adjacent cottage. 'Jude!' said a voice timidly—Sue's voice. 'It is you—is it not?'

'Yes, dear!'
(25) 'I haven't been able to sleep at all, and then I heard the rabbit, and couldn't help thinking of what it suffered, till I felt I must come down and kill it! But I am so glad you got there first....They ought not to be allowed to set these steel traps, ought they!'

Jude had reached the window, which was quite a low one, so that she was visible down to her waist. She let go of the casement stay and put her hand upon his, her moonlit face regarding him
(30) wistfully.

'Did it keep you awake?' he said.

'No—I was awake.'

'How was that?'

'O, you know—now! I know you, with your religious doctrines, think that a married woman in
(35) the trouble of a kind like mine commits a mortal sin in making a man the confidant of it, as I did you. I wish I hadn't, now!' [. . . .].

'I wish you were happy, whatever I may be!'

'I *can't* be! So few could enter into my feeling—they would say 'twas my fanciful fastidiousness, or something of that sort, and condemn me....It is none of the natural tragedies of love that's love's usual
(40) tragedy in civilized life, but a tragedy artificially manufactured for people who in a natural state would find relief in parting!....Jude, before I married him I had never thought out fully what marriage meant, even though I knew. It was idiotic of me—there was no excuse. I was old enough, and I thought I was very experienced. So I rushed on...with all the cock-sureness of the fool that I was!...I am certain one ought to be allowed to undo what one has done so ignorantly! I daresay it happens to lots of women; only
(45) they submit, and I kick....When people of a later age look back upon the barbarous customs and superstitions of the times that we have the unhappiness to live in, what *will* they say!' [. . . .].

Question Three

(Suggested time—40 minutes. This question counts as one-third of the total essay section score.)

Oftentimes in literature a character gradually becomes estranged from society due to some aspect of his/her nature or convictions, an estrangement that may have damaging consequences either for the individual or for the society itself. Choose a novel or play which features a character who has become estranged from the society in which he/she exists. Then, in a carefully well-organized, indicate the impetus behind the estrangement and the damaging effects this alienation has upon the individual or the society around him/her. You may choose from the list below or use another novel or play of recognized literary merit.

The Catcher in the Rye	*Winesburg, Ohio*
Medea	*The Metamorphosis*
The Scarlet Letter	*The Power and the Glory*
Jude the Obscure	*A Man For All Seasons*
The Stranger	*Invisible Man*
The Elephant Man	*The Hairy Ape*
On the Road	*Oliver Twist*
Stranger in a Strange Land	*Hedda Gabler*
Wise Blood	*Down These Mean Streets*
The Hunchback of Notre Dame	*Hamlet*
A Portrait of the Artist as a Young Man	*Bartleby the Scrivener*
The Awakening	*Ethan Frome*

Sample Examination One: Explications and Answers

Passage One: Abraham Cowley's "The Thief"

Abraham Cowley's "The Thief" explores a familiar poetic theme—that of a lover suffering the pangs of romantic love—one that is omnipresent in sonneteers from Thomas Wyatt to William Shakespeare. Here, however, the speaker does not bemoan an unrequited love that is figuratively represented by an elusive hind or a distant port, but laments the emotional distress engendered by a realized one.

Using the conceit of a thief, the speaker in the poem endeavors to convey the toll this relationship has exacted on him. In the opening stanza the beloved is seen as distracting the speaker from both business and pleasure during the day, and robbing him of sleep during the night. So powerful is the beloved's lure that the speaker confesses that the prayers he normally would direct to God have with a "wild idolatry" (line 6) been misdirected to his beloved. Aware of the price of such earthly obsession, the speaker helplessly inquires, "Ah, lovely thief, what wilt thou do? / What, rob me of heaven too?" (lines 3-4). This question is buttressed by the query that opens the second stanza, "Is it a sin to love, that it should thus / Like an ill conscience torture us?" (lines 8-9), the speaker again associating love with wrongdoing. In lines 10-14 the speaker depicts himself as a fugitive, a man whose mind is continually haunted by the face and shape of his beloved with such intensity it is as if he has committed a conscience-plaguing murder. In the third stanza the speaker endeavors to distract his mind with reading, but this too proves a fruitless endeavor since he finds that "[her] name all the letters make; / Whate'er 'tis writ, I find that there, / Like points and commas everywhere" (lines 16-18). So plagued is he by this 'happy state' that he likens himself to Midas, whose hasty and foolish wish to turn everything into gold caused him more grief than happiness.

In the fourth and final stanza, however, the speaker seems more resigned to his state. His rhetorical question, "What do I seek, alas, or why do I / Attempt in vain from thee to fly?" (lines 22-23), seems to acknowledge the futility of his lot, while his subsequent observation, "For, making thee my deity, / I gave thee then ubiquity" (lines 24-25), admits his awareness that he himself has engendered this problem. Those familiar with Chaucer's "The Wife of Bath's Tale" will recognize that, like the knight in the good Wife's story, the speaker has surrendered the mastery to his beloved, and if his "pains resemble hell" (line 26) they are a damnation brought upon him by himself. The poem's epigrammatic closure, "The divine presence there too is, / But to torment men, not to give them bliss" (lines 27-28), captures the cruel irony that all sublunary lovers know too well: that love hurts, sometimes more when you are in it than when you are out of it.

1. The "thief" in the poem is the speaker's **(D) beloved**.

   As is common in many early poems, the speaker is smitten by a woman. However, unlike many of the early sonnets in which the speaker is the victim of unrequited love, the speaker in this poem is tormented by an obsession with his beloved, one so acute that it torments him while he is awake or asleep. So strong is the speaker's obsession for his beloved that he admits to making her his "deity" (line 24) and, in so doing, giving her "ubiquity" (line 25), or complete control over him. Choice D reflects this best.

2. According to the speaker, the "thief" in the poem does all of the following EXCEPT **(E) make him ponder suicide**.

   The speaker states "Thou robst my days of business and delights / Of sleep thou robst my nights" (lines 1-2), suggesting that he can neither focus on his work nor get any rest. This confirms choices A and B. He also states, "Ah, lovely thief, what wilt thou do? / What, rob me of heaven too? / Thou even my prayers dost steal from me; / And I with wild idolatry / Begin, to God, and end them all to thee" (lines 3-7). This suggests that even when he tries to pray his distracted thoughts turn to his beloved. Moreover, he asks in lines 8-9, "Is it a sin to love, that it should thus / Like an ill conscience torture us?," suggesting that though he is "guiltless" he feels as if he has done something wrong. This information confirms choices C and D. Choice E is nowhere apparent in the passage.

3. The primary dilemma confronting the speaker is his **(B) deleterious attraction to his beloved**.

   As has been suggested in the explanation of question #1, the speaker's obsession with his beloved has had a deleterious effect upon his work, his play, his sleep, even his chance at salvation. Even when he reads, he cannot take his mind off this woman, saying that "[her] name all the letters make" (line 16). So tormented is he that he states "My pains resemble hell in this" (line 26).

4. The speaker questions all of the following EXCEPT **(C) his own level of culpability**.

   Lines 3-4, "Ah, lovely thief, what wilt thou do? / What, rob me of heaven too?," confirm A, while line 9, "Like an ill conscience torture us," validates B. Line 15, "From books I strive some remedy to take," supports D, while lines 22-23, "why do I / Attempt in vain from thee to fly?," prove E. The speaker, however, clearly states in line 11, "(None guiltless e'er was haunted so)," making C the exception.

5. In the second stanza, the speaker emphasizes the extent of his torment through all of the following EXCEPT **(E) metonymy**.

   "Like an ill conscience" in line 9 is a simile, while "Still, still" (line 12) exemplifies repetition. "(None guiltless e'er was haunted so)" in line 11 is a parenthetical comment, while lines 13-14, "And still thy shape does me pursue, / As if, not you me, but I had murdered you," exemplify irony. This validates choices A, B, C and D. Choice E, metonymy, is not evident in the second stanza.

6. Lines 10-14 and 15-18 are primarily intended to bring out what aspect of the thief's nature? **(A) her omnipresence**.

   Lines 10-14 suggest that the speaker cannot get his beloved's face out of his mind, while lines 15-18 imply that even when he tries to lose himself in reading, he sees her name in the letters written on each page. Choice A reflects this idea best.

7. The speaker's allusion to Midas (lines 20-21) emphasizes his own **(C) myopic foolhardiness**.

   The speaker's allusion to Midas, whose wish that everything he touched be turned to gold proved rash and foolhardy when he saw his food and daughter so transformed, suggests that he is painfully conscious of his own stupidity in permitting his obsession with his beloved to transform all the other aspects of his life into unhappiness. Choice C most accurately reflects this.

8. The word "ubiquity," as it is used in line 25, is BEST interpreted as **(A) omnipotence**.

   The speaker admits that by worshipping his beloved as if she were a deity, he has made her into an all-powerful presence, one that holds sway over all the other aspects of his existence. This is best represented by choice A.

9. In which of the following lines does the speaker offer the strongest admonition to the reader? **(C) line 19**.

   In line 19, "Me blest for this let no man hold," the speaker sends out a clear message to all other men that the state he is in is hardly a pleasurable one, but rather his own private hell.

10. All of the following may be considered highly ironic EXCEPT **(E) the title of the poem and the alleged actions of the speaker's beloved**.

    The speaker intends to pray to God but ends up making his beloved a deity. The speaker cannot take his mind off his beloved, yet he sees her shape as pursuing him. He deifies his love, yet he says his "pains resemble hell" (line 26). He willingly grants her "ubiquity," yet he suggests she torments him. This information validates choices A, B, C and D as ironies. The title of the poem and the poem's central conceit are metaphorical but not ironic.

11. Which of the following is NOT characteristic of the poet's style? **(D) highly imagistic descriptions of suffering**.

    The central conceit of love's being a thief, the seven-line stanzas of irregular length but of a definite iambic meter, rhetorical questions such as "What, rob me of heaven too?" (line 4) and "What do I seek, alas, or why do I / Attempt in vain to fly?" (lines 22-23), and words such as "heaven" (line 4), "prayers" (line 5), "conscience" (line 9) and "deity" (line 24) are all characteristic of the author's style, confirming the presence of A, B, C, and E and leaving choice D as the exception.

12. The tone of the poem is BEST classified as **(B) exasperated**.

The speaker seems about ready to give up, particularly in expressions such as "What do I seek, alas, or why do I / Attempt in vain to fly?" (lines 22-23). He tries to remedy his situation through work, sleep, prayer and reading, but can find no escape from his romantic obsession. Choice B expresses this best.

Passage Two: From Louise Erdrich's *Tracks*

The second selection in Sample Examination Two, an excerpt from noted Native American author Louise Erdrich's novel *Tracks*, focuses about a card game that ominously escalates into something more dangerous. Set in an Ontario butcher shop described by the narrator as "part killing shed, part store," the passage opens with a young, attractive but equally clever Chippewa woman named Fleur's having won thirty dollars over several weeks of playing cards with the shop workers. Fleur's success at a man's game irritates the other players, in particular Lily who, the narrator indicates, had been kept at bay until now by Pete, the owner of the shop. However, in the sweltering heat of an August night, with her aegis Pete's having left for the cooler ambience of Minnesota, Fleur finds herself in a more hostile and more vulnerable position.

The atmosphere established in the opening paragraph is a stifling one: the air motionless, the heat and humidity so intense that no one at the card table can move and cards and walls are damp to the touch. Fleur, who is still at work boiling hogheads in the back room, contributes heat of a different kind, her "green dress, drenched, wrapped [around] her like a transparent sheet" (lines 14-15). Impatient to recoup some of his lost money, Lily bellows "'Ain't that enough now'" (line 24) to Fleur, who is busy in the back, collecting scraps loosened from the hogheads by the boiling water that she turns with a paddle. When she joins the game, her skin smoking, the room is filled with palpable tension, including the growling animus of the small dog that Lily cradles in his lap.

When the game commences, Lily, with "a roll of money in his pocket" (line 36), immediately raises the ante. The phrase, he "had been stalking this night for weeks" (line 35), reflects both his eagerness to recover his losses and the lust for Fleur that had heretofore been checked by Pete. As the game develops, Fleur is said to play "unevenly" (line 43), winning enough to stay in the game, losing enough to entice them to swell the pot. Erdrich's terse, declarative sentences and her description of the body language of Lily's dog magnify the tension:

> The game went on. The dog was stiff now, poised on Lily's knees, a ball of vicious muscle with its yellow eyes slit in concentration. It gave advice, seemed to sniff the lay of Fleur's cards, twitched and nudged. Fleur was up, then down, saved by a scratch. Tor dealt seven cards, three down. The pot grew, round by round, until it held all the money. Nobody folded. Then it all rode on one last card and they went silent [. . . .] (lines 45-55).

As Fleur picks up her final hand, the author uses synaesthesia—the merging of two sensory images (in this case touch and sound) in "The heat lowered like a bell" (line 56)—to capture the deafening nature of the room's silence. Though this is momentarily relieved by Lily's smirking rhetorical query to his dog, "'You reckon that girl's bluffing?'" (line 61), and his overconfident reply, "'Me too'" (line 63), Lily's pushing of all his remaining bills and coins into the center of the table once more ratchets up the tension.

When the turned cards favor Fleur, the antithetical fortunes of the two main characters are readily apparent. As Erdrich describes,

> Lily looked once, looked again, then he squeezed the dog like a fist of dough and slammed it on the table.
>
> Fleur threw out her arms and swept the money close, grinning that same wolf grin that she'd used on me, the grin that had them. She jammed the bills inside her dress, scooped the coins in waxed white paper that she tied with string (lines 66-74).

Verbs such as "squeezed" (line 67) and "slammed" (line 68) convey the frustration of Lily's defeat, while phrases such as "swept the money close" (lines 69-70) and "jammed the bills inside her dress" (line 72) capture the elation of Fleur's triumph. Moreover, Fleur's "wolf grin" (lines 70-71) reinforces the implication that she has been conning them all along. Lily's burr-choked request for another round, a request almost impeded by the extremity of his irritation, is ignored by Fleur, who complacently yawns and returns to her work in the back room.

Though the cut used here does not include the vindictive action that follows, the selection from Erdrich's novel provides an interesting descriptive and narrative challenge. This and the irony of Fleur's triumph, her "turning the tables" on the workers who see her as a gullible mark, provide an interesting prose challenge for the Advanced Placement English student.

13. The atmosphere in the room in which the card game is played is BEST described as **(C) sultry**.

Lines 7-18 state that "the heat [was] so bad no one could move [. . .]," while lines 9-12 describe how "The cards sweat, limp in their fingers, the table was slick with grease, and even the walls were warm to the touch. The air was motionless." Choice C reflects this best.

14. The events that take place are seemingly recounted by **(D) an unidentified youth**.

Though the novel obviously clarifies who is telling the story, the only clues to the nature of the narrator occur in lines 25-29 in which the narrator states "The stump of a dog trembled in his lap, alive with rage. It never smelled me or noticed me above Fleur's smoky skin. The air was heavy in the corner, and pressed Russell and me down." This suggests that the narrator and his/her companion Russell are small enough to conceal or position themselves unobtrusively in a corner. This and the clear admiration the narrator shows for Fleur's cleverness suggests he/she is of a younger age.

15. The oppressive heat causes all of the following EXCEPT **(E) the other players to become irritable**.

Lines 9-10 recount how the cards "sweat," while line 12 indicates how the air was "motionless." Lines 14-16 describe Fleur's dress as "drenched, wrapp[ing] her like a transparent sheet. A skin of lakeweed," while Lily is observed saying in lines 24-25, "'Ain't that enough now?' 'We're waiting.'" This information validates choices A, B, C and D. Nowhere do the other players display any impatience, making E the exception.

16. The narrator implies which of the following about Fleur? **(D) That she lures the men into a more risky wager**.

This is readily apparent in lines 40-45, "'Ante a dollar then,' said Fleur, and pitched hers in. She lost, but they let her scrape along, a cent at a time. And then she won some. She played unevenly, as if chance were all she had. She reeled them in.'"

17. Lines such as "Let's up the ante" (line 34) and "Let's show" (line 63) are likely intended to convey Lily's **(B) brash confidence that he will win back his losses**.

The passage indicates in line 4 that Fleur had already won thirty dollars from the men playing cards. Line 35 also indicates that Lily "had been stalking this night for weeks." Clearly, Lily wishes to raise the pot and win back his losses, a fact further verified by his wagering all his bills and coins on the last hand. He is particularly buoyed by the fact that Fleur has lost some hands early in the game and believes she is ultimately bluffing.

18. The author mirrors Lily's changing fortunes and attitude through which of the following?

> I. The demeanor and body language of his dog.
> II. The changing size of the pot on the table.
> III. The facial expressions of the other card players.

(C) I and II.

When Fleur is holding up the game, the dog is seen trembling, "alive with rage" (line 26). When Lily is winning, the dog is said to be "stiff [. . .] poised on Lily's knees, a ball of vicious muscle with its yellow eyes slit in concentration" (lines 45-48). The narrator further states that "It gave advice, seemed to sniff the lay of Fleur's cards, twitched and nudged" (lines 48-50). Later, it whines (line 62) to suggest its agreement with Lily that Fleur is bluffing. This validates I. The pot, which at first is limited to a few cents, "grew, round by round, until it held all the money" (lines 52-53). This corroborates the correctness of II. Other than Fleur's winning grin, no mention is made of the expressions on the faces of the other players.

19. The narrator likely describes Lily's voice as "choked with burrs" (line 76) to illustrate his **(E) ire**.

Since "burrs" are irritating nettles, it is pretty clear that Lily is furious at the outcome of the game, so angry that he can barely talk.

20. Which of the following pairs of words captures the impression of Fleur that the author MOST wishes to convey to the reader? **(C) cunning and conniving**.

Fleur is said to have a "wolf grin" (lines 70-71), suggestive of animal-like cunning. Moreover, she is described as playing "unevenly" (line 43) in order to entice the men into wagering more aggressively. She is also said to have "reeled them in" (lines 44-45). This is best represented by choice C.

21. The author draws an ironic and incongruous connection between the two principal characters in the episode through which of the following? **(B) their names**.

Fleur is French for flower while Lily is a flower. This connection is ironic because they are antagonists.

22. The passage subtly intimates which of the following?

    I. That after collecting her winnings Fleur will resign from her arduous job.
   II. That the "real game" (line 33) does not necessarily involve card-playing.
  III. That, as a result of her winning, Fleur may be a victim of violence.

(D) II and III.

The passage has some subtle undertones, the first evidenced by lines 3-6, "A month running, Fleur had won thirty dollars and only Pete's presence had kept Lily at bay." This suggests that Lily is a threat to Fleur. The narrator also indicates that Lily "had been stalking this night for weeks" (line 35). The word "stalking" has a predatory connotation, and while part of this is clearly his desire to get back his losses, the intimation is that he plans to do so through the card game or, if necessary, by other means. This, coupled with the description of Fleur's drenched and skin-tight attire (lines 14-16), lends the scene a subtle eroticism that is reminiscent of the card game in *A Streetcar Named Desire*.

23. Which of the following demonstrates the literary device known as synaesthesia? **(E) "The heat lowered like a bell." (line 56)**.

This technique combines two disparate senses in a uniquely imagistic way. Here, heat (feeling) is described in terms of a bell (sound).

24. Which of the following is NOT characteristic of the author's style? **(E) ubiquitous symbols of imminent death**.

Erdrich's style is very much like that of Ernest Hemingway, primarily characterized by terse, simple sentences and succinct dialogue—e.g., "The game went on" (line 45), "Nobody folded" (line 53), "The heat lowered like a bell" (line 56). This tends to place the focus squarely on the events at the card table (A). As was delineated in the explanation to question #18, the dog, seated on Lily's lap for the duration of the card game, almost functions as another character (B). At the conclusion of the game, Lily slams the dog on the table while Fleur hungrily sweeps up her winnings, jamming them inside her dress (C). Finally, the passage has only a single exchange of dialogue, the other lines being voiced by Lily in moments of impatience or as rhetorical questions (D). Though there are some skulls being boiled by Fleur in the back room, there are no ubiquitous symbols of death in the passage. This makes choice E the exception.

Passage Three: Edward Hirsch's "After the Last Practice"

Edward Hirsch's "After the Last Practice" may seem to some a surprising choice with its masculine football bent and its clearly greater appeal to a reading audience that is old enough to be nostalgic, but if the actual AP English exam can include a prose passage about the Cuban boxer Bernie Paret and a poem about a young girl's imaginary steed, it seemed quite legitimate to include Hirsch's poem both as an interesting piece of literature and as a counterpoise to the other content of the book. Hirsch's poem, ostensibly a colorful collage of high school football memories recalled by older men around a campfire in the woods, gradually evolves into something more than nostalgia—a consciousness of lost youth, of lost innocence, and of the stealthy but inexorable encroachment of age and death.

The first fourteen stanzas of the poem provide a highly imagistic potpourri of the world of high school football, plunging the reader into the sights, smells, sounds and feelings of the gridiron. The rituals of pre-game preparation—of coaches intently diagramming plays on blackboards, of players pulling on jerseys, scraping their spikes on concrete, slamming their forearms into lockers, or pounding the shoulder-pads of teammates, of the antithetical mingling of anxious queasiness and equally anxious adrenaline; the archetypal Middle American setting of flat Midwestern fields stretching endlessly into the horizon, of the cold crispness of a typical November afternoon with the smell of burning leaves permeating the air, of family and sweethearts crowding the stands and lifting their ecstatic roar of support; the painful price of gladiatorial combat—the bruised arms, blackened eyes, aching muscles and torn ligaments, of the emotional ecstasy of "breaking loose from a tackle / And romping for daylight, for the green / Promised land of the end zone" (lines 70-72) and the agony of the "Thirteen-hour drive home after [having] bruised / A collarbone on the last play of the game / The whole bus encased in silence like a glass / Jar [. . .]" (lines 80-83)—all are recalled with a curious mixture of pride, exhilaration, and confusion. As the speaker admits, "not / One of us could explain why he had done it. / What use now is the language of traps / And draws, of power-sweeps and desperate on-side / Kicks, of screen passes, double reverses?" (lines 62-66). And yet, as his friend remarks, there were moments when he "felt as if [he] would explode with happiness, / As if [he] would never falter, waver, or die [. . .]" (lines 77-78).

The final three stanzas present a polar image—one of men of indeterminate age (but whose boyhoods have clearly been left behind) gathered like grim specters around a sputtering and smoldering campfire. Veiled by the night and the "ghostly woodsmoke" (line 86), they once more huddle together "as if [they] were partly warriors / And partly Boy Scouts ringed around the flame, / Holding [their] helmets in [their] arms and trying / To understand an old appetite for glory" (lines 87-90). Trapped like Polynices in some indeterminate nether world—some mapless matrix between boyhood and adulthood, between adolescence and maturity—they gradually fall silent, unable to comprehend how quickly glory fades, lives vanish. In many ways this scene recalls early Anglo-Saxon poems such as "The Seafarer" and "The Wanderer," whose protagonists, finding their lord and friends killed, their mead-halls and villages wasted, roam aimlessly, searching for direction and *guerdon*. As the fire, a mirror of their own gradual disintegration, "[glowers] down to embers and ashes, / To red bits of nothing" (lines 96-97), so they feel themselves "burning, burning, burning, burning…" (line 98). The song that someone intones in the final line, while perhaps a typical campfire ditty, should probably be seen as a metaphorical dirge, like Don McLean's anthematic tribute to the "day the music died." The friends are painfully conscious that their "raging, innocent, violent, American / Boyhoods [are] gone now, vanished forever / Like the victories and the hard losses" (lines 91-93); however, they seem clueless as to how those voids may be filled.

Hirsch's poem reminds me of the many colleagues I have known over the years who eagerly anticipated retirement only to find that, once they had attained it, they had an abundance of time on their hands which they did not know how to fill. There are only so many holes of golf one can play before that too becomes hackneyed. I also think here of Tom Buchanan in *The Great Gatsby*, who the narrator Nick Carraway observes "had achieved such an acute, limited excellence at twenty-one that everything afterward savor[ed] of anti-climax." Nick further notes how he felt Tom would "drift on forever seeking a little wistfully for the dramatic turbulence of some irrecoverable football game." Hirsch's poem ultimately suggests that though high school athletics may provide fond memories of gridiron glory, these cannot become the sum and substance of one's life. The poem ends with an embarrassingly poignant silence since, their memories of high school having been resurrected and revisited, the friends have essentially nothing left to say.

25. The main focus of the poem involves the **(B) fleeting nature of youth and glory**.

From the word "remember" in line 1 it is apparent that the poem is about the past, and as the companions contribute more specific memories it is apparent that it is about the world of high school football. However, it is not until relatively late in the poem that the theme of lost youth and glory fully emerges. Despite the bruises and more serious injuries, the tedious bus rides and arduous practices, the stomach-churning anxiety and nervous jitters, it is clear from lines such as "the green / Promised land of the end zone" (lines 71-72) and "I felt as if I would explode with happiness, / As if I would never falter, waver, or die…" (lines 77-78) that these were the halcyon days, days of youth and glory and triumph. Beginning with line 85, however, the tone of the poem changes as the companions, recognizing their age and position in life, sit about the campfire "Holding [their] helmets in [their] arms and trying / To understand an old appetite for glory, / [Their] raging, innocent, violent, American / Boyhoods gone now, vanished forever / Like the victories and the hard losses" (lines 89-93). The fire that sputters and glowers down into ashes and the speaker's comment that they were "burning, burning, burning, burning…" (line 98) symbolize this as well.

26. The tone of the poem is BEST labeled **(E) nostalgic**.

Nostalgia suggests a yearning for the past, for a time when things were better than they are at present. Though no specifics are provided as to the present economic or social successes of the companions, their preoccupation with their high school football days and their yearning for the triumph and glory of the high school gridiron suggests that this was the best time of their lives.

27. All of the following help to reinforce the sensory nature of the first two stanzas EXCEPT **(E) "the tension mounting all day [. . .]" (line 10)**.

Sensory imagery features words that appeal to the senses. The onomatopoeic "crack" of the shoulderpads (A), the multicolored bruises that "blossom" on the players' arms (B), the "faint, medicinal smell" of ointment in the locker room (C), and the onomatopoeic "hiss" of the steaming showers (D) all qualify in this regard. Choice E does not.

28. The most common feeling displayed by the players *before* the contest is **(B) apprehension**.

The speaker talks about the "tension mounting all day" (line 10), how it was manifest in the "sound of spikes clattering / Across the locker room floor, the low banter / Of the last players pulling on their jerseys, / Our middle-linebacker humming to himself / And hammering a forearm against the lockers [. . .]" (lines 11-15). He also remembers how "a huge pit opened up in your stomach / And the steady buzz of a crowd in the distance / Turned into a minor roaring in your skull [. . .]" (lines 21-23) as well as how "The jitters never disappeared until the opening / Kickoff [. . .]" (lines 25-26). Choice B captures this best.

29. The sixth and seventh stanzas of the poem (lines 31-42) do which of the following?

   I. Provide a measure of local color by introducing the reader to a specific geographical setting.

  II. Imagistically reinforce the friends' enduring camaraderie.

 III. Symbolically mirror the teammates' vanishing youth.

(E) I, II and III.

The sixth stanza introduces us to the Midwestern setting of endless golden cornfields set against a dark November sky (I). The seventh stanza, in particular line 37, "The smoky glow of faces around a small fire," imagistically buttresses the boys' enduring friendship (II). Moreover, the wooden fence posts and miles of empty cornfields that they pass in the team bus can be seen as symbols of passing time (III); hence, the selection of E as the best answer.

30. Lines 44-45—"Jesus, someone said, I never thought it would end / Like this, without pads, without hitting anybody"—are primarily intended to **(A) intimate subtly that the players' adult lives have been anticlimactic**.

The phrase "'I never thought it would end like this'" suggests disappointment, an outcome that is somehow polar to what they expected. The closing words "'without pads, without hitting anybody'" possibly imply that they have not made any impact as adults, that their best days are behind them.

31. The memories presented in lines 46-61 **(A) celebrate individual character and toughness**.

These lines present a catalog of endured pain and injury, of "getting blindsided by a bone-wrenching tackle" (line 47), of suffering and tolerating ligament tears and ankle sprains and black eyes, of enduring grueling 'two-a-days' in the summer heat. This is best represented by choice A.

32. The diction and imagery in stanzas twelve and thirteen (lines 67-78) are suggestive of all of the following EXCEPT **(D) transience and mortality**.

The memories of a "sharp cut" (line 67), of executing a perfect play, breaking free of a tackle, and "romping for daylight, for the green / Promised land of the end zone" (lines 71-72) confirm A, B, and C. The memories of seeing his girlfriend "in the stands at midfield— / [with] everyone around her… chanting and shouting" (lines 74-75), and of feeling "as if [he] would explode with happiness, / As if [he] would never falter, waver, or die…" (lines 77-78) confirm E. This makes D the exception.

33. The Boy Scout-warrior dichotomy, mentioned in lines 87-88, reinforces which of the following contrasts? **(B) youth and maturity**.

Being a Boy Scout is a childhood activity; hunting in the woods is an adult one.

34. The speaker's comment that they were all "burning, burning, etc" (line 98) may plausibly be interpreted as which of the following?

   I. Desiring to be young again.
   II. Rapidly passing into insignificance.
   III. Becoming irate over their lost youth.

(C) I and II.

Clearly the recollection of these high school memories makes them want to return to their "glory days" (I). At the same time, like the smoldering and sputtering fire, their adult lives are passing as quickly as wooden fence posts seen through a bus window (II). There is no sense of anger in the poem, only one of subdued reflection.

35. Which of the following contributes LEAST to the contemplative mood of the last three stanzas? **(B) the comparison "as if we were partly warriors / And partly Boy Scouts [. . .]" (lines 87-88)**.

The word "sputtering" suggests a fire about to go out. The terse sentences in choice C reinforce the deep subdued quiet that enfolds the companions as they sit about the campfire. The alliterative trio of "deep," "descended" and "disintegrated" also suggests a dying down, a dissolution. Much like the word "sputtering," the word "glowering" suggests fading light but no crackling sound. This validates choices A, C, D and E. Choice B contributes nothing in this regard.

36. In the course of the poem, the poet uses simile to depict each of the following EXCEPT **(C) the facial bruises that were the by-product of practice**.

The November sky is said to be "like a dome / Covering a chilly afternoon [. . .]" (lines 33-34), the windmills to move their blades "as if underwater [. . .]" (line 42). The quiet after a loss is said to be "like a glass / Jar, like the night itself [. . .]" (lines 82-83), while their boyhoods are said to vanish forever "Like the victories and the hard losses" (line 93). The speaker describes the facial bruises through the implied metaphor of a "black coin" (line 50).

37. When one considers the context in which it appears, which of the following is NOT intended to contribute to the transitory nature of the teammates' adolescent athletic experiences? **(A) "The smoky glow of faces around a small fire." (line 37)**.

As was expounded upon in the explanation to question #30, the compatriots voice in choice B their frustration over not having made an impact in life. The rhetorical question in choice C suggests that the complex plays they learned in football have had no relevance in their adult lives. Choices D and E suggest that they still burn for past glory. Choice A merely provides an image of camaraderie around a campfire.

38. Which of the following mirrors the diminishing significance of the individuals and their exploits on the football field?

    I. The ambiguity and inconsistency of their recollections.
    II. The poet's use of indefinite personal pronouns in lieu of names.
    III. The symbol of the sputtering and smoldering fire.

(D) II and III.

The sputtering and smoldering fire (III), directly connected to the companions by line 98, has already been sufficiently explicated. The fact that there are no names, only lines that begin with "Someone said" (line 1) and "Someone else remembered" (line 4), suggests that they have blurred into anonymity and insignificance (II). The clarity of their high school recollections eliminates I from consideration.

39. All of the following are stylistic traits of the poem EXCEPT **(D) a contrast between youth and infirmity**.

The recollections are made by different individuals in the poem, and the poem is filled with the language of football such as "desperate on-side / Kicks, screen passes, double reverses" (lines 65-66). These validate the presence of A and B. The description of players stretching, being taped, pulling on jerseys, etc. and the largely structured six line stanzaic pattern of free verse confirm C and E. There is no contrast between youth and infirmity in the poem.

Passage Four: From Ben Jonson's "On Style"

The final short-answer passage in Sample Examination One provides a stiff test for the young reader primarily because of its age. Still, despite its occasional rugged syntax and archaic diction, it is generally accessible and a good benchmark by which to determine a student's comfort level with literature from earlier centuries.

Like many others of his trade have done and continue to do, Jonson weighs in on the defining traits of good writers and good writing. His initial sentence—"For a man to write well there are required three necessaries—to read the best authors, observe the best speakers, and much exercise of his own style" (lines 1-4)—suggests that the key ingredients involve reading and listening to the best writers and regularly practicing one's own craft. Jonson places additional importance on careful selection of subject (and the genre most apropos to it) as well as diligent attention to diction and syntax. His advice that, "No matter how slow the style be at first, so it be labored and accurate; seek the best and be not glad of the forward conceits or first words that offer themselves to us, but judge of what we invent, and order what we approve" (lines 12-17), suggests that in order to effect the best possible product, a writer must be patient, self-critical and painstaking. In fact, he goes so far as to advocate rewriting passages that have already been written, claiming that "it helps the consequence, and makes the juncture better, it quickens the heat of imagination, that often cools in the time of setting down, and gives it new strength, as if it grew lustier by the going back" (lines 18-23). Using the analogy of a javelin toss by which "we force back our arms to make our loose the stronger" (lines 26-27), Jonson suggests that revisiting what one has written enables a writer to progress further with his argument or narrative. At the same time Jonson seems to be conscious of a "writer's groove" since he acknowledges that "if [the writer has] a fair gale of wind, I forbid not the steering out of [his] sail, so the favor of the gale deceive [him] not" (lines 28-30).

Still, Jonson cautions the writer against falling in love with the first words that readily come into his mind—"For all that we invent doth please us in the conception of our birth, else we would never set it down" (lines 30-32)—avowing that the safest course is always to "to return to our judgment, and handle over again those things the easiness of which might make them justly suspected" (lines 33-36). Suggesting that this is what the best writers have always done, Jonson compacts his advice into a concise paradox: "So that the sum of all is, ready writing makes not good writing, but good writing brings on ready writing" (lines 45-47). Jonson further warns writers against becoming over-confident, suggesting that "it is even then good to resist [this sense of self-satisfaction], as to give a horse a check sometimes with a bit, which doth not so much stop his course as stir his mettle" (lines 48-51). At the same time, Jonson antithetically urges that a writer must continually stretch his limits, "should more and more contend, lift and dilate [him]self; as men of low stature raise themselves on their toes, and so oft-times get even, if not eminent" (lines 53-56).

Jonson's closing comments then shift from writers in general to the novice writer, suggesting that he go to school on the works of writers of established reputation for lessons in subject and presentation:

> For the mind and memory are more sharply exercised in comprehending another man's things than our own; and such as accustom themselves and are familiar with the best authors shall ever and anon find somewhat of them in themselves, and in the expression of their minds, even when they feel it not, be able to utter something like theirs, which hath an authority above their own (lines 62-71).

Though a writer may have a predilection for a certain type of writing, Jonson staunchily maintains that he "must exercise all" (lines 75-76) and become adept at all different structures and genres. Drawing upon music for his concluding metaphor, Jonson observes that "For as in an instrument, so in style, there must be harmony and consent of parts" (lines 76-78). This implies that like an orchestra, in which various instruments playing various melodic lines combine in one harmonious whole, so the varied aspects of style—be they diction, syntax, figurative language or tone—must function in a similarly concordant manner.

Jonson's essay provides a short but eloquent primer on good writing which, despite is age, probably is equally applicable to teaching composition in the present day.

40. The author's tone is BEST characterized as **(E) didactic**.

From the very first sentence—"For a man to write well there are required three necessaries—to read the best authors, observe the best speakers, and much exercise of his own style" (lines 1-4)—Jonson's intent to instruct is abundantly clear. The passage is pretty much a primer for aspiring writers, a "how to" guide to becoming a writer and developing one's craft. Choice E captures this best.

41. In advancing his argument the author makes use of all of the following EXCEPT **(A) subtle sarcasm that reveals his disfavor of novice writers**.

Choice B is apparent in lines such as "Then take care, in placing and ranking both matter and words, that the composition be comely [. . .]" (lines 9-11) or "Repeat often what we have formerly written [. . .]" (lines 17-18), Choice C in his comparisons to jumping and javelin throwing (lines 23-27) and later to horseback riding (lines 49-51). Choice D is verified by the speaker's observation that "ready writing makes not good writing, but good writing brings on ready writing" (lines 45-47), Choice E in lines such as "For all that we invent doth please us in the conception of our birth, else we would never set it down" (lines 30-32). Nowhere does he suggest a distaste for novice writers.

42. The allusions to jumping and javelin throwing in lines 23-27 are primarily intended to buttress the author's conviction about the importance of **(B) repeating what one has previously written to strengthen it**.

Jonson suggests that repeating what one has already written "gives it new strength, as if it grew lustier by the going back" (lines 22-23). The allusions to broad-jumping and javelin throwing are made because in both sports the length of the jump or throw is determined by the force with which one makes it. The javelin toss seems the more apropos of the two since the length of the throw is directly proportional to how much we "force back our arms to make our loose the stronger" (lines 26-27).

43. Which of the following may safely be said about lines 28-30?

  I. They are an admonition against insufficiently thought out developments in the plot.
  II. They seemingly contradict the author's earlier comment that "No matter how slow the style be at first, so it be labored and accurate [. . .]." (lines 12-13).
  III. They reflect the author's concession that there may be moments when a writer must flow with his inspiration or rhythm.

(D) II and III.

Jonson's allusion to letting out more sail to take advantage of a favorable wind is mildly antithetical to his earlier admonition to young writers to proceed with deliberation and caution (II). However, it also suggests that there are moments when rules are to be broken (III). The "fair gale of wind" (line 28) symbolizes a time of rhythm or inspiration in which the writer finds the going easy. Even so, Jonson nevertheless cautions that "the safest is to return to our judgment, and handle over again those things the easiness of which might make them justly suspected" (lines 33-36).

44. The simile couched in lines 47-51 warns writers against becoming **(B) overconfident**.

The phrase "when we think we have got the faculty" (lines 47-48) translates roughly in contemporary terms into "when we think we have got the hang of it." It is in these moments that Jonson believes it is good to "give a horse a check sometimes with a bit, which doth not so much stop his course as stir his mettle" (lines 49-51)— in short, to rein ourselves in a bit. Choice B represents this idea best.

45. Lines 52-54, "Again, whither a man's genius is best able to reach, thither it should more and more contend [. . .]," suggest that when a writer is at the height of his creative powers he should **(D) be more daring in the scope and reach of his literary endeavors**.

The word "contend," in this context, is best read as "strive towards." The intimation here is that one should aspire as far as one's talents allow. The simile that follows—"as men of low stature raise themselves on their toes, and so oft-times get even, if not eminent" (lines 54-56)—alludes to men of shorter stature who raise themselves on their toes so they can look taller than their peers, essentially exceeding their natural limitations. Choice D reflects this best.

46. The author suggests that all writers—particularly novice ones—should "accustom themselves" (line 65) to the best authors for which of the following reasons?

   I. To discover some part of themselves in a more established writer's voice or material.
   II. To expose themselves to other styles and genres of writing.
   III. To utilize these authors' works as exemplars they might imitate.

(E) I, II and III.

Jonson's suggestion that by studying other writers novices may "find somewhat of them in themselves" (line 67) confirms I, while his suggestion that "though a man be more prone and able for one kind of writing than another, yet he must exercise all" (lines 73-76) validates II. III is evident in Jonson's observation that they may "in the expression of their minds, even when they feel it not, be able to utter something like theirs, which hath an authority above their own" (lines 68-71).

47. Which of the following does NOT paraphrase advice given by Jonson as to how best to effect good writing? **(C) Establish your own, unique style that has not been influenced by writers who have come before you**.

Choice A is confirmed by lines 5-6, "consider what ought to be written, and after what manner [. . .]," choice B by lines 9-11, "Then take care, in placing and ranking both matter and words, that the composition be comely." Choice D is supported by lines 16-17, "judge of what we invent, and order what we approve," and also lines 33-36, "But the safest is to return to our judgment, and handle over again those things the easiness of which might make them justly suspected." Choice E is backed by lines 47-51, "Yet, when we think we have got the faculty, it is even then good to resist it, as to give a horse a check sometimes with a bit, which doth not so much stop his course as stir his mettle" and also by lines 30-32, "For all that we invent doth please us in the conception of our birth, else we would never set it down." Choice C garners no support from the passage.

48. In the course of his essay, the author draws comparisons to all of the following EXCEPT **(B) government**.

   The comparisons to athletic competition (A) are evident in the aforementioned broad-jump and javelin throw in lines 23-27, the comparison to horseback riding (C) in lines 49-51. The comparison to sailing (D) is apparent in lines 28-30, "Yet, if we have a fair gale of wind, I forbid not the steering out of our sail, so the favor of the gale deceive us not," and the comparison to music (E) in the final three lines of the passage, "For as in an instrument, so in style, there must be harmony and consent of parts." There is no comparison made to government by the author.

49. In light of the context in which each word is embedded, which of the following would be the LEAST suitable replacement for one of the archaisms listed below? **(B) "common" for "forward" (line 14)**.

   While all of the other substitutions are plausible ones, the word "forward" in this context actually means "first to come to mind;" thus, B is the exception.

50. Ironically, a purist might find Jonson's opening sentence to be marred by which of the following? **(A) faulty parallelism**.

   Jonson somewhat awkwardly matches two infinitive phrases ("to read the best authors, [to] observe the best speakers") with a noun followed by a prepositional phrase ("exercise of his own style").

51. The passage ultimately makes what point about professional writers? **(B) They hone their craft by degrees**.

   The choice of B as the best answer is pretty much based on the passage as a whole since throughout the entire seventy-eight lines Jonson has indicated that good writing requires the reading of other writers, the imitation of their style, consideration of the appropriate content and genre of one's work, constant practice, revision, and a host of other "writing practices" that take time to master.

Explication of Free-Response Question One: Michael Waters' "The Mystery of the Caves"

Sometimes a deceptively simple piece may reveal itself to be much more complex than originally considered, and Michael Waters' poem, "The Mystery of the Caves," proves a fine example of that. This readily accessible, forty-line poem, proportionately divided into ten four-line stanzas, at first seems little more than a poem about a boy reading a story about a similarly aged boy lost in a cave, but further consideration of the poem reveals an undercurrent of mythological possibilities and troubling domestic strife.

In this task students were requested to examine "how the poet uses images and symbols to link the predicament of the lost boy to the domestic situation of the speaker." In some ways this poem seems filled with Pirandellian mirrors, the reader reading a story about a boy remembering a story he himself has read. The speaker describes how the boy-hero of the story "was lost, / wandering a labyrinth of caverns / filling stratum by stratum with water" (lines 2-4). The outcome for the hero was ambiguous: "would he float upward toward light? / Or would he somersault forever / in an underground black river?" (lines 6-8). The dilemma of the fictional hero quickly merges with the dilemma of the speaker, who reveals that "[his] mother was leaving again— / the lid of the trunk thrown open, / blouses torn from their hangers, / the crazy shouting among rooms" (lines 11-14). The scene the speaker is describing—an all-too-common one of domestic strife—represents his particular form of entrapment in an overwhelming domestic situation from which he sees no respite, no escape. The fact that his mother was leaving "again" implies that this scene has been repeated on more than one occasion, that the "crazy shouting among rooms" is the norm, not the exception.

Like his fictional counterpart who is seeking an escape from the rising water in the caves, the speaker finds it "impossible to see / which passage [leads] to safety" (lines 15-16). As the cave-trapped boy holds the wavering "yellow finger of flame" (line 17) of his last match, peering desperately into the darkness for any signs of an egress, the speaker finds himself in a hostile vortex of breaking perfume bottles and a mother caught in the violent hands of an angry and abusive father. As lines 23-25 suggest, the speaker feels equally helpless in his real and fictional worlds, too distant to help his desperate counterpart, too small to intercede on behalf of his hysterically sobbing mother. Lines 31-32, "I can't recall the whole story, / what happened at the end…," on one level suggest that the speaker has forgotten the outcome of the story, on another that he has partially repressed a painful memory.

The final two stanzas of the poem pull the fortunes of the speaker and the trapped boy in the story into even closer proximity. When the speaker says in lines 33-36

> Sometimes I worry that the boy
> is still searching below the earth
> for a thin pencil of light,
> that I can almost hear him

the reader wonders whether the boy he is searching for is the boy in the fictional story, or a youthful version of himself; whether the "thin pencil of light" that he mentions is a miraculous exit for his cave-bound companion, or his way out of the "My Papa's Waltz" situation he once found himself in. Are these painful memories of a distant past, or psychological demons of the present that he has yet to exorcise? Of particular interest is the word "pencil" since it offers a quite plausible interpretation that writing about these memories is his only way to eradicate them. Moreover, when the speaker suggests in lines 36-40 that he can almost hear the trapped boy

> through great volumes of water,
> through centuries of stone,
> crying my name among blind fish,
> wanting so much to come home

the reader feels his keen sense of alienation and abandonment ("among blind fish") as well as his frustrated desire for domestic bliss.

In terms of images and symbols, the student has quite a store from which to choose. As to the boy in the story, the "labyrinth of caverns" (line 3) may be seen as symbolizing the trappings of his situation, his inability to see any way out. The "underground black river" (line 8) serves a similar symbolic purpose, suggesting a powerful natural force which buffets him about and threatens to submerge him, one over which he can exert no control. The "One yellow finger of flame" (line 17), his solitary match, and the "thin pencil of light" (line 35) that he searches for above, represent his last hope of escape, while the fact that "The boy wasn't able to breathe" (line 23) suggests the growing desperation of his plight. These motifs of suffocation and drowning relate easily to the domestic situation of the speaker (abusive father, abandoning mother), a situation for which he is too small to have an answer. The image of the speaker's mother sitting "among bright islands of skirts / circling the rim of the bed" (lines 29-30) reinforces her isolation, while the images of "crazy shouting among rooms" (line 14) and his mother's "breaking miniature bottles" of perfume (lines 19-20) convey the contentiousness of the marriage. Moreover, the image of his "father gripping her, / but too tightly, by both arms" (lines 21-22) suggests his mother's helpless inability to do anything, making the reader wonder if the thrown-open trunk lid and smashing of miniature perfume bottles are merely an impotent histrionic display.

The theme of the journey home is an archetypal one, present in everything from the *Odyssey* to *The Hobbit*, though some like Thomas Wolfe have suggested that one "can't go home again." Whether home is a country, a domicile, or, as Warren coldly puts it in Frost's *The Death of the Hired Man*, "the place where, / when you have to go there, / They have to take you in," home remains for many a physical or psychological haven to which they are compelled to return, sometimes to recover bliss, other times to redress a wrong. Waters' poem also calls to mind the mythical Theseus following his string out of the labyrinth to safety. As someone whose own childhood was marred by similar scenes, this poem speaks very personally to me. I remember once equating my mother's crying after a particularly harrowing episode with my father to the incessant sirens I recall hearing as a first-grade student in 1960 when an airliner first plunged onto the streets of downtown Brooklyn—keening, agonizing, incessant ones. Waters' poem may be simple on the surface, but it has impressive depths that an ambitious student can enthusiastically plumb.

This question has been reprinted for your convenience.

Question One

(Suggested time—40 minutes. This question counts as one-third of the total essay section score.)

Read the following poem carefully. Then, in a well-organized essay, indicate how the poet uses images and symbols to link the predicament of the lost boy to the domestic situation of the speaker.

The Mystery of the Caves

I don't remember the name of the story,
but the hero, a boy, was lost,
wandering a labyrinth of caverns
filling stratum by stratum with water.

(5) I was wondering what might happen:
would he float upward toward light?
Or would he somersault forever
in an underground black river?

I couldn't stop reading the book
(10) because I had to know the answer,
because my mother was leaving again—
the lid of the trunk thrown open,

blouses torn from their hangers,
the crazy shouting among rooms.
(15) The boy found it impossible to see
which passage led to safety.

One yellow finger of flame
Wavered on his last match.
There was a blur of perfume,
(20) my mother breaking miniature bottles,

then my father gripping her,
but too tightly, by both arms.
The boy wasn't able to breathe.
I think he wanted me to help,

(25) but I was small, and it was late.
And my mother was sobbing now,
no longer cursing her life,
repeating my father's name

among bright islands of skirts
(30) circling the rim of the bed.
I can't recall the whole story,
What happened at the end…

Sometimes I worry that the boy
is still searching below the earth
(35) for a thin pencil of light,
that I can almost hear him

through great volumes of water,
through centuries of stone,
crying my name among blind fish,
(40) wanting so much to come home.

From *Parthenopi: New and Selected Poems* (BOA Editions, 2001).
Reprinted with permission of the author.

Scoring Rubric for Free-Response Question One: Michael Waters' "The Mystery of the Caves"

8-9   These papers not only convey their authors' keen understanding of the link between the predicament of the lost boy and the domestic situation of the speaker, but also their clear perception as to how the poet establishes this connection through imagery and symbolism. Well-conceived, well-developed, and well-organized, these papers are marked by frequent and accurate references to the text, by an admirable ability to synthesize thought, and by a mature control over the elements of composition. Though not perfect, they clearly indicate the students' ability to read poetry skillfully and to show how the literary elements of the poem support the poem's theme.

6-7   These essays exhibit a solid understanding of Waters' poem, but are less adept at responding to the question. This may be due to inconsistencies in textual understanding, to a lesser ability to comprehend the link between the predicament of the lost boy and the domestic situation of the speaker, and/or to a lesser ability to show how this connection is manifested by the images and symbols of the poem. Though these essays reflect their writers' abilities to convey their points clearly, they feature less fluency, development or cogency than 9-8 papers.

5   These papers respond to the question on the Waters' poem in superficial, formulaic, inconsistent or insufficiently supported ways. They may rely primarily on paraphrase, but may still convey an implicit understanding of the poem and the task. The papers are generally written in a satisfactory manner, with occasional errors in composition or mechanics that do not impede the reader's understanding. Nevertheless, these essays lack the organization, persuasiveness and development of upper-half papers.

3-4   These lower-half essays generally suggest an incomplete or overly simplistic understanding of the poem or task, an inability to comprehend the link between the predicament of the lost boy and the domestic situation of the speaker and/or to understand how this connection is manifested by the images and symbols of the poem. Their arguments are often characterized by a misreading of the text, a failure to provide adequate support, or insufficient control over the elements of composition. In some instances they may consist entirely of paraphrase and/or feature acute problems in organization, clarity, fluency or development.

1-2   These essays compound the shortcomings of 3-4 papers. They often contain many serious and distracting errors in grammar or mechanics that preclude any successful response to the prompt. Though these essays may attempt to show how the predicament of the lost boy and the domestic situation of the speaker are connected, they are severely limited by deficiencies in organization, clarity, fluency or development.

0   Papers scored a zero make no more than a passing reference to the task.

—   Papers given this score offer a blank or totally off-topic response.

Sample Student Essay One

Michael Waters' poem, "The Mystery of the Caves," is a masterful depiction of a small boy's confusion during his parents' vociferous fight contrasted with a book he is reading that portrays another young boy lost among the crevices of the earth. Through an array of images and symbols, Michael Waters correlates the boy's confounding situation to that of the lost boy in the story.

In the first five stanzas, Waters uses images of dark caverns and underground passages to connect the boy's disarrayed and disoriented situation to the predicament of the lost boy. The speaker is lost in his own head, trying to figure out why his parents are acting this way, with only a single flame to light the way. As explained in line 15, "The boy found it impossible to see which passage led to safety." The speaker cannot find the right passage to safety in his hostile home. Waters uses the images of torn clothes and trunks thrown open and "crazy shouting among rooms" to connect the chaotic house to a labyrinth of caverns. Both are extremely difficult to follow and seem to lead nowhere.

Michael Waters also uses symbols to represent both parallel narratives. For example, in line 7, the speaker says about the lost boy, "would he float upward toward light? Or would he somersault forever in an underground black river?" This is the same question he is asking about himself, only in his case he will somersault into his parents' divorce.

In the last five stanzas, the poem focuses on the story of the boy whose parents are fighting. The speaker explains how his mother is now sobbing, cursing his father's name and he is too young and too small to help. He feels helpless in his situation which is when he reconnects the night to the story of the lost boy. In line 31, the speaker says, "I can't recall the whole story, what happened at the end...". This is a symbol for his own situation. He does not know what will come of his parents' fight, or what will happen when it subsides. He then says, "Sometimes I worry that the boy is still searching below the earth for a thin pencil of light." He fears that he will be like the lost boy, searching for light in an otherwise dark and dismal childhood. This relates the speaker to the lost boy and makes their situations almost analogous in meaning.

In conclusion, the poem, "The Mystery of the Caves," is a brilliant work that effectively parallels the story of the lost boy to the story of a boy trapped under his parents' abusive fighting. Through the use of images and symbols, Michael Waters weaves both stories together and successfully links the two, which makes the poem even more powerful.

You Rate It!

1. How thorough a job did the student do in linking the predicament of the lost boy to the domestic situation of the speaker?

   _____

   _____

   _____

   _____

2. What images and/or symbols did the student identify? How effective were they in linking the predicaments of the two boys?

   _____

   _____

   _____

   _____

3. How well-organized and fluent was the student's paper? Was the student's overall argument a persuasive one?

   _____

   _____

   _____

   _____

4. On a 0-9 scale, how would you rate this response? Explain why.

   _____

   _____

   _____

   _____

Sample Student Essay Two

The poem "The Mystery of the Caves" eloquently links the peril of a young boy in a cavern with the situation of the real boy who is facing trouble in his family life. His mother has threatened to leave once more, and her and the father get into a fight, which ends with her sobbing. It is implied that the boy lives in an unstable family environment, and that he is perhaps reading this story about the young boy in the cavern to parallel his own life and make him feel better about the situation at hand. In fact, the lost boy in the caves truly represents the loss of the narrator's innocence, and the poet uses imagery and symbolism within both worlds to portray this.

When describing the real world of the narrator, the poet uses vivid imagery in order to create a sense of realism. However, he turns it into a memory by only choosing to accent several key things. Rather, the smaller details are mentioned, whereas the overall picture is generally either excluded, or only concisely mentioned. For example, it briefly states that the narrator's mother is leaving, but then goes into the finer details of the "blouses torn from their hangers" and the "crazy shouting" between the mother and father (11-14). Later, he mentions the "blur of perfume" from the mother smashing bottles, a minute detail which creates a more striking reality in the situation. Since the situation is a memory, the actual imagery has the qualities that a memory would. Most people do not remember things exactly, and often there will be one or two specific details that are more easily remembered than other parts of the situation. The narrator did not hear the specific words of the shouting, and therefore only stated it vaguely, but somehow remembered the mother repeating the name of the father (28). Shortly, the mother is sobbing amidst the clothing she has strewn from her trunk earlier, and the narrator uses vivid metaphor to enforce this imagery by calling the skirts "bright islands" (29). However, the true worth of this piece is measured by the way that the poet skillfully includes and intertwines the story of the young boy with the story of the narrator.

Within the world of the young boy, who is lost within a cavern, the poet uses grave symbolism and imagery to show the desperate situation. He sets up the situation by stating that the boy is lost amongst a maze-like cavern filling with water. Then, he states a simple series of rhetorical questions to state that he does not know whether or not the boy will survive. However, the diction he uses to describe the two choices clearly has connotation. For instance, he asks whether the boy will "float" to safety, something which implies lightness and a lack of suffering. On the other end of the spectrum, he asks whether the boy will "somersault forever in an underground black river," a question which holds grave power and implies, perhaps not death, but a lack of escape from the situation. The narrator wished to know the answer very much, but was interrupted in his reading by his mother throwing clothes into the trunk. However, as if this didn't happen at all, he continues telling the story of the boy, who cannot see where he is and lights a match. Then, once again, the story is interrupted by the arguing within the real world. Suddenly, the boy's situation has worsened, for he cannot breathe and, though he wishes for help, can find none. The narrator believes that he could be this source of help. The story never ends, however, because the narrator never finishes it. He assumes that perhaps the boy is still beneath the earth, searching for escape from the water, even though he would be presumably dead. The imagery of a young boy searching for that "pencil thin" light shows the hopelessness of his situation, and yet the fact that, throughout centuries he still cries for the narrator, creates an eerie surrealism to the scene overall. The poet uses the imagery in a powerful way to convey the different emotions of the boy within the cavern, and the boy in the real world.

Conclusively, the boy in the cavern and the boy in the real world must be somehow related. Due to the choppy nature of the poem, in which the narrative skips over between the two stories, it appears evident that the young boy calling for help is the victim of the arguments of the parents in the real world.

This young boy, lost within the cavern, living precariously, is actually the very innocence of the narrator. The narrator has fallen victim to the arguments of his parents and though he himself never expresses fear or remorse, it is his complete innocence which is hurt through the process, being buried underneath the callous facade that such a situation creates in a developing child. Therefore, the imagery that the narrator uses is a way to show how this boy was affected by the problems in his family life.

You Rate It!

1. How thorough a job did the student do in linking the predicament of the lost boy to the domestic situation of the speaker?

   _____

   _____

   _____

   _____

2. What images and/or symbols did the student identify? How effective were they in linking the predicaments of the two boys?

   _____

   _____

   _____

   _____

3. How well-organized and fluent was the student's paper? Was the student's overall argument a persuasive one?

   _____

   _____

   _____

   _____

4. On a 0-9 scale, how would you rate this response? Explain why.

   _____

   _____

   _____

   _____

Sample Student Essay Three

In poem "The Mystery of the Caves," Michael Waters explores the "caves" of his own childhood, specifically a painful and repressed memory involving a fight between his parents. Waters uses symbols that link his self-exploration to a young boy lost in a cave, as well as images that illustrate the nature of his domestic situation and involve the reader in an exploration of his past.

Waters uses symbolism as an alternative to explaining to the reader that he was exploring his mind to uncover the past. He describes his memory as an enormous, complex "labyrinth" which suggests that the memory that he describes shortly thereafter could have been easily lost and never recovered. Later in the poem Waters refers to a "passage" that would lead him to safety or the overcoming of this difficult memory. This connects to the symbolic conveyance of his mind and memory as a labyrinth of caves. In line 6, Waters wonders if the boy would "float upward towards the light," therefore reach salvation and go beyond the pain of the memory he has uncovered. On the following line the author suggests that perhaps the boy will instead "somersault forever in an underground black river". Waters deliberately uses the color black to convey a feeling of despair, or a loss of hope. In line 25, the author remembers himself as a boy and calls himself "small". The word works in many ways illustrating that he is physically young, but also demonstrating how insignificant he felt, and how though he wanted to help his mother he felt helpless. In the stanza preceding this line, the author suggests that as the memory slowly exposed itself piece by piece, the "boy" in the labyrinth of Waters' mind (Waters) began to suffocate or attempt to re-repress the remaining parts of the memory.

Waters uses a vast array of imagery to portray to the reader his domestic situation, as well as attempt to draw the readers further into their own pasts as he delves into his. The first taste of imagery in the poem is at the end of the first stanza, when he describes the caverns as "filling stratum by stratum with water." This suggests his overwhelming feeling of suffocation and his feeling that he must run quickly away from the danger of losing himself in the caves of his past. In the third and fourth stanzas, Waters vividly describes the way the clothes are scattered as his mother leaves "again". By focusing on the blouses "torn from their hangers" as well as the lid of the trunk "thrown open," Waters paints the reader a mental picture of the chaotic nature of his domestic situation. In line 19, Waters tells the reader of a "blur of perfume," this line serving to incite the reader to remember his own mothers' perfume, and therefore capture the reader's attention on a more personal level. This level of closeness that Waters gains with the reader allows the reader to follow him more intimately through his past.

The final two stanzas of the poem deliver to the reader Waters' emotions and true feeling that, while he explores the memories of his past, he will never uncover them all.

You Rate It!

1. How thorough a job did the student do in linking the predicament of the lost boy to the domestic situation of the speaker?

_____

_____

_____

_____

2. What images and/or symbols did the student identify? How effective were they in linking the predicaments of the two boys?

_____

_____

_____

_____

3. How well-organized and fluent was the student's paper? Was the student's overall argument a persuasive one?

_____

_____

_____

_____

4. On a 0-9 scale, how would you rate this response? Explain why.

_____

_____

_____

_____

Author's Response to Sample Student Essays on Michael Waters' "The Mystery of the Caves"

Sample Student Essay One:

This paper offers a very solid response to the prompt. The student immediately associates the boy's "disarrayed and disoriented situation" to that of the boy "lost among the crevices of the earth." He cites images of "torn clothes and trunks torn open" to show the turbulence of the marriage and connects "the chaotic house to a labyrinth of caverns." The student focuses upon the word "somersault" to connect the tumbling of the underground boy with his own sense of upheaval. He also links the "pencil of light" with his own search for light in a "dark and dismal childhood." The student's vocabulary ("vociferous," "confounding," "analogous") is sophisticated, and the paper itself has good unity and fluency, though further development would have yielded a higher score.

Author's Score: low 7

Sample Student Essay Two:

Though the second student's response is significantly longer, it is not necessarily better. This paper, while generally competent in both compositional skill and analytical insight, lacks the fluency of the previous response in conveying the connection between the situations of the two boys. Though not overtly addressing the symbolic, it does a pretty thorough job with the imagery, suggesting that the selectivity of detail by the speaker helps create the sense of blurred childhood memory that marks the poem. Though it is clear that the writer understands the link between the speaker and the boy trapped in the underground cavern, the paper is tarnished in spots by redundant language ("Then, he states a simple series of rhetorical questions to state [. . .]"), grammatical incorrectness ("her and the father"), and less than optimal word choice ("callous facade"). That said, this response is thorough and perceptive enough to nudge its way into the upper-half.

Author's Score: 6

Sample Student Essay Three:

This paper provides a useful reminder of the great variety that can exist within a given score point. In many ways this paper has elements of both of the previous ones, showing some of the strength of insight of the first and some of the weakness of language of the second. For much of the essay the writer takes a one-lane road—the idea of repressed memory—but travels down it in occasionally profound ways. His idea that the speaker's "mind and memory [are] a labyrinth of caves" is a good one as is his suggestion that the speaker may be trying to suppress this memory. The writer also scores well with his claim that the rapidly rising cave-waters symbolize the speaker's "overwhelming feeling of suffocation and his feeling that he must run quickly away from the danger of losing himself in the caves of his past." His use of the clothes and opened trunk to reflect the "chaotic nature of the domestic situation" and his seeing the black river as reflecting "despair" are also commendable. While there are some clumsy constructions ("symbolic conveyance," "re-repress") that detract from the fluency of the essay, the idea was a good one that the student sustained well enough to earn the benefit of the doubt.

Author's Score: 7

Explication of Free-Response Question Two: From Thomas Hardy's *Jude the Obscure*

The second selection, a prose passage from Thomas Hardy's 1895 novel *Jude the Obscure*, offers a very different literary challenge. In this episode Sue Brideshead, Jude's desired but inaccessible beloved, having returned to Marygreen for the funeral of Jude's aunt, spends the night at a neighboring widow's cottage in painful proximity to the house in which Jude is staying. During a mutually sleepless night—Sue's due to her unhappy marriage, Jude's to the frustration of unrequited love—they are each further discomfited by the occasional cry of a hare caught by the leg in a trap. As their task, students were asked to "discuss how the literary elements of the passage reveal[ed] the nature and predicament of both Jude and Sue."

The best responses to this question will recognize the symbol (or metaphor) of the trapped rabbit and relate it to Sue's unhappy wedlock. Sue's protestation that "'They ought not to be allowed to set these steel traps, ought they!'" (lines 26-27) clearly functions on both literal and figurative levels. The passage's final paragraph, in which Sue poignantly declares marriage "'a tragedy artificially manufactured for people who in a natural state would find relief in parting!...'" (lines 40-41), confirms the sense of entrapment she feels in her marriage to Phillotson (her husband in the novel). Though Sue bemoans her naïveté in so hastily committing to marriage, calling herself "'idiotic'" and a "'fool'" (lines 42-43), like Kate Chopin's protagonist Edna Pontellier she assumes the voice of *all* women bound to unhappy relationships by the strict moral conventions of the time: "'I daresay it happens to lots of women; only they submit, and I kick [. . .] When people of a later age look back upon the barbarous customs and superstitions of the times that we have the unhappiness to live in, what will they say!' [. . .]'" (lines 44-46). Moreover, she utters (for the time, at least) a heretical comment when she claims "'one ought to be allowed to undo what one has done so ignorantly!'" (lines 43-44). Figuratively, the narrator's graphic description of the trapped rabbit—if a 'bad catch' its hind leg-bone stripped of flesh; if a 'good catch' its foreleg bone shattered and its limbs ripped in two by its desperate efforts to escape—delineates an unhappy marriage as a tortuous, trapped existence; a *huit clos*, as Sartre would have it, from which the only liberation is death.

In terms of Jude the passage provides very different opportunities. For one he appears in a subordinate position in the episode, an impotent Romeo cloaked by the shadows outside the casement of Sue's window. Much as he'd saved the lives of earthworms as a child, he alleviates the concern Sue feels for the trapped rabbit by knocking it on the head and humanely ending its misery; however, he can do nothing to quell the misery of her marriage (other than serve as a confidant for her complaints) or to relieve the frustration and misery that he himself endures. (A Freudian criticism might make much of the fact that only Sue's upper half is revealed by the window). In an ironically romantic moment—in which Sue "let[s] go of the casement stay and put[s] her hand upon his, her moonlit face regarding him wistfully" (lines 29-30)—Jude finds, like the teacher mourning his dead student in Theodore Roethke's "Elegy for Jane," that he has "no rights in this matter, / Neither father nor lover."

The overall passage has a fatalistic tone, suggesting that, despite Cassius' confident avowal, the fault *is* indeed in the stars, not ourselves—or, if not, in the institutions and codes of conduct that circumscribe behavior and prevent individuals from pursuing their true desires. The astute student should see that both Jude and Sue are trapped "behind walls equally lonely and disheartened" (lines 2-3), and that in a bitterly ironic way their only avenue of escape is death.

This question has been reprinted for your convenience.

<u>Question Two</u>

(Suggested time—40 minutes. This question counts as one-third of the total essay section score.)

Read the following passage carefully. Then, in a well-organized essay, discuss how the literary elements of the passage reveal the nature and predicament of both Jude and Sue. In your essay, you may wish to consider such things as diction, choice of detail, symbolism, and tone.

In the lonely room of his aunt's house Jude sat watching the cottage of the Widow Edlin as it disappeared behind the night shade. He knew that Sue was sitting within its walls equally lonely and disheartened; and again questioned his devotional model that all was for the best.

He retired to rest early, but his sleep was fitful from the sense that Sue was so near at hand. At
(5)   some time near two o'clock, when he was beginning to sleep more soundly, he was aroused by a shrill squeak that had been familiar enough to him when he lived regularly at Marygreen. It was the cry of a rabbit caught in a gin. As was the little creature's habit, it did not soon repeat its cry; and probably would not do so more than once or twice; but would remain bearing its torture to the morrow, when the trapper would come back and knock it on the head.

(10)   He who in his childhood had saved the lives of the earthworms now began to picture the agonies of the rabbit from its lacerated leg. If it were a 'bad catch' by the hind-leg, the animal would tug during the ensuing six hours till the iron teeth of the trap had stripped the leg-bone of its flesh, when, should a weak-springed instrument enable it to escape, it would die in the field from the mortification of the limb. If it were a 'good catch,' namely, by the fore-leg, the bone would be broken, and the limb nearly torn in
(15)   two in attempts at an impossible escape.

Almost half-an-hour passed, and the rabbit repeated its cry. Jude could rest no longer till he had put it out of his pain, so dressing himself quickly he descended, and by the light of the moon went across the green in the direction of the sound. He reached the hedge bordering the widow's garden, when he stood still. The faint click of the trap as dragged about by the writhing animal guided him now, and
(20)   reaching the spot he struck the rabbit on the back of the neck with the side of his palm, and it stretched itself out dead.

He was turning away when he saw a woman looking out of the open casement at a window on the ground floor of the adjacent cottage. 'Jude!' said a voice timidly—Sue's voice. 'It is you—is it not?'

'Yes, dear!'

(25)   'I haven't been able to sleep at all, and then I heard the rabbit, and couldn't help thinking of what it suffered, till I felt I must come down and kill it! But I am so glad you got there first....They ought not to be allowed to set these steel traps, ought they!'

Jude had reached the window, which was quite a low one, so that she was visible down to her waist. She let go of the casement stay and put her hand upon his, her moonlit face regarding him
(30)   wistfully.

'Did it keep you awake?' he said.

'No—I was awake.'

'How was that?'

'O, you know—now! I know you, with your religious doctrines, think that a married woman in
(35)   the trouble of a kind like mine commits a mortal sin in making a man the confidant of it, as I did you. I wish I hadn't, now!' [. . . .].

'I wish you were happy, whatever I may be!'

'I *can't* be! So few could enter into my feeling—they would say 'twas my fanciful fastidiousness, or something of that sort, and condemn me....It is none of the natural tragedies of love that's love's usual
(40)   tragedy in civilized life, but a tragedy artificially manufactured for people who in a natural state would find relief in parting!....Jude, before I married him I had never thought out fully what marriage meant, even though I knew. It was idiotic of me—there was no excuse. I was old enough, and I thought I was very experienced. So I rushed on...with all the cock-sureness of the fool that I was!...I am certain one ought to be allowed to undo what one has done so ignorantly! I daresay it happens to lots of women; only
(45)   they submit, and I kick....When people of a later age look back upon the barbarous customs and superstitions of the times that we have the unhappiness to live in, what *will* they say!' [. . . .].

Scoring Rubric for Free-Response Question Two: From Thomas Hardy's *Jude the Obscure*

8-9 These papers feature not only a keen understanding of how the literary elements of the passage reveal the nature and predicament of both Jude and Sue, but also a clear perception as to how the author uses literary elements such as diction, choice of detail, symbolism, and tone to reveal it. Well-conceived, well-developed, and well-organized, these papers are marked by frequent and accurate references to the text, by an admirable ability to synthesize thought, and by a mature control over the elements of composition.

6-7 These essays exhibit a solid understanding of the nature and predicament of both Jude and Sue, but are less adept at showing how the author uses literary elements such as diction, choice of detail, symbolism, and tone to reveal it. This may be due to inconsistencies in textual understanding, to less persuasive and/or less frequent references to the text, and/or to less control over the elements of composition. Though these essays reflect their writers' abilities to convey their points clearly, they feature less fluency, development or cogency than 9-8 papers.

5 These papers respond to the question on the passage from *Jude the Obscure* in superficial, formulaic, inconsistent or insufficiently supported ways. They may rely primarily on paraphrase, but may still convey an implicit understanding of the passage and the task. The papers are generally written in a satisfactory manner, with occasional errors in composition or mechanics that do not impede the reader's understanding. Nevertheless, these essays lack the organization, persuasiveness and development of upper-half papers.

3-4 These lower-half essays generally suggest an incomplete or overly simplistic understanding of the passage or task, or an inability to comprehend the nature and predicament of both Jude and Sue and/or how the author uses literary elements to reveal it. Their arguments are often characterized by a misreading of the text, a failure to provide support from the text, or an insufficient control over the elements of composition. In some instances they may consist entirely of paraphrase and/or feature acute problems in organization, clarity, fluency or development.

1-2 These essays compound the shortcomings of 3-4 papers. They often contain many serious and distracting errors in grammar or mechanics that preclude any successful response to the prompt. Though these essays may attempt to show how the author uses literary elements to reveal the nature and predicament of both Jude and Sue, they are severely limited by deficiencies in organization, clarity, fluency or development.

0 Papers scored a zero make no more than a passing reference to the task.

— Papers given this score offer a blank or totally off-topic response.

Sample Student Essay One

Women's role in society constantly varies from time period to time period and from culture to culture. In some cases, the women lead in the community, while in others they are subjected to subservient and lesser roles. Regardless of their position, however, there has always been a relationship that exists between man and woman. Love is a constant throughout, independent of the marital status that women retain. However, oftentimes the social restrictions of the culture put obstacles in the way of relations between people. Here, the love of Jude and Sue is held captive by the shadow of the women's position in their society. Sue is not allowed to break through the bonds of her marriage, and therefore Jude is not allowed to be with her. Their struggle against the social decorum of the time period is depicted through the symbolism of the rabbit along with the desperate tone of the piece, which is backed by the author's choice of detail.

The symbolism of the rabbit is a key part of the narrative. Its pain and suffering is representative of the trials and tribulations that are brought up in Jude and Sue's predicament. The piece begins at night with Jude's hearing the cry of a trapped rabbit, ensnared by a trapper and left to its agony and suffering until the next morning. At the same time, Jude had been thinking of Sue alone in the house across the way and also trapped, only in her case by an unhappy marriage deemed unbreakable by the social standards of the day. Jude feels the urge to save the rabbit, just as he wishes he could save Sue. He ponders the fate of the rabbit, knowing that if it were a "bad catch" it would suffer far more than if it were a "good catch". Either way, however, its pain would be immense. This exemplifies the pain felt by Sue and the women of other unhappy marriages during the time. Fighting to get away into another life only leads to the anguish that comes from the automatic failure of an uphill battle to escape. Should a "weak-springed instrument" (being the trap of the rabbit or the broken marriage of the woman) enable one to escape, one is no better off. For the rabbit, the "wound" is too deep and the rabbit surely will die. For Sue, the social impact would be too great and her reputation would be ruined. There is, as proven through the symbolism of the rabbit, often no escape from the binds of cultural decorum.

The story progresses to say that Jude kills the rabbit to put it out of its misery. The only way for the animal to be saved is death as is there no way for the love of Sue and Jude to be preserved in a relationship. Sue comments at the end of the piece that "I daresay it happens to lots of women; only they submit, and I kick". While she knows that fake happiness is forced on other women as well, she sees that they simply give in to the burden and do not fight back. She may "kick," but there is no escaping "what marriage [means]": permanent unity.

The tone of this essay also depicts the burdens placed on Sue and Jude's relationship. Its wistfulness shows the longing of the two lovers and is depicted through the choice of detail the author employs. In the beginning, the author sets the scene by placing Jude in a "lonely room" from which he stares out the window towards Sue's house as it "disappeared behind the night shade." One can imagine the mist rising and the evanescence of the house, its fading fast. Jude watches it vanish, questioning whether or not "his devotional model was all for the best." Why does the author choose to include this detail? It supports the theme by adding a sense of distress and struggle. The house is disappearing quickly, and Jude must be content to watch it go, knowing he can do nothing but see his love fade into the shadows. This detail and imagery supports the idea of the social barrier placed on relationships of the time period, and depicts the power that they have over his life.

A second detail that sets the tone of the narrative is the author's use of time. Jude says that it takes a gruesome total of six hours for the "iron teeth of the trap [to strip] the leg bone [of the rabbit] of its flesh." This graphic piece adds even further to the desperate tone of the story. It shows the epic nature of the struggle to overcome a trap, be it the trap of the hunter or the trap of marriage. Finally, the detail used in the description of the window from which Sue calls out to Jude also adds to the tone. When Jude walks over to the window, "which is quite a low one, so that [Sue] was visible down to her waist," he is so near to her, and yet the one little wall makes them so far apart. They may be able to get close to each other emotionally, but they will never be able to come together all of the way due to Sue's inability to escape her marriage. Their love is a desperate and wishful situation that is blocked by the barrier of social culture.

By the end of this narrative, one is left with a clear image of the time period and its effect on the lives of Sue and Jude. Neither of them, though so in love, is able to break through the wall of propriety and begin a true relationship together. This feeling of distress and hopelessness is portrayed through the symbolism of the rabbit and the tone set by the choice of detail throughout the piece.

You Rate It!

1. How thorough a job did the student do in establishing the nature and predicament of both Jude and Sue?

_____

_____

_____

_____

2. What literary elements did the student identify? How well did they relate these to the situations of the two characters?

_____

_____

_____

_____

3. How well-organized and fluent was the student's paper? Was the student's overall argument a persuasive one?

_____

_____

_____

_____

4. On a 0-9 scale, how would you rate this response? Explain why.

_____

_____

_____

_____

Sample Student Essay Two

In works of prose, authors use multiple literary tools to convey the same aspect of the plot. As the story line progresses, both Jude and Sue are approached from many different angles in the passage. To convey their natures and predicaments, the author utilizes tone, symbolism, and diction.

In the passage, the tone evolves to convey deeper meaning behind the characters and their situations. The beginning of the passage is dark, confined and lonely. Night isolates Jude from the world around him, hoping to find solace, but instead finding himself restless. This restless tone is conveyed through the rapid, staggered rhetoric. The rabbit's cries are a shrill invasion of the isolation which Jude has forced upon himself. As the passage progresses, this tone evolves and is replaced by a softer attitude. Once the rabbit, a source of anxiety in the beginning of the story, is dead, Jude encounters Sue. The isolation and depressed tone are replaced by touch and intimacy as Sue comes into the story. The change in tone conveys Jude's feelings. Although the dialogue and narration insist on the contrary, the change in tone which Sue's entrance imparts on the story illustrates the love which Jude feels for Sue. In turn, this tone contrasts Jude's determination to maintain the separation from Sue which the darkness and walls of their homes provide.

The rabbit is used as a symbol in the passage to illustrate the conflict which both characters face and the nature in which they deal with these issues. The rabbit's cries of pain arouse both Jude and Sue, who come to its aid. This is similar to Sue and Jude's predicament; Sue, unhappy in her marriage, reached out to Jude for help. This put him in a socially compromising position, since to be the confidant of such information was against the "barbarous customs and superstitions" of the time. In turn, Jude forced himself to separate from Sue, who brought happiness into his life, leaving him painfully isolated. By helping the rabbit, Jude encountered Sue, making it harder to resist and maintain the distance he knew was needed between them. The rabbit, like Sue, was caught in a "steel trap;" Sue's trap was marriage, which society had set down as binding as steel. Jude knew he could not open the trap and let the rabbit go free, as he would have liked; the only solution was to put it out of its misery. Like the rabbit caught in the steel trap, Sue reached out to Jude, but Jude had no way to help her out except to let their relationship die.

Diction plays an enormous role in conveying the meaning behind the passage. In order to draw the parallel between the rabbit and Sue, Sue describes her decision to end her marriage as a "kick" instead of a submission, like most other women, to her unhappiness. This animal-like language draws a connection to the rabbit, as the human-like qualities given to the rabbit connect to Sue. The rabbit is given feeling through the language used to describe its pain; "agonies", "torture", and "mortification". Diction is also used to convey the pain of the separation between Jude and Sue. At the beginning of the passage, Sue is described as sitting "within the walls" of the house. Walls, unlike homes, have no way of escape, and do not provide the freedom of a home. The house disappears in the darkness, leaving the sentiment that it still exists among the darkness behind. The predicament is illuminated using this language.

Although complex, the predicament in the passage is understood through the literary elements used to convey it. Jude, although he understands that he must separate himself from Sue, is not willing to do so, and Sue is not willing to give up on the possibility of living out her life away from the unhappiness of her marriage. The use of tone, symbolism, and diction, all contribute to this understanding.

You Rate It!

1. How thorough a job did the student do in establishing the nature and predicament of both Jude and Sue?

_____

_____

_____

_____

2. What literary elements did the student identify? How well did they relate these to the situations of the two characters?

_____

_____

_____

_____

3. How well-organized and fluent was the student's paper? Was the student's overall argument a persuasive one?

_____

_____

_____

_____

4. On a 0-9 scale, how would you rate this response? Explain why.

_____

_____

_____

_____

Sample Student Essay Three

In an excerpt from Thomas Hardy's book <u>Jude the Obscure</u>, the author uses several literary elements to highlight the innocent, kindly nature, and trapped, yet familiar predicament of the protagonist, Jude, and his cousin/sweetheart Sue. These literary elements include the symbolism of the captured rabbit, the repetition of certain meaningful words, and the tone of the piece, which is largely represented through the imprisoning but familiar setting.

The captured rabbit is quite obviously strongly symbolic of both the nature and predicament of Jude and Sue. Both characters are caught in a marital trap as strong, for them, as any rabbit gin of iron teeth. Nothing that they do can free them of the religious bonds of matrimony, just as none of the suffering the rabbit will put itself though can break its trap. But similarly, neither of them can submit to the fate they have been sentenced to. The rabbit will keep struggling until it kills itself, and Jude and Sue will continue to torment themselves with ideas of what could have been and make their married (or separated) lives tortured because of an inability to separate from their past experiences and give in to the present.

The repetition of words offers a similar representation of the situation. Repeating certain words, such as "lonely" and "cry", emphasizes the feelings of the characters. All three characters in the excerpt are alone in their own situation. Jude cannot properly be with Sue, and all that he can do for the rabbit is send it off to another world. Yet no physical barriers separate them. He can still hear the rabbit's cry and feel Sue's loneliness. Therefore, the repetition emphasizes not what is there, but what is missing. The characters can feel one another's pain and try to innocently and openly remedy it, but cannot get past the physical because of the mental barriers in their way.

The tone of Hardy's excerpt is just as depressing as the meaning of the repetition. It is largely represented by the setting; a setting of cold, darkness and confinement. It is ominous, emphasizing the loneliness of the characters, the inefficiency and dimness of the moonlight, and yet the familiarity of the setting and situation. Jude, Sue, and even the rabbit are unfortunate. It is the night after a funeral and by no fault of their own beyond naivete and lack of judgment, they are being besieged with more death and sorrow. But perhaps the most ironic turn of events is that every bit of their predicament is so predictable and familiar, even to them. The entire scene occurs in their home village, surrounding events such as death, rabbit catching, and the church sanctity of divorce (or lack thereof) which had always been stable, unmoving pillars in their lives. The very familiarity of the setting gives the passage a tone of reliability and dependence. This is the way things are, the way life goes. But the night and the loneliness brought in with it bring in the other aspect. Despite the familiarity of their situation, despite the innocence of their original intentions, they are part of a very dire predicament which can never lead to complete happiness as long as they continue to adhere to the religious values with which they were raised from childhood.

Thomas Hardy manages to say a lot in his excerpt from <u>Jude the Obscure</u>, using various literary elements such as symbolism, repetition, and tone/setting. He portrays the nature of his main characters, Jude and Sue, as well as the difficulties they face in their feelings for each other, combined with their positions in life. He shows how neither can be happy in their confined positions, but yet none of the past can be changed, just as the rabbit will never be able to escape the iron jaws of its trap unharmed.

You Rate It!

1. How thorough a job did the student do in establishing the nature and predicament of both Jude and Sue?

_____

_____

_____

_____

2. What literary elements did the student identify? How well did they relate these to the situations of the two characters?

_____

_____

_____

_____

3. How well-organized and fluent was the student's paper? Was the student's overall argument a persuasive one?

_____

_____

_____

_____

4. On a 0-9 scale, how would you rate this response? Explain why.

_____

_____

_____

_____

Author's Response to Sample Student Essays on *Jude the Obscure*

Sample Student Essay One:

While not exemplifying the smoothest writing, this paper responds to the prompt with thoroughness and accuracy. It recognizes the analogous relationship between the rabbit caught in the trap and Sue's entrapment in her loveless marriage. Moreover, it endeavors with some measure of success to connect Sue's plight to the position of all women in that time period, perceptively alluding to "social restrictions" and "the binds of cultural decorum." It notices the bleak irony shared by women and the rabbit, how "Fighting to get away into another life only leads to the anguish that comes from the automatic failure of an uphill battle to escape." It somewhat surprisingly focuses on the widow's house being obscured by nightfall, noting how "Jude must be content to watch it go, knowing he can do nothing but see his love fade into the shadows." It also does something unique in its focus on the long time that the rabbit has to endure its agony, claiming that "It shows the epic nature of the struggle to overcome a trap, be it the trap of the hunter or the trap of marriage." The writer further notices the irony of Jude's proximity to Sue, how though separated only by a low wall, "Their love is a desperate and wishful situation that is blocked by the barrier of social culture." Though tainted in spots by rough syntax, this is a case where one must reward the writer for what he or she did well, which was substantial

Author's Score: 8

Sample Student Essay Two:

The second student sample is a bit problematic. The writer of this essay is not without insight. The student perceives the connection between Sue and the trapped rabbit, makes some accurate observations about the "dark, confined, and lonely" tone of the passage, recognizes Jude's impotence in terms of being able to effect any change in Sue's marriage, and uses the passage's diction to further cement the connection between Sue and the entrapped hare. At the same time, the essay's introductory paragraph does not provide clear direction, the organization of the essay seems rather random, and the syntax (e.g., "Night isolates Jude from the world around him, hoping to find solace, but instead finding himself restless.") suffers occasional lapses. In this case, though the thought propels this into the upper-half, the compositional shortcomings deter it from rising very far in it.

Author's Score: 6

Sample Student Essay Three:

The third student essay also is a bit inconsistent. Its opening paragraph, which offers the carefully laid out trinity of "the symbolism of the captured rabbit, the repetition of certain meaningful words, and the tone of the piece [. . .]", also is a bit muddled by cumbersome phrases such as "the imprisoning but familiar setting." A sentence such as "Nothing that they do can free them of the religious bonds of matrimony, just as none of the suffering the rabbit will put itself though can break its trap," makes it seem that the student thinks Jude and Sue are married. This confusion is further abetted by sentences such as "The rabbit will keep struggling until it kills itself, and Jude and Sue will continue to torment themselves with ideas of what could have been and make their married (or separated) lives tortured because of an inability to separate from their past experiences and give in to the present." The writer scores some points with his discussion of diction, but is clearly off-target in his claim that "no physical barriers separate them." Though the discussion of tone and setting at first seems promising, muddled sentences, such as

"The entire scene occurs in their home village, surrounding events such as death, rabbit catching, and the church sanctity of divorce (or lack thereof) which had always been stable, unmoving pillars in their lives," hinder comprehension of the writer's point. Though having too much analysis for it to be sentenced to the lower half, the failure to maintain a clear, fluent argument keeps this from being promoted into the upper one.

Author's Score: 5

Explication of Free-Response Question Three: An Estranged Character

The final free-response task in Sample Examination One asked students to select a character who "gradually becomes estranged from society due to some aspect of his/her nature or convictions, an estrangement that may have damaging consequences either for the individual or for the society itself." After identifying such a character, students were asked to write an essay in which they "indicate[d] the impetus behind the estrangement and the damaging effects this alienation [had] upon the individual or the society around him."

Finding a character who is estranged should not have proved too difficult for students since the causes of estrangement—race, creed, gender, political belief or action, sexual orientation, physical appearance, to name a few—provide a wide range of possibilities. For example, students could delve into Greek tragedy to show how Medea—brought to Greece from her homeland by Jason who, having fathered two children with her, abandons her to marry the king's daughter—feels isolated and alone; or how Antigone's bold decision to defy Creon's edict and bury her brother Polynices makes her, by the king's decree, an enemy of the state. Or students might look at how physically deformed characters such as Pomerantz's "elephant man," Rostand's Cyrano, and Flannery O'Connor's grotesque Hazel Motes are ostracized by the community around them. The strong feminine convictions of Chopin's Edna Pontellier or Ibsen's Nora and Hedda Gabler; the political stance of Thomas More in *A Man for All Seasons*, or the religious conviction (albeit an unsteady one) of the whisky priest in *The Power & the Glory*; even Bartleby's exasperating "I prefer not to" provide excellent examples of texts and characters that would answer the question successfully.

As to the damaging effects this estrangement has upon the individual and/or the society around him, in some cases the individual is killed or elects suicide, in others he is confined to a prison or sanatorium. In more positive instances, such as in *On the Road* or *The Scarlet Letter*, the individuals blissfully revel in their estrangement or, by their good works, are gradually accepted back into society, though these seem to be exceptional cases. My expectation is that students should enjoy this question and have little difficulty finding an appropriate work with which to respond to it.

This question has been reprinted for your convenience.

<u>Question Three</u>

(Suggested time—40 minutes. This question counts as one-third of the total essay section score.)

Oftentimes in literature a character gradually becomes estranged from society due to some aspect of his/her nature or convictions, an estrangement that may have damaging consequences either for the individual or for the society itself. Choose a novel or play which features a character who has become estranged from the society in which he/she exists. Then in a well-organized essay, indicate the impetus behind the estrangement and the damaging effects this alienation has upon the individual or the society around him/her. You may choose from the list below or use another novel or play of recognized literary merit.

The Catcher in the Rye	*Winesburg, Ohio*
Medea	*The Metamorphosis*
The Scarlet Letter	*The Power and the Glory*
Jude the Obscure	*A Man For All Seasons*
The Stranger	*Invisible Man*
The Elephant Man	*The Hairy Ape*
On the Road	*Oliver Twist*
Stranger in a Strange Land	*Hedda Gabler*
Wise Blood	*Down These Mean Streets*
The Hunchback of Notre Dame	*Hamlet*
A Portrait of the Artist as a Young Man	*Bartleby the Scrivener*
The Awakening	*Ethan Frome*

Scoring Rubric for Free-Response Question Three: An Estranged Character

8-9   These papers select an appropriately estranged character, provide clear reason(s) for his/her estrangement, and illustrate the effects that this isolation has upon the character and/or the society around him/her. Well-conceived, well-developed, and well-organized, these papers are marked by frequent and accurate references to the text, by an admirable ability to synthesize thought, and by a mature control over the elements of composition. Though not perfect, they clearly indicate the students' ability to repond to the prompt with fluency and cogency.

6-7   These essays select an appropriately estranged character, but are less adept at identifying the reasons for the estrangement or at showing how this isolation negatively impacts the character and/or the society around him/her. These papers may make less persuasive or less frequent references to the text, and/or illustrate less control over the elements of composition. Though these essays reflect their writers' abilities to convey their points clearly, they feature less fluency, development or cogency than 9-8 papers.

5   These papers respond to the question about an estranged character in superficial, formulaic, inconsistent or insufficiently supported ways. They may rely primarily on paraphrase, but may still convey an implicit understanding of the task. The papers are generally written in a satisfactory manner, with occasional errors in composition or mechanics that do not impede the reader's understanding. Nevertheless, these essays lack the organization, persuasiveness and development of upper-half papers.

3-4   These lower-half essays generally suggest an incomplete or overly simplistic understanding of the work or task, fail to provide convincing reasons for the estrangement, or fail to show how this isolation negatively impacts the character and/or the society around him/her. Their arguments are often characterized by a failure to provide support from the text, or an insufficient control over the elements of composition. In some instances they may consist entirely of paraphrase and/or feature acute problems in organization, clarity, fluency or development.

1-2   These essays compound the shortcomings of 3-4 papers. They often contain many serious and distracting errors in grammar or mechanics that preclude any successful response to the prompt. Though these essays may identify an estranged character, they are severely limited by deficiencies in organization, clarity, fluency or development.

0   Papers scored a zero make no more than a passing reference to the task.

—   Papers given this score offer a blank or totally off-topic response.

Sample Student Essay One

The human is a very social being. He desires to surround himself with others, thus making isolation a very severe punishment. In Nathaniel Hawthorne's The Scarlet Letter, *Hester Prynne is subject to this sentence after having a child with a man other than her husband. Immediately following the placement of a scarlet "A" on her chest, Hester becomes estranged from society and must be as self-sufficient as possible so she can survive. What becomes clear is the fact that isolation makes people yearn for company, as Hester does for Arthur Dimmesdale, the father of her child. However, her estrangement eventually destroys the souls of both her child and Dimmesdale, leaving Hester completely desolate.*

Hester becomes isolated after a scarlet letter is placed on her chest due to her adultery with another man. Hester is married to Roger Chillingworth, but they part for a few years as he travels and learns, planning to meet when this journey is complete. In this time, however, Hester falls in love with Reverend Arthur Dimmesdale and gives birth to a child soon after. When the public discovers this, she is punished by being forced to stand on a scaffold and drown in her own shame. Hester stands alone, holding her child, Pearl, for the Reverend is unable to confess with her at this time. By forcing her to wear the letter "A" for her crime of adultery, the society makes it obvious to any outsider that she has committed this crime, making the townspeople quick to mock her and ostracize her from society. On one particular occasion, young children find it appropriate to throw mud at the daughter, Pearl, and whisper about her and her mother. While it is Hester's choice to live on the outskirts of town after becoming an outcast, the public has almost rendered this necessary because the torment Hester would be forced to handle by living in town each day would be unbearable.

Hester's life changes drastically when she is estranged for she must use her independence and personal strength to survive even as she is losing everyone she loves. Hester supports herself by selling work she sews to the townspeople, but they by no means accept her because of this. Though this talent is usually respectable, Hester is still looked down upon and excluded even in her efforts to help the poor. This makes Hester desperate for affection, and although she does her best to support herself and raise her child, neither she nor Dimmesdale can live without each other completely. To satisfy this desire, Hester meets secretly with Dimmesdale in the woods at night. She is willing to risk the exposure of her secret to be with the person she loves, showing that no person can happily live alone but must find some way to be with others or fall apart. In Hester's case, however, Dimmesdale and Pearl internally deteriorate, leaving her unable to find affection.

Ironically, Dimmesdale becomes estranged as well despite his inability to admit to his crime. Although society does not know the truth and has yet to force him into isolation, he becomes so depressed that he physically deteriorates and is engrossed in his shame. He and Hester show a desire to reunite and break the isolation by planning an escape, but Dimmesdale has become so lonely from her absence that this becomes impossible. He finally realizes that he must be with her completely and admit his wrongdoing to the public, but by the time he confesses, his health has become so poor that he passes away.

While Hester's isolation is destroying Dimmesdale, it is also taking hold of Pearl with its incredible hands. Pearl is unable to communicate with other children and is therefore missing necessary social skills. Having no one her own age to play with, Pearl creates friends in her mind and focuses the rest of her energy on the one thing that sparks her attention: the scarlet letter on her mother's chest. Pearl begins to absorb its evil and to remind Hester daily that it represents her crime. Because of this, Hester becomes very distant from Pearl and at times thinks of her as maligned. Just like Hester, Pearl simply longs for love but the estrangement does not allow this, so her heart dies along with Hester's.

With estrangement comes a series of problems, including a longing for love that is not fulfilled. Hester's wrongdoings force her into isolation and make her stronger for a short while, but as her estrangement from society negatively affects both Dimmesdale and Pearl, she soon loses the two people that she loves and becomes even more isolated than at the start of the novel. Perhaps the human is too reliant on the warmth of others to save herself when others are absent, which brings a quick demise when others are gone.

You Rate It!

1. How thorough a job did the student do in identifying an estranged character and providing reason(s) for the character's estrangement?

_____

_____

_____

_____

2. How successfully did the student illustrate the damaging effects of the estrangement upon the individual or upon his/her society?

_____

_____

_____

_____

2. How well-organized and fluent was the student's paper? Was the student's overall argument a persuasive one?

_____

_____

_____

_____

4. On a 0-9 scale, how would you rate this response? Explain why.

_____

_____

_____

_____

Sample Student Essay Two

Offred, the protagonist of Margaret Atwood's <u>The Handmaid's Tale</u>, goes through a complete estrangement from what is considered proper society when her secular country turns into the strictly Christianized Republic of Gilead. The events surrounding this impetus, its direct effects on her, and the resulting mental damage suffered by Offred illustrate the harm a separation from society can cause, even if it is the society that is at fault for the incident.

The Republic of Gilead is formed through a complete change of societal values. Secularism is exchanged for religious extremism as women are returned to their primeval roles as mothers and housekeepers, and men to their positions of landlords and rulers, as well as strict guardsmen of biblical morality. As a wife to a man in his second marriage, this vault completely confounds Offred's original lifestyle. By no fault of her own beyond her gender and position in life, Offred is separated from her husband and daughter (as second marriages become illegitimatized), loses all her political rights, and is forced into the role of a walking uterus, or handmaid, for old and most often sterile married men. No longer allowed to read, write, or even talk without permission, Offred must find a way to meet her new surroundings.

When her life started Offred was a responsible, fun-loving woman. She worked, took care of her husband and daughter, and relaxed with her friends. She worried over little things, but was for the most part fairly content with her position in life. After the political upheaval and her acclimation to her new roles, Offred herself does not change. She has all of the same memories and potential. However, in reaction to her surroundings, aspects of her personality become more pointed. Her love of companionship turns into an intense loneliness as she craves the company she now lacks. Without friends or family Offred becomes more introspective and learns to focus on the happy past as opposed to the dismal present and even worse future. And as a result of this lack of camaraderie and bleak future, Offred becomes incredibly desperate for anything that will spice up her life. She takes risks, ranging from sexual encounters to forbidden conversations to underground parties, all for the sake of something to do and some vent for her pent-up emotions.

Unfortunately, such actions can be very dangerous in an authoritarian society. Any misstep holds grave potentials for Offred to be caught by immorality squadrons and sent off for torture or forced labor among nuclear waste, both of which result in an almost guaranteed death. And, of course, there is that misstep. A smudge of lipstick indicating her presence in a place she should not have visited leads to a van to take her away. Due to underground connections Offred is actually not immediately placed in captivity and may have actually escaped altogether, but nothing can change the effects of her experiences on herself. The intense boredom and longing for freedom can be heard in every paragraph of her narrative, as well as the yearning for the child and husband she had to leave behind. Whether Offred made it to freedom or not, her inability to fit into her new society caused her intense pain and grievances.

Offred, of <u>A Handmaid's Tale</u>, did not choose her society. It chose her to endure dictates which she could not believe in. And because of this separation from society, because Offred could not adapt to the ways of the Republic of Gilead, she suffered mental harm that no time could take away. She may have even been killed.

You Rate It!

1. How thorough a job did the student do in identifying an estranged character and providing reason(s) for the character's estrangement?

_____

_____

_____

_____

2. How successfully did the student illustrate the damaging effects of the estrangement upon the individual or upon his/her society?

_____

_____

_____

_____

2. How well-organized and fluent was the student's paper? Was the student's overall argument a persuasive one?

_____

_____

_____

_____

4. On a 0-9 scale, how would you rate this response? Explain why.

_____

_____

_____

_____

Sample Student Essay Three

The 1920s were a time of prosperity and of generally good humor; it was the age of flappers and jazz, in which almost everyone was partying. The "Lost Generation," disliking the actions of those around them, was a group of writers and poets, many of whom have written works of great caliber. One of the members of the small society was Ernest Hemingway, whose book <u>The Sun Also Rises</u> actually depicts the life of a member of society who does not fit in. Jake Barnes was a soldier in World War I who is now searching for his place in life, but despite his efforts, remains quite detached from the society around him.

Jake Barnes is excluded from the fun-loving society around him by his inescapable past and experiences. The efforts of World War I have maimed him not only physically, but have mentally separated him from the people around him. He feels that there is so much more to life now (aside from the silly chatter that people entertain themselves with) due to the things he has seen. Being in the war gave him the opportunity to see many horrific things that have changed his views of life significantly. Incapable of finding a place for himself in the United States when the war ended, the story begins with Jake living in Paris with several shallow friends and a former nurse with whom he was romantically involved during the War. Though he has friends now, he has a vast aperture to fill in his life due to what he has seen, and attempts to use alcohol to buffer the pain. Ironically, this only makes it worse for himself, and it is very often that Jake ends a day by crying himself to sleep. There doesn't seem to be anyone in the world that he can relate to, even the people who have been through it with him, because just as he tries to keep his sorrow hidden, so do those around him. There seems to be no escaping this consuming truth, that the war has permanently separated him from the rest of the world. All around him the world has remained the same jovial place, but within him a greater truth has been found about the nature of life and death. This knowledge has permanently separated Jake Barnes from the average society of the 1920s.

Due to physical injuries, Jake has also been separated not only from the society around him, but even from his intimate circle of friends. One of these friends was Lady Brett Ashley, who served as a nurse during the war. Her and Jake live a close life, and are often romantically involved with each other. However, Jake's infertility, caused by the war, will always keep her just out of reach. This is because she desires men in a more sexual than emotional way, because she feels that she cannot fill her life any other way. She uses sex and alcohol to take the edge off of life, hoping that eventually she can fill the emptiness that she herself feels. However, all of her affairs and second marriages cannot help her forget the fact that she loves Jake, and that he loves her to extreme ends. The two endlessly tell each other this truth, but will never truly be together because, though they share similar wounds, they are incurable by contact with their own kind. However, due to them, they are incapable of normal social interaction. Therefore, it would seem that they are stuck in a proverbial trench within themselves, battling to discover who out there is hiding truth with superficial prattle, and who truly has no knowledge to hide.

Jake continues to yearn for Brett throughout the novel, but receives no real confirmation of a relationship. Due to his injuries, they cannot have sex, something which is very important to Brett. And due to her fleeting personality, and her knack for travel, there is no possibility of a true romance. Kissing is as far as the couple can truly go—unsatisfying and passionate kissing that makes Jake mourn. The problem is that Jake has been separated from his world in more than just a mental way. He has been separated because of his wounds, and because of how they have impacted his romantic life.

Summarily, Jake Barnes is a desperate character in American literature. The horrors of war have forever detached him from the society that he wishes to be accepted in. There is no way for him to enjoy the "Roaring '20s," because he knows exactly what led to the gaiety of those around him: the death of many he cared for, and the injury of his very psyche. War has permanently corrupted his view of the world around him, and Jake is tied inexorably to the world in which he lives.

You Rate It!

1. How thorough a job did the student do in identifying an estranged character and providing reason(s) for the character's estrangement?

_____

_____

_____

_____

2. How successfully did the student illustrate the damaging effects of the estrangement upon the individual or upon his/her society?

_____

_____

_____

_____

2. How well-organized and fluent was the student's paper? Was the student's overall argument a persuasive one?

_____

_____

_____

_____

4. On a 0-9 scale, how would you rate this response? Explain why.

_____

_____

_____

_____

Author's Response to Sample Student Essays on An Estranged Character

Sample Student Essay One:

This competent and well-developed response chooses an appropriate character—Hester Prynne from Nathaniel Hawthorne's *The Scarlet Letter*—with which to respond to the prompt. The writer clearly identifies the reason for Hester's estrangement (adultery) and the immediate price she pays for it (ignominious exhibition on the scaffold, the stigma of the scarlet A, and ostracism from the Puritan community). Moreover, the writer pursues the effect of Hester's ostracism on the characters most dear to her, her lover Dimmesdale and her daughter Pearl, showing how the burden of his inability to confess mentally destroys the former, and how the taunts and meanness of the children in the community depress the latter. The author also examines Hester's acute loneliness, suggesting that "She is willing to risk the exposure of her secret to be with the person she loves [because] no person can happily live alone but must find some way to be with others or fall apart." The student's observation that, "Perhaps the human is too reliant on the warmth of others to save herself when others are absent, which brings a quick demise when others are gone," offers a sapient closing aphorism. While this essay lacks the compositional élan of the finest papers, it does an extremely thorough job of addressing all aspects of the question and is appropriately rewarded for doing so.

Author's Score: 8

Sample Student Essay Two:

The second sample essay also chooses an appropriate novel with which to answer the question—*The Handmaid's Tale* by Margaret Atwood. It notes key differences in that Offred, the novel's protagonist, is more victim than transgressor and that her ostracism is a result of political circumstances (in this case, a fictional takeover by religious conservatives who perceive women's primary role as childbearing). The writer tidily sums up the consequences of Offred's estrangement in the sentence "By no fault of her own beyond her gender and position in life, Offred is separated from her husband and daughter (as second marriages become illegitimatized), loses all her political rights, and is forced into the role of a walking uterus, or handmaid, for old and most often sterile married men." The student suggests the impact such isolation has upon Offred's nature when she observes how "as a result of this lack of camaraderie and bleak future Offred becomes incredibly desperate for anything that will spice up her life. She takes risks, ranging from sexual encounters to forbidden conversations to underground parties, all for the sake of something to do and some vent for her pent up emotions." The writer further observes that through these dangerous actions, Offred exposes herself to punishment, noting that "Any misstep holds grave potentials for Offred to be caught by immorality squadrons and sent off for torture or forced labor among nuclear waste, both of which result in an almost guaranteed death." This paper also responds well to the assigned task, though it on occasion too readily assumes that the reader is intimately familiar with the novel's plot and has occasional lapses in diction and phrasing ("vault;" "pointed;" "Offred must find a way to meet her new surroundings").

Author's Score: 7

Sample Student Essay Three:

The third sample essay also chooses a highly appropriate character—Jake Barnes of Ernest Hemingway's *The Sun Also Rises*. Though this essay takes awhile to get started (we are three paragraphs in before we learn that Jake's wartime injuries have left him impotent), it ultimately gets the job done as well, showing how Jake's infertility estranges him from the woman he loves (Brett Ashley) and from love itself. The writer also hints at the fact that Brett has her own emotional void and sagely observes how "The two endlessly tell each other this truth, but will never truly be together because, though they share similar wounds, they are incurable by contact with their own kind." Unlike the novels discussed in the previous two essays, the estrangement here is physical on two levels: the expatriate scene of post-World War I Paris, and Jake's inability to engage in sexual relations. Even so, the greater estrangement in Hemingway's novel is emotional since characters such as Jake, Brett and others that the writer does not mention cannot seem to connect to others in anything but the most meaningless ways. The student writer uses a wonderfully insightful turn-of-phrase when she writes "they are stuck in a proverbial trench within themselves, battling to discover who out there is hiding truth with superficial prattle, and who truly has no knowledge to hide." Though this essay has some moments of awkward syntax, it nevertheless remains a strong, upper-half paper.

Author's Score: 7

Sample Examination II

Questions 1-14. Refer to the following poem.

Any Woman to a Soldier

The day you march away—let the sun shine.
Let everything be blue and gold and fair,
Triumph of trumpets calling through bright air,
Flags slanting, flowers flaunting—not a sign
(5)   That the unbearable is now to bear,
      The day you march away.

The day you march away—this I have sworn,
No matter what comes after, that shall be
Hid secretly between my soul and me
(10)   As women hide the unborn—
You shall see brows like banners, lips that frame
Smiles, for the pride those lips have in your name.
You shall see soldiers in my eyes that day—
      That day, O soldier, when you march away.

(15)   The day you march away—cannot I guess?
There will be ranks and ranks, all leading on
To one white face, and then—the white face gone,
And nothing left but a gray emptiness—
Blurred moving masses, faceless, featureless—
(20)   The day you march away.

You cannot march away! However far,
Farther and faster still shall I have fled
Before you; and that moment when you land,
Voiceless, invisible, close at your hand
(25)   My heart shall smile, hearing the steady tread
      Of your faith-keeping feet.

First at the trenches I shall be to greet;
There's not a watch I shall not share with you;
But more—but most—there where for you the red,
(30)   Drenched, dreadful, splendid, sacrificial field lifts up
Inflexible demand,
      I will be there!

My hands shall hold the cup.
My hands beneath your head
(35)   Shall bear you—not the stretcher bearer's—through
All anguish of the dying and the dead;
With all your wounds I shall have ached and bled,

73

Waked, thirsted, starved, been fevered, gasped for breath,
Felt the death dew;
(40)   And you shall live, because my heart has said
To Death
That Death itself shall have no part in you!

—Grace Ellery Channing-Stetson

Grace Ellery Channing-Stetson, "Great Poems by American Women",
Dover Publications 1998

1. The appeal made by the speaker in stanza one is primarily prompted by her

   (A) patriotic zeal
   (B) unwillingness to face the reality of her beloved's departure
   (C) stoic defiance in the face of impending defeat
   (D) prescient fear of her beloved's possible death
   (E) determination to inspire the troops

2. Which of the following is NOT an accurate observation about the second stanza?

   (A) It reinforces the masked disappointment felt by the speaker in stanza one.
   (B) It compares the speaker's premonition to pregnancy.
   (C) It shifts from natural imagery to facial description.
   (D) It utilizes dashes to convey an important private thought.
   (E) It contains an overt statement about the speaker's opposition to war.

3. The rhetorical question in stanza three does all of the following EXCEPT

   (A) reveal the speaker's knowledge of the exact date of the army's departure
   (B) reflect the speaker's frustration in finding her beloved's face amid the marching ranks
   (C) suggest the transience of the speaker's and her beloved's parting moment
   (D) indicate the emotional void felt by the speaker upon her beloved's departure
   (E) imply the source of the speaker's intuition: the experience of all war-bereft women

4. The "one white face" (line 17) is most likely the face of

   (A) the speaker
   (B) the soldier
   (C) a commanding officer
   (D) death
   (E) God

5. The speaker stylistically complements the hasty and impersonal nature of her parting from her beloved through all of the following EXCEPT

   (A) the uniform anonymity of the marching ranks
   (B) a symbolic change in color
   (C) a series of adjectives that imply her fading consciousness of her beloved's appearance
   (D) onomatopoeic description of the marching feet
   (E) images of rapid movement

6. The primary difference between the fourth stanza and the previous three is the speaker's

   (A) sudden revelation of her acute emotional angst
   (B) obstinate refusal to accept her beloved's deployment
   (C) fanciful reverie that she will anticipate her beloved at the front line or in heaven
   (D) stalwart belief that he will return unharmed
   (E) fervent plea for her beloved to desert

7. The words "Voiceless, invisible" (line 24) come closest to modifying which of the following?

   (A) "I" (line 22)
   (B) "you" (line 23)
   (C) "moment" (line 23)
   (D) "heart" (line 25)
   (E) "feet" (line 26)

8. Lines 25-26, "My heart shall smile, hearing the steady tread / Of your faith-keeping feet," possibly suggest that the speaker is gratified that her beloved has done which of the following?

   I. Maintained his love for her.
  II. Returned home unharmed.
  III. Entered into heaven.

   (A) I only
   (B) III only
   (C) I and II
   (D) I and III
   (E) I, II, and III

9. In stanza five the speaker's stalwart faithfulness is enhanced by all of the following EXCEPT

   (A) an inversion that emphasizes an adverb
   (B) negation
   (C) implied metaphor
   (D) graphically descriptive adjectives
   (E) a climactic affirmation

10. The BEST interpretation of the word "Inflexible" (line 31) is

   (A) obstinate
   (B) intolerable
   (C) stringent
   (D) irrevocable
   (E) imperious

11. In the final two stanzas the speaker is figuratively depicted as a(n)

   (A) soldier
   (B) nurse
   (C) mourner
   (D) penitent
   (E) martyr

12. Ultimately, the speaker's attitude toward her beloved's entrance into battle is BEST classified as

   (A) maternal
   (B) solicitous
   (C) romantic
   (D) deterministic
   (E) pragmatic

13. The poem's primary theme concerns the

   (A) power of love
   (B) horrors of battle
   (C) sadness of separation
   (D) importance of religious faith
   (E) inevitability of death

14. Of the following, which can NOT be seen as figuratively alluding to the soldier's possible death in battle?

   (A) "Flags slanting, flowers flaunting [. . .]" (line 4)
   (B) "the unbearable is now to bear [. . .]" (line 5)
   (C) "the white face gone [. . .]" (line 17)
   (D) "that moment when you land, / Voiceless, invisible [. . .]" (lines 23-24)
   (E) "Inflexible demand [. . .]" (line 31)

Questions 15-27. Refer to the following passage.

Journeying down the Rhone on a summer's day, you have perhaps felt the sunshine made dreary by those ruined villages which stud the banks in certain
(5) parts of its course, telling how the swift river once rose, like an angry, destroying god, sweeping down the feeble generations [. . .] and making their dwellings a desolation. Strange contrast, you may have
(10) thought, between the effect produced on us by these dismal remnants of commonplace houses which in their best days were but the sign of a sordid life belonging in all its details to our own vulgar era, and the effect
(15) produced by those ruins on the castled Rhine which have crumbled and mellowed in such harmony with the green and rocky steeps that they seem to have a natural fitness, like the mountain-pine—nay, even
(20) in the day when they were built they must have had this fitness, as if they had been raised by an earth-born race who had inherited from their mighty parent a sublime instinct of form. And that was a
(25) day of romance! If those robber-barons were somewhat grim and drunken ogres, they had a certain grandeur of the wild beast in them; they were forest boars with tusks, tearing and rending, not the ordinary
(30) domestic grunter; they represented the demon forces forever in collision with beauty, virtue, and the gentle uses of life [. . . .]. That was a time of colour, when the sunlight fell on glancing steel and floating
(35) banners; a time of adventure and fierce struggle—nay, of living, religious art and religious enthusiasm, for were not cathedrals built in those days and did not great emperors leave their Western palaces
(40) to die before the infidel strongholds in the sacred East? Therefore it is that these Rhine castles thrill me with a sense of poetry; they belong to the grand historic life of humanity and raise up for me the vision of
(45) an epoch. But these dead-tinted, hollow-eyed angular skeletons of villages on the Rhone oppress me with the feeling that human life—very much of it—is a narrow, ugly, groveling existence which even
(50) calamity does not elevate, but rather tends to exhibit in all its bare vulgarity of conception; and I have a cruel conviction that the lives these ruins are traces of were

part of a gross sum of obscure vitality that
(55) will be swept into the same oblivion with generations of ants and beavers.
   Perhaps something akin to this oppressive feeling may have weighed upon you in watching this old-fashioned family
(60) life on the banks of the Floss, which even sorrow hardly suffices to lift above the level of the tragic-comic. It is a sordid life, you say, this of the Tullivers and Dodsons—irradiated by no sublime principles, no
(65) romantic visions [. . .] moved by none of those wild, uncontrollable passions which create the dark shadows of misery and crime; without that primitive rough simplicity of wants, that hard submissive ill-paid toil,
(70) that childlike spelling-out of what nature has written, which gives its poetry to peasant life [. . .] Observing these people narrowly, even when the iron hand of misfortune has shaken them from their
(75) unquestioning hold on the world, one sees little trace of religion, still less of a distinctly Christian creed. Their belief in the Unseen, so far as it manifests itself at all, seems to be rather of a pagan
(80) kind [. . .]. You could not live among such people; you are stifled for want of an outlet towards something beautiful, great, or noble; you are irritated with these dull men and women, as a kind of population out of
(85) keeping with the earth on which they live, with this rich plain where the great river flows forever onward and links the small pulse of the old English town with the beatings of the world's mighty heart. A
(90) vigorous superstition that lashes its gods or lashes its own back seems to be more congruous with the mystery of the human lot than the mental condition of these emmetlike[1] Dodsons and Tullivers [. . . .].

_____

[1] ant-like

15. The speaker's primary purpose in the opening paragraph is to

    (A) depict the results of a devastating calamity
    (B) contrast the archaeological ruins along two different rivers
    (C) speculate as to the reasons for these peoples' disappearance
    (D) depict the rustic beauties of the natural setting
    (E) offer an affinity for the dullness of the Tullivers and Dodsons

16. The speaker's depiction of the disparate ruins along the Rhone and the Rhine rivers effects all of the following contrasts EXCEPT

    (A) realism and romance
    (B) sordidness and grandeur
    (C) transience and permanence
    (D) stasis and adventure
    (E) obscurity and prominence

17. Which of the following does NOT help to establish the acute contrast between the Rhine River castle dwellers and their Rhone River counterparts?

    (A) "glancing steel and floating banners" (lines 34-35) and "dead-tinted, hollow-eyed angular skeletons" (lines 45-46)
    (B) "forest boars with tusks" (lines 28-29) and "domestic grunter" (line 30)
    (C) "time of adventure and fierce struggle" (lines 35-36) and "narrow, ugly, groveling existence" (lines 48-49)
    (D) "grand historic life of humanity" (lines 43-44) and "a gross sum of obscure vitality" (line 54)
    (E) "Western palaces" (line 39) and "infidel strongholds in the sacred East" (lines 40-41)

18. Which of the following does the speaker offer as reason(s) for his preference for the Rhine River ruins?

    I. Their harmonious integration with the natural landscape.
    II. Their status as Christian symbols.
    III. Their recollection of the adventurous age during which they were constructed.

    (A) I only
    (B) II only
    (C) I and III
    (D) II and III
    (E) I, II and III

19. The speaker depicts the eradication of the Rhone River community as a(n)

    (A) unfortunate consequence of their locale
    (B) challenging trial of their fortitude and perseverance
    (C) divine deterrent to further expansion along the riverside
    (D) understandable by-product of their lack of hardiness
    (E) caprice of a vengeful deity

20. Lines 24-25, "And that was a day of romance!," do which of the following?

    I. Emphatically declare that the speaker's position is incontrovertible.
    II. Introduce a counterpoint to the dreary Rhone River ruins.
    III. Indirectly indict the generally dull reality of the present.

    (A) I only
    (B) II only
    (C) I and III
    (D) II and III
    (E) I, II and III

21. The primary shift effected by the transitional sentence in lines 57-62 involves

    (A) topographical location
    (B) a shift in tense from the past to the literary present
    (C) the degree of misfortune experienced by the inhabitants
    (D) the speaker's attitude towards the inhabitants
    (E) the audience addressed by the speaker

22. The speaker's description of the Tullivers and the Dodsons suggests that they

    (A) are characterized by intellectual curiosity
    (B) manifest shifts in temperament that often turn violent
    (C) are taxed by the onerousness of their labor
    (D) are largely passionless and prosaic
    (E) reflect an endearing rural simplicity

23. So damning is the speaker's second paragraph description of the Tullivers and the Dodsons that she places them on a level beneath all of the following EXCEPT

    (A) idealistic visionaries
    (B) impassioned criminals
    (C) exploited laborers
    (D) unrefined peasants
    (E) robber barons

24. The speaker's final observation about the Tullivers and the Dodsons (lines 89-94) is intended to

    (A) censure their heathenism
    (B) criticize their belief in corporal punishment
    (C) satirize their insignificance
    (D) marvel at their tenacity
    (E) empathize with their penury

25. The author's attitude towards the Tullivers and the Dodsons is BEST classified as

    (A) bewildered
    (B) empathetic
    (C) derisive
    (D) apologetic
    (E) admiring

26. The speaker's tone throughout the passage is

    (A) highbrow and erudite
    (B) intimate and reflective
    (C) admonishing and moralistic
    (D) perplexed and inquisitive
    (E) regretful and nostalgic

27. The passage is most likely part of a(n)

    (A) novel of manners
    (B) travelogue
    (C) formal essay
    (D) autobiography
    (E) historical record

Questions 28-41. Refer to the following poem.

Ode to the West Wind

I.

O wild West Wind, thou breath of Autumn's being,
Thou, from whose unseen presence the leaves dead
Are driven, like ghosts from an enchanter fleeing.

Yellow, and black, and pale, and hectic red,
(5) Pestilence-stricken multitudes: O thou
Who chariotest to their dark wintry bed

The wingèd seeds, where they lie cold and low,
Each like a corpse within its grave, until
Thine azure sister of the Spring shall blow

(10) Her clarion o'er the dreaming earth, and fill
(Driving sweet buds like flocks to feed in air)
With living hues and odours plain and hill:

Wild Spirit, which art moving everywhere:
Destroyer and preserver; hear, oh hear!

II.

(15) Thou on whose stream, mid the steep sky's commotion,
Loose clouds like earth's decaying leaves are shed,
Shook from the tangled boughs of Heaven and Ocean,

Angels of rain and lightning: there are spread
On the blue surface of thine aery surge,
(20) Like the bright hair uplifted from the head

Of some fierce Maenad, even from the dim verge
Of the horizon to the zenith's height,
The locks of the approaching storm. Thou dirge

Of the dying year, to which this closing night
(25) Will be the dome of a vast sepulchre,
Vaulted with all thy congregated might

Of vapours, from whose solid atmosphere
Black rain, and fire, and hail will burst: oh, hear!

III.

Thou who didst waken from his summer dreams
(30) The blue Mediterranean, where he lay
Lulled by the coil of his crystalline streams,

Beside a pumice isle in Baiae's bay,
And saw in sleep old palaces and towers
Quivering within the wave's intenser day,

(35)   All overgrown with azure moss and flowers
         So sweet, the sense faints picturing them! Thou
         For whose path the Atlantic's level powers

         Cleave themselves into chasms, while far below
         The sea-blooms and the oozy woods which wear
(40)   The sapless foliage of the ocean, know

         Thy voice, and suddenly grow grey with fear,
         And tremble and despoil themselves: oh, hear!

                         IV.

         If I were a dead leaf thou mightest bear;
         If I were a swift cloud to fly with thee;
(45)   A wave to pant beneath thy power, and share

         The impulse of thy strength, only less free
         Than thou, O uncontrollable! If even
         I were as in my boyhood, and could be

         The comrade of thy wanderings over Heaven,
(50)   As then, when to outstrip thy skiey speed
         Scarce seemed a vision; I would never have striven

         As thus with thee in prayer in my sore need.
         Oh, lift me as a wave, a leaf, a cloud!
         I fall upon the thorns of life! I bleed!

(55)   A heavy weight of hours has changed and bowed
         One too like thee: tameless, and swift, and proud.

                         V.

         Make me thy lyre, even as the forest is:
         What if my leaves are falling as its own!
         The tumult of thy mighty harmonies

(60)   Will take from both a deep, autumnal tone,
         Sweet though in sadness. Be thou, Spirit fierce,
         My spirit! Be thou me, impetuous one!

         Drive my dead thoughts over the universe
         Like withered leaves to quicken a new birth!
(65)   And, by the incantation of this verse,

         Scatter, as from an unextinguished hearth
         Ashes and sparks, my words among mankind!
         Be through my lips to unawakened earth

         The trumpet of a prophecy! O, Wind,
(70)   If winter comes, can Spring be far behind?

                         —Percy Bysshe Shelley

28. Which of the following is NOT used by the speaker to describe the power of the wind in the opening section of the poem?

    (A) apostrophe
    (B) synecdoche
    (C) paradox
    (D) oxymoron
    (E) simile

29. In the initial section of the poem the speaker compares the wind to all of the following EXCEPT

    (A) a plague
    (B) a charioteer
    (C) a corpse
    (D) a sorcerer
    (E) a trumpeter

30. The word which BEST depicts the first section of the poem is

    (A) allusive
    (B) allegorical
    (C) satirical
    (D) imagistic
    (E) ironic

31. Lines 15-23 in the second section of the poem are characterized by an imagistic merger of

    (A) the arboreal and the celestial
    (B) the beautiful and the squalid
    (C) the heavenly and the infernal
    (D) the natural and the synthetic
    (E) the classical and the contemporary

32. The phrase, "the wave's intenser day" (line 34), refers to the

    (A) cleaving chasms stirred by the rising winds
    (B) bright reflection of the sun off the water
    (C) superior force of the ocean to the wind
    (D) lazy tides that have lulled the bay waters to sleep
    (E) brilliant blue waters of the Mediterranean

33. The fourth section of the poem introduces which of the following?

    I. The speaker's belief that he is as powerful as the wind.
    II. The speaker's consciousness of his affinity with nature.
    III. The speaker's awareness that the trappings of his existence have worn and weighted him down.

    (A) I only
    (B) III only
    (C) I and II
    (D) II and III
    (E) I, II and III

34. The fourth section of the poem introduces a tone that is BEST labeled

    (A) wistful longing
    (B) abject despair
    (C) stoic resignation
    (D) reverential awe
    (E) sentimental nostalgia

35. In lines 47-54 the speaker could perhaps be comparing himself to what classical figure?

    (A) Sisyphus
    (B) Icarus
    (C) Prometheus
    (D) Apollo
    (E) Orpheus

36. In the fifth and final section of the poem, the speaker figuratively expresses concern over his

    (A) health
    (B) isolation
    (C) aging
    (D) rashness
    (E) despondency

37. The fifth section of the poem figuratively differs from the first section of the poem in its introduction of which of the following images/symbols?

    (A) magic
    (B) music
    (C) the cycle of nature
    (D) autumn
    (E) fire

38. In the concluding section, the speaker asks the west wind for

    (A) eternal youth
    (B) poetic inspiration
    (C) musical ability
    (D) romantic bliss
    (E) widespread fame

39. The emotional appeal of the final two sections is buttressed by the speaker's use of all of the following EXCEPT

    (A) a tone of imploration
    (B) imperatives that urge immediate action
    (C) exclamations that convey the gravity of his condition
    (D) diction that links the speaker with the wind
    (E) radical changes in the poem's rhythm

40. Which of the following does NOT contribute to the impressive structural unity of the poem?

    (A) a pervasive seasonal motif
    (B) integrated sonnet-like sections
    (C) symbols of death and regeneration
    (D) religious imagery and allusions
    (E) the choric invocation of the wind

41. This poem is likely a product of which of the following literary epochs?

    (A) Medieval
    (B) Elizabethan
    (C) Romantic
    (D) Victorian
    (E) Modern

Questions 42-52. Refer to the following passage.

When Miss Emily Grierson died, our whole town went to her funeral: the men through a sort of respectful attention for a fallen monument, the women mostly out of
(5) curiosity to see the inside of her house, which no one save an old man-servant—a combined gardener and cook—had seen in at least ten years.

It was a big, squarish frame house that had
(10) once been white, decorated with cupolas and spires and scrolled balconies in the heavily lightsome style of the seventies, set on what had been our most select street. But garages and cotton gins had encroached and obliterated
(15) even the august names of that neighborhood; only Miss Emily's house was left, lifting its stubborn and coquettish decay above the cotton wagons and the gasoline pumps—an eyesore among eyesores. And now Miss Emily had
(20) gone to join the representatives of those august names where they lay in the cedar-bemused cemetery among the ranked and anonymous graves of Union and Confederate soldiers who fell at the battle of Jefferson.
(25) Alive, Miss Emily had been a tradition, a duty, and a care; a sort of hereditary obligation upon the town, dating from that day in 1894 when Colonel Sartoris, the mayor—he who fathered the edict that no Negro woman should
(30) appear on the streets without an apron—remitted her taxes, the dispensation dating from the death of her father on into perpetuity. Not that Miss Emily would have accepted charity. Colonel Sartoris invented an involved tale to
(35) the effect that Miss Emily's father had loaned money to the town, which the town, as a matter of business, preferred this way of repaying. Only a man of Colonel Sartoris' generation and thought could have invented it, and only a
(40) woman could have believed it.

When the next generation, with its more modern ideas, became mayors and aldermen, this arrangement created some little dissatisfaction. On the first of the year they
(45) mailed her a tax notice. February came, and there was no reply. They wrote her a formal letter, asking her to call at the sheriff's office at her convenience. A week later the mayor wrote her himself, offering to call or send his car for
(50) her, and received in reply a note on paper of an archaic shape, in a thin, flowing calligraphy in faded ink, to the effect that she no longer went out at all. The tax notice was also enclosed, without comment.
(55) They called a special meeting of the Board of Aldermen. A deputation waited upon her, knocked at the door through which no visitor had passed since she ceased giving china-painting lessons eight or ten years earlier. They
(60) were admitted by the old Negro into a dim hall from which a stairway mounted into still more shadow. It smelled of dust and disuse—a close, dank smell. The Negro led them into the parlor. It was furnished in heavy, leather-covered
(65) furniture. When the Negro opened the blinds of one window, they could see the leather was cracked; and when they sat down, a faint dust rose sluggishly about their thighs, spinning with slow motes in the single sun-ray. On a
(70) tarnished gilt easel before the fireplace stood a crayon portrait of Miss Emily's father.

They rose when she entered—a small, fat woman in black, with a thin gold chain descending to her waist and vanishing into her
(75) belt, leaning on an ebony cane with a tarnished gold head. Her skeleton was small and spare; perhaps that was why what would have been merely plumpness in another was obesity in her. She looked bloated, like a body long
(80) submerged in motionless water, and of that pallid hue. Her eyes, lost in the fatty ridges of her face, looked like two small pieces of coal pressed into a lump of dough as they moved from one face to another while the visitors
(85) stated their errand.

She did not ask them to sit. She just stood in the door and listened quietly until the spokesman came to a stumbling halt. Then they could hear the invisible watch ticking at the
(90) end of a gold chain.

Her voice was dry and cold. "I have no taxes in Jefferson. Colonel Sartoris explained it to me. Perhaps one of you can gain access to the city records and satisfy yourselves."
(95) "But we have. We are the city authorities, Miss Emily. Didn't you get a notice from the sheriff, signed by him?"

"I received a paper, yes," Miss Emily said. "Perhaps he considers himself the sheriff...I
(100) have no taxes in Jefferson."

"But Miss Emily—"

"See Colonel Sartoris." (Colonel Sartoris had been dead almost ten years.) "I have no taxes in Jefferson. Tobe!" The Negro appeared.
(105) "Show these gentlemen out [. . . .]."

42. The sentence that comprises all of the opening paragraph is primarily intended to establish which aspect of Emily Grierson's character?

    (A) her gregarious nature
    (B) her eccentricity
    (C) her social stature
    (D) her reclusiveness
    (E) her paralysis

43. The description of Emily Grierson's house does all of the following EXCEPT

    (A) parallel in its physical decline her status as a "fallen monument"
    (B) reflect the deleterious effect of mercantilism upon the once-fashionable neighborhood
    (C) suggest via its gloomy interior an archetypal Gothic setting
    (D) account for Miss Emily's withdrawn nature
    (E) mirror in its endurance Miss Emily's own obstinate existence

44. Miss Emily's financial 'arrangement' with the town was likely a product of

    (A) her father's meritable tenure as a public servant
    (B) her father's gross mismanagement of funds
    (C) Colonel Sartoris' empathy for her orphaned condition
    (D) Colonel Sartoris' dishonorable designs upon her
    (E) Miss Emily's own skill as a negotiator

45. In light of the speaker's description of the interior of Miss Emily's house, which of the following details provides the most definitive clue as to the motive behind her reclusive behavior?

    (A) the moldy entranceway
    (B) the cracked leather furniture
    (C) the drawn blinds
    (D) the crayon portrait of her father
    (E) the gloomy and ominous stair

46. It may be inferred from the tone of the speaker that the BEST equivalent for the phrase "more modern" (lines 41-42) would be

    (A) hopelessly impractical
    (B) financially pragmatic
    (C) artistically avant-garde
    (D) politically radical
    (E) strikingly imaginative

47. Miss Emily's implacable nature is primarily established by her

    (A) dark, recessed eyes
    (B) hidden but ticking timepiece
    (C) repeated refrain, "I have no taxes in Jefferson"
    (D) snide remark about the sheriff
    (E) imploration to Tobe to "Show these gentlemen out [. . . .]."

48. The physical description of Miss Emily in lines 72-85 most fittingly depicts her as a(n)

    (A) fallen woman
    (B) prophetess
    (C) *femme fatale*
    (D) madonna
    (E) grotesque

49. Which of the following does NOT play a role in the invented and involved tale concocted by Colonel Sartoris?

    (A) Miss Emily's poverty
    (B) Miss Emily's hubris
    (C) Colonel Sartoris' chivalry
    (D) Colonel Sartoris' charity
    (E) the townspeople's gratitude

50. Which of the following second paragraph phrases clearly foreshadows the physical description of Miss Emily in lines 79-85?

    (A) "heavily lightsome style" (lines 11-12)
    (B) "encroached and obliterated even the august names of that neighborhood" (lines 14-15)
    (C) "stubborn and coquettish decay" (line 17)
    (D) "eyesore among eyesores" (lines 18-19)
    (E) "ranked and anonymous graves" (lines 22-23)

51. A Freudian, or psychological, approach to the passage would show the LEAST interest in

    (A) the crayon portrait of Miss Emily's father
    (B) Miss Emily's pallid hue and bloated frame
    (C) Miss Emily's funereal attire
    (D) Miss Emily's ebony cane and invisible gold watch
    (E) Miss Emily's graceful and flowing handwriting

52. Which of the following does the speaker NOT do?

    (A) describe an idiosyncratic character
    (B) provide an anecdotal explanation
    (C) establish a regional setting
    (D) present a humorous stalemate
    (E) satirize a gentrified lifestyle

Section II

Question One

(Suggested time—40 minutes. This question counts as one-third of the total essay section score.)

Read the following passage carefully. Then, in a well-organized essay, discuss how the author uses literary techniques to convey the speaker's singular relationship with his chimney. In your essay, you may wish to consider such things as diction, figurative language, syntax and tone.

I and my chimney, two gray-headed old smokers, reside in the country. We are, I may
say, old settlers here; particularly my old chimney, which settles more and more every day.
   Though I always say, *I and my chimney*, as Cardinal Wolsey[1] used to say, *I and my King*,
yet this egotistic way of speaking wherein I take precedence of my chimney, is hardly borne out
(5)   by the facts; in everything, except the above phrase, my chimney taking precedence over me.
   Within thirty feet of the turf-sided road, my chimney—a huge, corpulent old Harry VIII
of a chimney—rises full in front of me and all my possessions. Standing well up a hillside, my
chimney, like Lord Rosse's[2] monster telescope, swung vertical to hit the meridian moon, is the
first object to greet the approaching traveler's eye, nor is it the last which the sun salutes. My
(10)   chimney, too, is before me in receiving the first-fruits of the seasons. The snow is on its head ere
on my hat; and every spring, as in a hollow beech tree, the first swallows build their nests in it.
   But it is within doors that the pre-eminence of my chimney is most manifest. When in the
rear room, set apart from that object, I stand to receive my guests (who, by the way, call more, I
suspect, to see my chimney than me), I then stand, not so much before, as, strictly speaking,
(15)   behind my chimney, which is, indeed, the true host. Not that I demur. In the presence of my
betters, I hope I know my place [. . . .].
   My chimney is grand seignior here—the one great domineering object, not more of the
landscape, than of the house; all the rest of which house, in each architectural arrangement, as
may shortly appear, is, in the most marked manner, accommodated, not to my wants, but to my
(20)   chimney's, which, among other things, has the centre of the house to himself, leaving but the odd
holes and corners to me [. . . .].
   Most houses here, are but one and a half stories high; few exceed two. That in which I
and my chimney dwell, is in width nearly twice its height, from sill to eaves—which accounts for
the magnitude of its main content [. . .].
(25)   The frame of the old house is of wood—which but the more sets forth the solidity of the
chimney, which is of brick. And as the great wrought nails, binding the clapboards, are unknown
in these degenerative days, so are the huge bricks in the chimney walls. The architect of the
chimney must have had the pyramid of Cheops before him; for, after that famous structure, it
seems modeled [. . .] From the exact middle of the mansion it soars from the cellar, right up through
(30)   each successive floor, till, four feet square, it breaks water from the ridgepole of the roof, like an
anvil-headed whale, through the crest of a billow. Most people, though, liken it, in that part, to a
razeed[3] observatory, masoned up [. . . .].

---

[1] influential churchman made Lord Chancellor by Henry VIII in 1515

[2] designer and builder of the 19th century's largest telescope

[3] razed; torn down

Question Two

(Suggested time—40 minutes. This question counts as one-third of the total essay section score.)

The impact of one author or literary work upon another may be unconscious or deliberate. The following two poems, written some seventy years apart by an Irishman and an American, strongly suggest that the former poem inspired or influenced the latter. Read each poem carefully. Then, in a well-organized essay, discuss how the two authors use a similar scene to provoke a strikingly different response. In your essay, you may wish to consider such things as diction, theme, choice of detail, figurative language and tone.

The Wild Swans at Coole

The trees are in their autumn beauty,
The woodland paths are dry,
Under the October twilight the water
Mirrors a still sky;
(5)   Upon the brimming water among the stones
Are nine-and-fifty swans.

The nineteenth autumn has come upon me
Since I first made my count;
I saw, before I had well finished,
(10)   All suddenly mount
And scatter wheeling in great broken rings
Upon their clamorous wings.

I have looked upon these brilliant creatures,
And now my heart is sore.
(15)   All's changed since I, hearing at twilight,
The first time on this shore
The bell-beat of their wings above my head,
Trod with a lighter tread.

Unwearied still, lover by lover,
(20)   They paddle in the cold
Companionable streams or climb the air;
Their hearts have not grown old;
Passion or conquest, wander where they will,
Attend upon them still.

(25)   But now they drift on the still water,
Mysterious, beautiful;
Among what rushes will they build,
By what lake's edge or pool
Delight men's eyes when I awake some day
(30)   To find they have flown away?

—William Butler Yeats (1916, 1919)

The Great Scarf of Birds

Playing golf on Cape Ann in October,
I saw something to remember.
Ripe apples were caught like red fish in the nets
of their branches. The maples
(5) were colored like apples
part orange and red, part green.
The elms, already transparent trees,
seemed swaying vases full of sky. The sky
was dramatic with great straggling V's
(10) of geese streaming south, mare's-tails above
     them.
Their trumpeting made us look up and around.
The course sloped into salt marshes,
and this seemed to cause the abundance of birds.

As if out of the Bible
(15) or science fiction,
a cloud appeared, a cloud of dots
like iron filings which a magnet
underneath the paper undulates.
It dartingly darkened in spots,
(20) paled, pulsed, compressed, distended, yet
held an identity firm: a flock
of starlings, as much one thing as a rock.
One will moved above the trees
the liquid and hesitant drift.

(25) Come nearer, it became less marvelous,
more legible, and merely huge.
"I never saw so many birds!" my friend exclaimed.
We returned our eyes to the game.
Later, as Lot's wife must have done,
(30) in a pause of walking, not thinking
of calling down a consequence
I lazily looked around.

The rise of the fairway above us was tinted,
So evenly tinted I might not have noticed
(35) But that at the rim of the delicate shadow
The starlings were thicker and outlined the flock
As an inkstain in drying pronounces its edges.
The gradual rise of green was vastly covered:
I had thought nothing in nature could be so broad
     but grass.

(40) And as
I watched, one bird,
prompted by accident or will to lead,
ceased resting; and, lifting in a casual billow,
the flock ascended as a lady's scarf,
(45) transparent, of gray, might be twitched
by one corner, drawn upward and then,
decided against, negligently tossed toward a chair:
the southward cloud withdrew into the air.

Long had it been since my heart
(50) had been lifted as it was by the lifting of that
     great scarf.

—John Updike (1989)

<u>Question Three</u>

(Suggested time—40 minutes. This question counts as one-third of the total essay section score.)

Frequently in literature, a novel or play focuses around a pair of "counterparts," characters who seem inseparably bound by situation or by fate. This mutual involvement, which may range from the acute interdependence of soul-mates to the polar hostility of rivals, is often used to further the work's larger literary purpose. From the novels and plays you have read, choose a work that features such a pair of "counterparts." Using your knowledge of the work, clarify the nature of the characters' relationship and indicate in what way their intimate involvement makes an important contribution to the work as a whole. You may choose from the list below or use another novel or play of recognized literary merit.

Waiting for Godot	*Of Mice and Men*
Crime and Punishment	*Jude the Obscure*
The Scarlet Letter	*Julius Caesar*
Romeo and Juliet	*The Adventures of Huckleberry Finn*
Frankenstein	*J.B.*
Death in Venice	*On the Road*
Billy Budd	*Cry, the Beloved Country*
Othello	*Dr. Jekyll and Mr. Hyde*
The Mill on the Floss	*Wuthering Heights*
Les Miserables	*Amadeus*
The Sound and the Fury	*Billy Budd*
The Importance of Being Earnest	*The Power & the Glory*

Sample Examination Two: Explications and Answers

Passage One: "Any Woman to a Soldier" by Grace Ellery Channing-Stetson

The first selection in Sample Examination One was a real find, and after working on it for the last year or so, I find it in many ways to be as fine a war poem as Wilfred Owen's "Dulce Et Decorum Est." Channing-Stetson's poem, seen through the eyes of a woman whose beloved has been called away to war, takes the reader through an imagined reverie, from the triumphant day of his departure to the dreadful moment of his death on the battlefield. Throughout this journey the speaker confidently proclaims that her powerful and unshakeable love for her husband will guide him safely through all peril, in the end defying even the death that has come to claim him.

In the opening three stanzas of the poem, the speaker's emphasis is on the positive, on maintaining a stalwart front though the news that her beloved has been summoned to fight is clearly devastating to her. She buoyantly declares in lines 1-4 "The day you march away—let the sun shine. / Let everything be blue and gold and fair, / Triumph of trumpets calling through bright air, / Flags slanting, flowers flaunting [. . .]," insisting that everything be celebratory and upbeat despite the sobering fact that "the unbearable is now to bear" (line 5). She insists in lines 11-13 that he shall see "brows like banners, lips that frame / Smiles, for the pride those lips have in [his] name. / [He] shall see soldiers in [her] eyes that day—." In the last image the speaker's eyes form a mirror, presenting not tears but a martial reflection of rank upon rank of troops marching proudly off to war. This image carries over into stanza three in which the seemingly endless legion of soldiers leads to but a momentary and fleeting glimpse of her beloved, who passes quickly, his "white face gone," replaced by a "gray emptiness" (lines 17-18). Though the speaker maintains a supportive façade, the impact of her beloved's departure is manifest in the choric repetition of the phrase "the day you march away" at the beginning and end of each of the first three stanzas.

The emotional plea "You cannot march away!," voiced by the speaker in line 21, marks the transition in the poem from the specter of faraway war to its realistically grim proximity. The line actually serves two purposes. On one level, it exposes the emotional angst that the speaker has been suppressing; on another, it initiates the speaker's poignant but romantic belief that the strength of her love and devotion will somehow see him safely through this calamity. The speaker romantically conceives that no matter how physically distant from her the war takes him, she will nonetheless remain "close at [his] hand," imagining how "[her] heart shall smile, hearing the steady tread / Of [his] faith-keeping feet" (lines 25-26). However, this stanza can also be seen as foreshadowing the soldier's death ("Voiceless, invisible") and entrance into the afterlife ("steady tread / Of [his] faith keeping feet), where she will faithfully greet him as a devoted (in both connotations) wife.

The final three stanzas are comprised of a reverie in which the speaker imagines herself present at all the diverse scenes of battle—greeting her beloved in the trenches, standing vigilant watch with him, there even when "the red, / Drenched, dreadful, splendid, sacrificial field lifts up / Inflexible demand [. . .]" (lines 29-31). Though the subsequent two stanzas, with their images of a bleeding soldier being carried on a litter through a corpse-strewn battlefield, suggest that the speaker's beloved has been wounded, the phrase "Inflexible demand" (line 31) may be seen as connoting the ultimate sacrifice, death. In fact, there are several potential foreshadowings of the beloved's death (e.g., the "one white face;" his gradual fading away in the speaker's consciousness in stanza three), but the speaker's conviction in lines 40-42, "And you shall live, because my heart has said / To Death / That Death itself shall have no part in you!," seems to suggest an unshakeable belief that he will survive the war and return to her. However, this can just as easily be perceived as a romantic denial of an inevitable and bleak reality. An additional ambiguity is provided by the phrase "faith-keeping feet" in line 26, which can be seen as faith in his beloved, faith in his survival, or faith in a heavenly reward. The last interpretation offers the possibility that the reunion of speaker and soldier is not to take place in this world but in the after-life; that the speaker can only vicariously experience her beloved's suffering because she cannot physically be there to see him die. No matter which way one reads it, the poem provides a wonderfully insightful glimpse into the complexity of emotions that run through a woman left bereft, if not by death, by the call to duty of her beloved.

1. The appeal made by the speaker in stanza one is primarily prompted by her **(D) prescient fear of her beloved's possible death**.

The speaker appeals to the sun to be shining and for "everything to be blue and gold and fair" (line 2); for a glorious trumpet and flag-flourishing departure on the day her beloved must march away to battle. She more subtly adds that there should be "not a sign / That the unbearable is now to bear [. . .]" (lines 4-5). The somewhat euphemistic word "unbearable" clearly represents the bleak possibility that she is seeing her beloved for the last time, that he is marching off to his death. Her appeal seems to be a denial of this dark premonition.

2. Which of the following is NOT an accurate observation about the second stanza? **(E) It contains an overt statement about the speaker's opposition to war**.

Similar to the first stanza, lines 11-13—"You shall see brows like banners, lips that frame / Smiles, for the pride those lips have in your name. / You shall see soldiers in my eyes that day"—mask the disappointment the speaker feels at her beloved's deployment. Her claim in lines 7-10— "this I have sworn, / No matter what comes after, that shall be / Hid secretly between my soul and me / As women hide the unborn"—offers an implied metaphor drawn from maternity. This information confirms choices A and B. The change in focus from the sunshine, blue skies and flowers of the opening stanza to the brows, lips and eyes of the second confirms C, while the use of dashes to convey the speaker's secret thought validates D. There is no suggestion in these two stanzas that the speaker opposes the war on principle.

3. The rhetorical question in stanza three does all of the following EXCEPT **(A) reveal the speaker's knowledge of the exact date of the army's departure**.

Line 15, "The day you march away—cannot I guess?," suggests that the speaker is already conscious of the imminence of her beloved's deployment. It also implies that, having probably seen such departures before, she knows how difficult it will be to find her beloved's face among the ranks upon ranks of passing soldiers as well as how short-lived her contact with his face will be. The question also foreshadows the emotional void—that "gray emptiness"—that she will quickly experience once he has marched out of her ken. Moreover, it intimates her womanly intuition, her communal sense that this is the lot of all women whose husbands are sent off to war; that the "Blurred moving masses, faceless, featureless—" (line 19) are the faces of other husbands and lovers leaving behind women just like herself. This validates choices B, C, D and E. That the speaker knows the *exact* date of the army's deployment is pretty much eliminated by the speculative tone of her refrain, which refers to some undefined future moment.

4. The "one white face" (line 17) is most likely the face of **(B) the soldier**.

Since the speaker is scouring the ranks of passing soldiers for her beloved, and the "one white face" she sees is quickly gone with "nothing left but a gray emptiness—" (line 18), it is logical to presume that this is the face of her beloved.

5. The speaker stylistically complements the hasty and impersonal nature of her parting from her beloved through all of the following EXCEPT **(D) onomatopoeic description of the marching feet**.

Line 19, "Blurred moving masses, faceless, featureless—," confirms both A and C, while diction such as "ranks and ranks," "leading on," "Blurred," and "moving" (lines 16-19) validates E. The change in the speaker's description of her beloved from "one white face" (innocence?) to gray (the pallor of death?) confirms B. Onomatopoeia is not evident in these lines.

6. The primary difference between the fourth stanza and the previous three is the speaker's **(C) fanciful reverie that she will anticipate her beloved at the front line or in heaven**.

While the poem's first three stanzas focus on the speaker's attempt to deal with her beloved's departure, line 21, "You cannot march away!," reveals her impassioned and unwilling reluctance to part with him. Though the reality of his deployment is inexorably confirmed by his marching past, the speaker embarks upon a reverie in which she imagines herself outracing him to the front lines to be there the moment he embarks (ostensibly from a troop ship). Though he will be "Voiceless, invisible"—perhaps debarking quietly and covertly under cover of nightfall—she will be "close at [his] hand" (line 24), essentially acting as a guardian spirit.

There is, however, another plausible reading of this stanza. If one chooses to perceive the adjectives "Voiceless, invisible" as modifying "you" in a spiritual way (meaning her beloved has been killed and is a disembodied spirit), then the speaker is greeting him not on the front line, but in heaven or an after-life. Support for this is provided by her joy at the "faith-keeping feet" (line 26) that got him there. While I like this reading very much, it is more difficult to reconcile with the scenes of battle in stanzas five, six and seven, in which the speaker nurses her beloved through injury, fever, and starvation, as well as with the speaker's confrontational and defiant final words "And you shall live, because my heart has said / To Death / That Death itself shall have no part in you!" (lines 40-42). Being a hopeless romantic myself—I just love that line in *Gatsby*, "Can't repeat the past? Why, of course you can!"—I buy into the emotional adamancy of the speaker. We are, after all, dealing with *literature*, and ambiguity is a writer's best friend; thus, the selection of choice C, which allows for both possibilities.

7. The words "Voiceless, invisible" (line 24) come closest to modifying which of the following? **(B) "you" (line 23)**.

This is a deceptively challenging grammatical question. One would readily assume that the adjectives in line 24 describe the speaker since, in her reverie, it is she who is the imaginary presence that has fled before him to be at his side. Yet these adjectives are separated from the "I" in line 22 by a semi-colon and by the phrase "and that moment when you land" (line 23). Coming on the heels of "when you land," it would seem that they are describing the soldier. As has been suggested in the explanation of the previous question, this could refer either to the covert nature of his regiment's landing or could perhaps allude to his entrance into a post-death afterlife. Though it could be argued that the pronoun "I" should be understood here, and that the words describe the speaker's own silent and unsent presence–or that lines 25-26, "[her] heart shall smile, hearing the steady tread / Of [his] faith-keeping feet," support her invisible guardianship–this claim is primarily founded upon conjecture.

8. Lines 25-26, "My heart shall smile, hearing the steady tread / Of your faith-keeping feet," possibly suggest that the speaker is gratified that her beloved has done which of the following?

      I. Maintained his love for her.
     II. Returned home unharmed.
   III. Entered into heaven.

   (D) I and III.

   The choice of D as the correct answer is consistent with the explanation of the answers to the previous two questions. If one reads stanza four literally, I must be chosen; if one reads the stanza figuratively, III becomes the choice. II is quickly ruled out by the wounds he suffers on the battlefield.

9. In stanza five the speaker's stalwart faithfulness is enhanced by all of the following EXCEPT **(B) negation**.

   Choice A is supported by line 27, "First at the trenches I shall be to greet," which emphasizes how fast the speaker will outstrip the marching troops, choice C by the "splendid, sacrificial field" (line 30) which recalls the altar of sacrifice, the transubstantiation of the physical into the spiritual. Choice D is apparent in "red, / Drenched, dreadful" (lines 29-30), choice E in the speaker's affirmation, "I will be there!" (line 32). Though students may see line 28 as exemplifying negation, this does not qualify as describing something by what it is not; rather, this is an example of emphasis, the speaker suggesting that she will be with him on every single watch.

10. The BEST interpretation of the word "Inflexible" (line 31) is **(D) irrevocable**.

    The phrase "Inflexible demand" is a euphemism for death since the soldier's moment of death cannot be negotiated. Choice D represents this best.

11. In the final two stanzas the speaker is figuratively depicted as a(n) **(B) nurse**.

    This is readily apparent in lines 33-39, in which the speaker is seen helping him drink, cradling his head, bearing him on a stretcher, and essentially seeing him safely through injury, fever, starvation and ubiquitous death.

12. Ultimately, the speaker's attitude toward her beloved's entrance into battle is BEST classified as **(C) romantic**.

    Clearly, the speaker cannot *literally* do these things. A key to focus on here is her closing claim that "you shall live, because my heart has said / To Death / That Death itself shall have no part in you!" (lines 40-42). It is the speaker's *heart* that wants to believe that the strength of her love will insure his safety. In the end, the speaker's attitude is romantic in both senses of the word: the fact that she feels deeply for him, and the fact that the things she imagines herself doing are simply unrealistic.

13. The poem's primary theme concerns the **(A) power of love**.

This is consistent with the explanation of the previous question; the speaker truly believes that the strength of her love will see her beloved safely home to her or insure their reunion in the afterlife.

14. Of the following, which can NOT be seen as figuratively alluding to the soldier's possible death in battle? **(A) "Flags slanting, flowers flaunting [. . .]" (line 4)**.

While the other four choices each present either an image (C, D) or a euphemism (B, E) for death, choice A describes the heroic day of his departure.

Passage Two: From George Eliot's *The Mill on the Floss*

The passage from George Eliot's *The Mill on the Floss* that comprises the second selection in this sample examination offers the student a unique opportunity to relate character and setting. The speaker in the passage establishes a contrast between the ruins of villages along the Rhone River and the remnants of castles along the Rhine. In the first case, these ruins are said to be depressing, the "sunshine made dreary by those ruined villages which stud the banks in certain parts of its course, telling how the swift river once rose, like an angry, destroying god, sweeping down the feeble generations [. . .] and making their dwellings a desolation" (lines 3-9). The speaker refers to these ruins in disdainful fashion, as the "dismal remnants of commonplace houses which in their best days were but the sign of a sordid life belonging in all its details to our own vulgar era [. . .]" (lines 11-14), claiming that "these dead-tinted, hollow-eyed angular skeletons of villages on the Rhone oppress [her] with the feeling that human life— very much of it—is a narrow, ugly, groveling existence which even calamity does not elevate, but rather tends to exhibit in all its bare vulgarity of conception" (lines 45-52). The diction throughout these examples suggests insignificance, bleakness, barbarity and cadaverousness. In contrast, the speaker's description of the castled ruins along the Rhine is nostalgic, uplifting, and romantic, suggesting that even though they too have fallen into ruin, they have "crumbled and mellowed in such harmony with the green and rocky steeps that they seem to have a natural fitness, like the mountain-pine [. . .]" (lines 16-19). Though admitting that they were built by "robber-barons" (line 25), the speaker nevertheless insists these artisans must have had "a certain grandeur of the wild beast in them; they were forest boars with tusks, tearing and rending, not the ordinary domestic grunter [. . .]" (lines 27-30). She insists that they belonged to a "a time of colour, when the sunlight fell on glancing steel and floating banners; a time of adventure and fierce struggle [. . .]" (lines 33-36), comparing them to the great cathedrals that were erected in this era and claiming that "these Rhine castles thrill [her] with a sense of poetry; they belong to the grand historic life of humanity and raise up for [her] the vision of an epoch" (lines 41-45). While nostalgically viewing these castles and their long-gone inhabitants as belonging to a golden age of spirituality and chivalry, she somewhat superciliously looks down on the Rhone ruins as "part of a gross sum of obscure vitality that will be swept into the same oblivion with generations of ants and beavers" (lines 54-56).

In the second paragraph the speaker shifts from a reflection on the ruins along two German rivers to the dwellings along the fictional river Floss. These, she indicates, have more in common with their Rhone counterparts than their Rhine ones, calling the old-fashioned family life along the Floss a "sordid" one (lines 59-62). Alluding to two particular families, the Tullivers and the Dodsons (ostensibly characters in the novel), she refers to them as being

> irradiated by no sublime principles, no romantic visions [. . .] moved by none of those wild, uncontrollable passions which create the dark shadows of misery and crime; without that primitive rough simplicity of wants, that hard submissive ill-paid toil, that childlike spelling-out of what nature has written, which gives its poetry to peasant life [. . .] (lines 64-72).

This less than flattering description paints these families as dull, unimaginative, irreligious peoples somewhat "out of keeping with the earth on which they live, with this rich plain where the great river flows forever onward and links the small pulse of the old English town with the beatings of the world's mighty heart" (lines 84-89). Referring to them as "emmetlike" (line 94), or ant-like, the speaker uses words such as "dull" (line 83) and "stifled" (line 81), suggesting that their passionless and stolid nature is deflating and depressing. Though the passage gives little insight into the subsequent plot of the novel, it is readily clear that the Tullivers and Dodsons are to be seen as beings whose existence is tenuous and insignificant like their Rhone River counterparts before them.

15. The speaker's primary purpose in the opening paragraph is to **(B) contrast the archaeological ruins along two different rivers**.

This is established in the long opening paragraph and is apparent as early as the opening sentence in which the speakers observes "Journeying down the Rhone on a summer's day, you have perhaps felt the sunshine made dreary by those ruined villages which stud the banks in certain parts of its course, telling how the swift river once rose, like an angry, destroying god, sweeping down the feeble generations [. . .] and making their dwellings a desolation" (lines 1-9). The speaker contrasts these sordid ruined villages with "the effect produced by those ruins on the castled Rhine which have crumbled and mellowed in such harmony with the green and rocky steeps that they seem to have a natural fitness, like the mountain-pine [. . .]" (lines 14-19).

16. The speaker's depiction of the disparate ruins along the Rhone and the Rhine rivers effects all of the following contrasts EXCEPT **(C) transience and permanence**.

Whereas the dwellers in the Rhone villages suffered a "narrow, ugly, groveling existence which even calamity [did] not elevate [. . .]" (lines 48-50) and led a life that was "irradiated by no sublime principles, no romantic visions [. . .]" (lines 64-65), their Rhine counterparts are said to belong to "a time of colour, when the sunlight fell on glancing steel and floating banners; a time of adventure and fierce struggle [. . .]" (lines 33-36) and to thrill the speaker with "a sense of poetry" (line 42). This confirms choice A. While the Rhone ruins are said by the speaker to be "dismal remnants of commonplace houses which in their best days were but the sign of a sordid life belonging in all its details to our own vulgar era [. . .]" (lines 11-14), their grand Rhone counterparts seem "as if they had been raised by an earth-born race who had inherited from their mighty parent a sublime instinct of form" (lines 21-24). This validates choice B. The speaker perceives the lot of the Rhone village dwellers to be "part of a gross sum of obscure vitality that will be swept into the same oblivion with generations of ants and beavers" (lines 54-56), while viewing the lives of the Rhine castle-dwellers as belonging to "a day of romance!" (lines 24-25), "the grand historic life of humanity" (lines 43-44). This supports choices D and E. Since the edifices of both cultures are in ruins, choice C has no validity.

17. Which of the following does NOT help to establish the acute contrast between the Rhine River castle dwellers and their Rhone River counterparts? **(E) "Western palaces" (line 39) and "infidel strongholds of the sacred East" (lines 40-41)**

Choice A contrasts images of chivalric romance with cadaverous ones, choice B contrasts a near-mythical animal with an ordinary barnyard sow. Choices C and D both contrast lives of adventure and accomplishment with lives of insignificance and struggle,. Choice E, however, is not a reference to ruins along the two rivers, but a reference to edifices in the Holy Land during the period of the great Crusades.

18. Which of the following does the speaker offer as reason(s) for his preference for the Rhine River ruins?

    I. Their harmonious integration with the natural landscape.
    II. Their status as Christian symbols.
    III. Their recollection of the adventurous age in which they were constructed.

(C) I and III.

The speaker notes that unlike the sordid hovels which "stud the banks" (line 4) of the Rhone River, the castled Rhine River ruins "have crumbled and mellowed in such harmony with the green and rocky steeps that they seem to have a natural fitness, like the mountain-pine [. . .]" (lines 16-19). This validates I. III gains credence from the speaker's commentary in lines 19-32, "nay, even in the day when they were built they must have had this fitness, as if they had been raised by an earth-born race who had inherited from their mighty parent a sublime instinct of form. And that was a day of romance! If those robber-barons were somewhat grim and drunken ogres, they had a certain grandeur of the wild beast in them; they were forest boars with tusks, tearing and rending, not the ordinary domestic grunter; they represented the demon forces forever in collision with beauty, virtue, and the gentle uses of life [. . . .]." II draws no support from the passage.

19. The speaker depicts the eradication of the Rhone River community as a(n) **(E) caprice of a vengeful deity**.

This is derived directly from the speaker's observation in lines 5-9, "how the swift river once rose, like an angry, destroying god, sweeping down the feeble generations [. . .] and making their dwellings a desolation."

20. Lines 24-25, "And that was a day of romance!," do which of the following?

    I. Emphatically declare that the speaker's position is incontrovertible.
    II. Introduce a counterpoint to the dreary Rhone River ruins.
    III. Indirectly indict the generally dull reality of the present.

(E) I, II and III.

The "And that" (as well as the exclamation point) with which the speaker punctuates the sentence confirms I. This sentence also initiates the subsequent description of the aesthetic sensibilities of the Rhine castles, their "certain grandeur" (line 27) and "sense of poetry" (line 42), validating II. III gains support through the nostalgic tone, which suggests that this age, "belong[s] to the grand historic life of humanity and raise[s] up for [her] the vision of an epoch" (lines 43-45)

21. The primary shift effected by the transitional sentence in lines 57-62 involves **(B) a shift in tense from the past to the literary present**.

Though many students will jump at A, the entirety of the speaker's opening paragraph is a remembrance, a flashback to a trip to the Continent. However, a careful reading of lines 57-62 reveals that the speaker is, as has been her wont since the opening line of the passage, addressing her *reading audience*. She has used the flashback to trips along the two German rivers to set up an analogous situation to the fictional world of the Floss-dwelling Tullivers and Dodsons. Choice B reflects this best.

22. The speaker's description of the Tullivers and the Dodsons suggests that they **(D) are largely passionless and prosaic**.

The speaker's description of the Tullivers and the Dodsons is surely an unflattering one. For example, she says they are

> irradiated by no sublime principles, no romantic visions [. . .] moved by none of those wild, uncontrollable passions which create the dark shadows of misery and crime; without that primitive rough simplicity of wants, that hard submissive ill-paid toil, that childlike spelling-out of what nature has written, which gives its poetry to peasant life [. . .]" (lines 64-72).

Later, speaking to her readers, she adds that

> You could not live among such people; you are stifled for want of an outlet towards something beautiful, great, or noble; you are irritated with these dull men and women, as a kind of population out of keeping with the earth on which they live, with this rich plain where the great river flows forever onward and links the small pulse of the old English town with the beatings of the world's mighty heart (lines 80-89).

This suggests that they are unimaginative and provincial, out of touch with the intellectual developments of the big city, London. The speaker figuratively contrasts the energy level of the two through "small pulse" and "mighty heart." In the passage's final line she compares their intellect to that of ants. It is choice D that presents these characteristics best.

23. So damning is the speaker's second paragraph description of the Tullivers and the Dodsons that she places them on a level beneath all of the following EXCEPT **(E) robber barons**.

The speaker's claim that they are "irradiated by no sublime principles, no romantic visions [. . .]" validates A, her observation that they are "moved by none of those wild, uncontrollable passions which create the dark shadows of misery and crime [. . .]" supports B. That they are "without that primitive rough simplicity of wants, that hard submissive ill-paid toil, that childlike spelling-out of what nature has written, which gives its poetry to peasant life [. . .]" supports both C and D, leaving E as the exception.

24. The speaker's final observation about the Tullivers and the Dodsons (lines 89-94) is intended to **(C) satirize their insignificance**.

The speaker suggests that even a primitive, superstitious culture that flagellated itself or blamed some unseen gods for its constant misfortune would be "more congruous with the mystery of the human lot than the mental condition of these emmetlike Dodsons and Tollivers [. . .]" (lines 91-94). The addition of the word "emmetlike" compares these people to ants, suggesting they are small-minded and virtually insignificant.

25. The author's attitude towards the Tullivers and the Dodsons is BEST classified as **(C) derisive**.

This may be easily derived by consulting the explanation of questions #22, #23 or #24.

26. The speaker's tone throughout the passage is **(B) intimate and reflective**.

The speaker continually addresses the reader in the second person, as a confidant; as someone who shares both her penchant for travel and her overall highbrow tastes. However, she does not merely scorn the sordid villages that dot the Rhine or the provincial lives of the Floss-dwellers; rather, she reflects on their existence, ruminating on their response to hardship and misfortune, mystified by their lack of aesthetic and intellectual sensibilities. Choice B reflects this best,

27. The passage is most likely part of a(n) **(A) novel of manners**.

The novel of manners examines the customs, values, and mindset of a particular class or group of people in a particular era or place. The commentary on the Tullivers and Dodsons seems to suggest that this passage is part of one.

Passage Three: Percy Bysshe Shelley's "Ode to the West Wind"

The third selection in the second sample examination is a recognizable one, Percy Bysshe Shelley's "Ode to the West Wind." The inclusion of this oft-anthologized poem was prompted by a desire to select something from the Romantic period that was challenging but accessible. Shelley's highly imagistic paean to the west wind met this need perfectly. Filled with seasonal and nature motifs and replete with figurative language, Shelley's poem provides a nice primer for introducing the developing AP student to Romantic poetry.

Divided into five movements or sections, each consisting of a sonnet-like fourteen lines, Shelley's poem addresses the wind in much the same way writers of classical epics appealed to the Muses for inspiration. In the first section of the poem, the speaker uses apostrophe, invoking the West Wind (whom he characterizes in diverse ways) to hear his appeal. The speaker alternately describes the wind as: the "breath of Autumn's being" (line 1); "an enchanter" (line 3) who drives the multicolored dead leaves of the season before him; a charioteer who carries the "winged seeds" to their "dark wintry bed" in the soil (lines 6-7); and a trumpeter whose resounding horn wakens the slumbering buds to the spring season (lines 9-12). Labeling it paradoxically as "Destroyer and preserver" (line 14), the speaker calls upon the wind to hear his cry.

The poem's second movement changes from the fall season to the fomation of a storm over the ocean. The poet maintains some semblance of the seasonal motif of section one, referring to the clouds as "earth's decaying leaves" (line 16) and the process of cloud formation over the water as the "tangled boughs of Heaven and Ocean" (line 17). The imposing thunderheads are compared in a simile/allusion to "the bright hair uplifted from the head / Of some fierce Maenad" (lines 20-21), their aery tendrils said to be the "locks of the approaching storm" (line 23). The poet than switches to diction associated with death. The storm is said to be the "dirge / Of the dying year" (lines 23-24), the sky is the "dome of a vast sepulchre" (line 25). The third section extends the impact of the gathering celestial storm to the tranquil ocean below it. The Mediterranean, personified as a slumbering youth lost in pleasant reverie, is awakened by the thunder of the approaching storm that rouses him from his dreams and "Cleave[s]" his tranquil waters into "chasms" (line 38). So potent is the storm that even the "sea-blooms and the oozy woods" (line 39) on the ocean floor sway before it in fealty.

In the fourth and fifth sections the speaker connects the images of leaf, cloud and wave that dominate the opening three sections to his own situation. All three elements of nature are impacted by the wind, and the speaker yearns for such an intimate communion. In what may be a vague allusion to Icarus, he appeals to the wind to return him to his boyhood when he was "The comrade of [its] wanderings over Heaven" (line 49). The poignant appeal—"Oh, lift me as a wave, a leaf, a cloud! / I fall upon the thorns of life! I bleed!" (lines 53-54)—recalls at once the fallen Icarus, cast down from his ecstatic flight, and, more vaguely, the sufferings of Jesus. Here the speaker sees himself chained down by "A heavy weight of hours" (line 55), deflated by Wordworth's "too much with us" world. Unable to enjoy the wind's limitless freedom and conscious of his increasing age ("What if my leaves are falling as its own!"), the speaker implores the wind to make him its "lyre, even as the forest is" (line 57). By asking to become the wind's lyre, a stringed instrument used by the bards or first poets, the speaker is asking for poetic inspiration. He implores the wind to "Drive [his] dead thoughts over the universe / Like withered leaves to quicken a new birth!" (lines 63-64); to "Scatter, as from an unextinguished hearth / Ashes and sparks, my words among mankind!" (lines 66-67); to "Be through [his] lips to unawakened earth / The trumpet of prophecy!" (lines 68-69). In each case the speaker is the passive vehicle that must be energized by the wind's natural force, and in each case the wind breathes new life into something dead or inactive. Through this return to the images of the opening stanza (the dead leaves of the fall and the trumpet of the spring), the poet achieves impressive structural and thematic closure, concluding with the optimistic rhetorical question "O, Wind, / If winter comes, can Spring be far behind?" (lines 69-70).

28. Which of the following is NOT used by the speaker to describe the power of the wind in the opening section of the poem? **(D) oxymoron**.

The speaker addresses the "wild West Wind" (apostrophe), calls it the "breath of Autumn's being" (synecdoche), and labels it "Destroyer and preserver" (paradox). This validates choices A, B and C. It is said to drive the buds "like flocks" of sheep (simile), confirming E. This leaves D as the exception.

29. In the initial section of the poem the speaker compares the wind to all of the following EXCEPT **(C) a corpse**.

The wind strikes down the leaves like a "Pestilence" (A), "chariotest to their dark wintry bed / The winged seeds [. . .]" (B), drives the dead leaves like "an enchanter" (D), and blows its "clarion over the dreaming earth [. . .]" (E). The" corpse" in line 8 refers to each individual seed that lies dormant in the ground until spring.

30. The word which BEST depicts the first section of the poem is **(D) imagistic**.

Though there are many different examples of figurative language at work in the opening stanza, imagery dominates. The "Yellow, and black, and pale, and hectic red" leaves provide a wonderful collage of fall colors; the "unseen presence" of the "wild West wind" blows the rustling leaves in every direction as if they were compelled by a sorcerer to fly. It also disseminates the seeds until its "azure sister," Spring, "blow[s] / her clarion horn o'er the dreaming earth" and wakens them to life. The "sweet buds" then fill the entire landscape "With living hues and odours." The diction in this section appeals to sight, sound and scent, making D the appropriate choice.

31. Lines 15-23 in the second section of the poem are characterized by an imagistic merger of **(A) the arboreal and the celestial**.

The speaker describes how "mid the steep <u>sky</u>'s commotion / <u>Loose clouds</u> like earth's <u>decaying leaves</u> are shed, / Shook from the <u>tangled boughs</u> of <u>Heaven</u> and Ocean [. . .]." He goes on to describe how these clouds "are spread on the <u>blue surface</u> of thine <u>aery surge</u>," later referring to them as "the <u>locks</u> of the approaching storm." As the underlined words display, the author merges diction that has to do with trees with diction that involves the sky.

32. The phrase, "the wave's intenser day" (line 34), refers to the **(B) bright reflection of the sun off the water**.

The "day" refers to the sun which is "Quivering" (line 34) on the quietly rolling waves of the Mediterranean. That it is the "wave's intenser day" suggests that the light is being brilliantly reflected by the crystal blue waters of the sea.

33. The fourth section of the poem introduces which of the following?

    I. The speaker's belief that he is as powerful as the wind.

    II. The speaker's consciousness of his affinity with nature.

    III. The speaker's awareness that the trappings of his existence have worn and weighted him down.

(D) II and III.

That the speaker suggests that in his boyhood he was the "comrade of [the wind's] wanderings over Heaven" (line 49) and later refers to himself as "One too like [the wind]" (line 56) confirms II. III is validated by the speaker's admission that "A heavy weight of hours has changed and bowed / One too like thee" (lines 55-56). Nowhere does he claim to be as powerful (I); rather, he invokes the wind to lift him "as a wave, a leaf, a cloud!" (line 53).

34. The fourth section of the poem introduces a tone that is BEST labeled **(A) wistful longing**.

This is pretty much derived from lines 43-47, "If I were a dead leaf thou mightest bear; / If I were a swift cloud to fly with thee; / A wave to pant beneath the power, and share / The impulse of thy strength, only less free / Than thou, O uncontrollable!," in which the speaker clearly longs to have the freedom and strength that the wind enjoys.

35. In lines 47-54 the speaker could perhaps be comparing himself to what classical figure? **(B) Icarus**.

Icarus, the mythological boy who soared too close to the sun on his father's waxen wings and, as a result, plummeted to a watery death, may very well be the allusion here. The speaker wishes to be lifted by the wind, to soar with it in flight, to be "The comrade of [its] wanderings over Heaven" (line 49). However, he also says "I fall upon the thorns of life! I bleed!" (line 54), suggesting that his mortality prevents him from such lofty exhilaration. While the allusion is not a definitive one, the penchant for Romantic poets to allude to classical mythology at least makes it a plausible one.

36. In the fifth and final section of the poem, the speaker figuratively expresses concern over his **(C) aging**.

This is derived directly from line 58, "What if my leaves are falling as its own!," which could figuratively refer to the seasons of his own life or literally to his losing his hair. Phrases such as "withered leaves" (line 64) and "ashes" (line 67) also suggest aging and approaching death.

37. The fifth section of the poem figuratively differs from the first section of the poem in its introduction of which of the following images/symbols? **(E) fire**.

Magic (the enchanter), music (the clarion), the cycle of nature (the motif of the shifting seasons) and autumn ("thou breath of Autumn's being") are all visible in the opening and closing sections of Shelley's ode. Fire (E) is not.

38. In the concluding section, the speaker asks the west wind for **(B) poetic inspiration**.

When the speaker asks the wind to "Drive [his] dead thoughts over the universe / Like withered leaves to quicken a new birth" (lines 63-64), and to "Scatter, as from an unextinguished hearth / Ashes and sparks, my words among mankind!" (lines 66-67), he is referring to his creativity which, like the leaves, has dried up, like the fire has nearly gone out. The wind here is seen as an invigorating, inspirational force that can bring renewed life.

39. The emotional appeal of the final two sections is buttressed by the speaker's use of all of the following EXCEPT **(E) radical changes in the poem's rhythm**.

The tone of imploration (A) is evident in lines such as "Oh, lift me as wave, a leaf, a cloud!" (line 53) and "Make me thy lyre, even as the forest is" (line 57). Imperatives (B) are evident in lines 57 ("Make"), 61 ("Be"), 63 ("Drive"), 66 ("Scatter") and 68 ("Be"). Exclamations that convey the gravity of his condition (C) are apparent in line 54, "I fall upon the thorns of life! I bleed!," while diction linking the speaker with the wind is evident in lines such as "Drive my dead thoughts over the universe" (line 63) and "Scatter, as from an unextinguished hearth / Ashes and sparks, my words among mankind!" (lines 66-67). There are no dramatic changes in the poem's rhythm.

40. Which of the following does NOT contribute to the impressive structural unity of the poem? **(D) religious imagery and allusions**.

The motif of the seasons is to a greater or lesser degree imbued in all five sections of the poem, each of which is comprised of a sonnet-like fourteen lines. Symbols of death and regeneration—the foliage, the flowers, the hearth—are present throughout the poem as are apostrophes asking the wind to "hear" the speaker's appeal. This information validates choices A, B, C, and E. There is, however, little support for D in the poem.

41. The poem is likely a product of which of the following literary epochs? **(C) Romantic**.

One of the skills all AP students should develop is a sense of what characterizes the major poetic movements. In this case, the speaker's intimate communion with nature, the hint in section four of the growing encroachment of the industrial world, and the classical allusions to a Maenad and Baiae's bay should be sufficient to identify this as a product of the Romantic period.

Passage Four: From William Faulkner's "A Rose for Emily"

The concluding passage in Sample Examination Two is drawn from the opening pages of William Faulkner's well-known short story, "A Rose for Emily." In preparing students for the AP English Literature and Composition exam, many teachers expose their students to various types of literary criticism—feminist, Marxist, New Historicist, or psychological. While it is not mandatory that a teacher do so, nor crucial that a student be thoroughly adept at mastering modes of literary criticism, viewing a book through a particular critical lens is a college-level skill that almost always elevates the quality of student papers. Discussing *The Awakening* or *The Scarlet Letter* through a feminist lens, or *The Jungle* or *Death of a Salesman* through a Marxist one enables the student to set the work against the social and economic background of the time in which it was written, often generating rich insights that separate the essay from the rapidly increasing pack. The passage from "A Rose for Emily" offers both teacher and student, if they are unfamiliar, an opportunity to expose themselves to psychological criticism through the death of Emily Grierson, the story's protagonist and the town's most idiosyncratic spinster.

The speaker of the passage indicates that when Miss Emily died, everyone in the town attended her funeral, as if she were a "fallen monument" (line 4), some sort of local curiosity. The astute reader may, in the speaker's description of Miss Emily's house, recognize the distinctly ornate Gothic architecture— "cupolas and spires and scrolled balconies" (lines 10-11), even if he is not yet cognizant of the other Gothic or psychological baggage with which the story is laden. To begin with, the word "fallen," when applied to a woman, usually connotes either a loss of virginity or a pregnancy, and the speaker indicates that the Grierson house, which "had once been white" (lines 9-10), now "lift[ed] its stubborn and coquettish decay above the cotton wagons and the gasoline pumps—an eyesore among eyesores" (lines 16-19). Many times in Gothic literature the house stands for the mind, and the use of a very feminine adjective ("coquettish") to describe the decay of the Grierson mansion should immediately raise some antennae. Coupled with Miss Emily's idiosyncratically reclusive behavior—no one except a solitary Negro man-servant had seen her house's interior in at least ten years—these details suggest that there is something unusual about Miss Emily Grierson.

Further piquing the reader's curiosity is the strange dispensation Miss Emily enjoys from paying taxes. The speaker reveals how upon her father's death Miss Emily had become "a tradition, a duty, and a care; a sort of hereditary obligation upon the town" (lines 25-27), and how Colonel Sartoris, the mayor during her father's time, had "invented an involved tale to the effect that Miss Emily's father had loaned money to the town, which the town, as a matter of business, preferred this way of repaying" (lines 34-37). So romantic and preposterous was this rationale that the speaker observes that "Only a man of Colonel Sartoris' generation and thought could have invented it, and only a woman could have believed it" (lines 38-40). The ensuing paragraphs recount the amusing rejection the next generation of mayors and aldermen receive when they attempt to collect tax from Miss Emily, who rebuffs them by letter and in person, telling them she has "no taxes in Jefferson" (lines 91-92) and advising them to see the long-dead Colonel Sartoris if they are in need of further explanation.

When the deputation of aldermen first enters the house (lines 59-63), they are admitted into a dimly-lit, dank, and dusty interior "from which a stairway mounted into still more shadow" (lines 61-62). This latter detail, a frequent characteristic of the Gothic house, suggests something guarded, a hidden secret. In fact, everything in the room suggests disuse—the leather of the sofa is cracked, the blinds dust-covered, a gilt easel "tarnished" (line 70). On this last object is propped the first intriguing psychological symbol, "a crayon portrait of Miss Emily's father" (lines 70-71). This immediately hints at the possibility of an Oedipal complex, especially in light of her father's premature death.

When Miss Emily enters, she does so dressed in black and "leaning on an ebony cane with a tarnished gold head" (lines 75-76), a gold object that bears material similarity to the easel (Is it a cane that belonged to her father?). She also has a "thin gold chain descending to her waist and vanishing into her belt" (lines 73-75), another object that could well have belonged to her father. Like the brooding and black-clothed Hamlet, Miss Emily seems still to be mourning her father's death years after his passing. Moreover, Miss Emily's physical description immediately identifies her as a grotesque; she is somewhat deformed, and the speaker notes how "Her skeleton was small and spare; perhaps that was why what would have been merely plumpness in another was obesity in her. She looked bloated, like a body long submerged in motionless water, and of that pallid hue" (lines 76-81). Like Poe's Madeline Usher, Emily Grierson's physical features suggest internal illness, and in Gothic fiction this is commonly precipitated by some type of mental disease or moral corruption.

While the reader really needs to read the entire Faulkner story to solve the riddle of Emily Grierson fully, there are enough hints planted in these opening paragraphs to at least offer a peek into her mysterious world. Though at passage's end Miss Emily has her servant show the deputation summarily out, students may actually benefit from reading the rest of this story which provides an excellent vehicle for the teacher wanting to give his/her class an introduction to the Gothic without doing an entire novel. Coupled with a few Edgar Allan Poe stories ("The Fall of the House of Usher;" "The Black Cat") and perhaps something as short as Robert Louis Stevenson's *Dr. Jekyll and Mr. Hyde*, Faulkner's story can open a whole new critical world to AP students and add yet one more implement to their analytical toolbox.

42. The sentence that comprises all of the opening paragraph is primarily intended to establish which aspect of Emily Grierson's character? **(D) her reclusiveness**.

This answer choice is pretty much determined by the fact that the entire town turns out for her funeral and by the curiosity of the women to see the inside of her house "which no one save an old man-servant—a combined gardener and cook—had seen in at least ten years" (lines 5-8).

43. The description of Emily Grierson's house does all of the following EXCEPT **(D) account for Miss Emily's withdrawn nature**.

While the speaker says in the opening paragraph that the men attended Miss Emily's funeral "through a sort of respectful attention for a fallen monument [. . .]" (lines 3-4), Miss Emily's house is described in similar fashion as a "big, squarish frame house that had once been white [. . .]" (lines 9-10) and which was now "lifting its stubborn and coquettish decay above the cotton wagons and the gasoline pumps—an eyesore among eyesores" (lines 16-19). This validates choice A. Choice B is supported by the speaker's observation that though Miss Emily's house had been "set on our most select street [. . .] garages and cotton gins had encroached and obliterated even the august names of that neighborhood" (lines 12-15). Later descriptions of the interior, such as "It smelled of dust and disuse—a close, dank smell" (lines 62-63) and "when they sat down, a faint dust rose sluggishly about their thighs, spinning with slow motes in the single sun-ray" (lines 67-69), provide proof of choice C, while the author's observation that "Miss Emily's house was left, lifting its stubborn and coquettish decay above the cotton wagons and the gasoline pumps [. . .]" (lines 16-18) supports E. Though other factors may, the house itself does not account for Miss Emily's withdrawn nature.

44. Miss Emily's financial 'arrangement' with the town was likely a product of **(C) Colonel Sartoris' empathy for her orphaned condition**.

The speaker indicates in lines 25-32 that "Alive, Miss Emily had been a tradition, a duty, and a care; a sort of hereditary obligation upon the town, dating from that day in 1894 when Colonel Sartoris, the mayor—he who fathered the edict that no Negro woman should appear on the streets without an apron—remitted her taxes, the dispensation dating from the death of her father on into perpetuity." This suggests that, knowing her father had prematurely died, Colonel Sartoris was looking out for Miss Emily's financial welfare.

45. In light of the speaker's description of the interior of Miss Emily's house, which of the following details provides the most definitive clue as to the motive behind her reclusive behavior? **(D) the crayon portrait of her father**.

Choices A, B, C and E are all *consequences* of another action. A close reading of the text shows that Emily Grierson has not gotten over the death of her father. Years after his death she dresses in black, seemingly wears his gold timepiece, and leans upon what appears to be a man's ebony cane, These details, coupled with the preserved crayon portrait of the father, all point to a severe Oedipal complex.

46. It may be inferred from the tone of the speaker that the BEST equivalent for the phrase "more modern" (lines 41-42) would be **(B) financially pragmatic**.

Clearly, the chivalric generosity of Colonel Sartoris in granting Emily Grierson a dispensation from all tax liability belongs to a long gone age. The "more modern" mayors and aldermen want their tax dollars and are determined to collect them until they are stymied by Miss Emily's idiosyncratic obstinacy.

47. Miss Emily's implacable nature is primarily established by her **(C) repeated refrain, "I have no taxes in Jefferson."**

This refrain, uttered in three separate places and silently voiced in her dismissal of their correspondence, shows that no matter how efficient the tax collectors of the town have become, they will not get Miss Emily's money.

48. The physical description of Miss Emily in lines 72-85 most fittingly depicts her as a(n) **(E) grotesque**.

The "grotesque" in literature is a term applied to bizarre, unnatural, often freakish characters. In Gothic fiction these characters may be physically deformed or may, like Stevenson's Mr. Hyde, have some twisted inner deformity that seems to resonate through their character in a greater way than mere dwarfishness. The speaker's description of Miss Emily's physical features—"Her skeleton was small and spare; perhaps that was why what would have been merely plumpness in another was obesity in her. She looked bloated, like a body long submerged in motionless water, and of that pallid hue. Her eyes, lost in the fatty ridges of her face, looked like two small pieces of coal pressed into a lump of dough as they moved from one face to another while the visitors stated their errand" (lines 76-85)—falls into this category. She is described in terms of a corpse.

49. Which of the following does NOT play a role in the invented and involved tale concocted by Colonel Sartoris? **(B) Miss Emily's hubris**.

That Miss Emily has been orphaned and left to raise money by giving painting lessons certainly establishes her financial distress (A), while the speaker's observation that, "Alive, Miss Emily had been a tradition, a duty, and a care; a sort of hereditary obligation upon the town, dating from that day in 1894 when Colonel Sartoris, the mayor—he who fathered the edict that no Negro woman should appear on the streets without an apron—remitted her taxes, the dispensation dating from the death of her father on into perpetuity" (lines 25-32), supports the townspeople's gratitude (E). Choices C and D are both implicit in the tale that Colonel Sartoris concocts to explain the reason for the dispensation. Choice B has nothing to do with it.

50. Which of the following second paragraph phrases clearly foreshadows the physical description of Miss Emily in lines 79-85? **(C) "stubborn and coquettish decay" (line 17)**.

Both words, but particularly the second due to its feminine connotation, are equally applicable to Miss Emily's character and her obstinate refusal to remit any taxes.

51. A Freudian, or psychological, approach to the passage would show the LEAST interest in **(E) Miss Emily's graceful and flowing handwriting**.

As has been made clear in the overall explication of the passage and the explanation of question #45, all of the details or articles listed in choices A, B, C and D would lend themselves to a Freudian or psychological analysis of the passage. Choice E would not.

52. Which of the following does the speaker NOT do? **(E) satirize a gentrified lifestyle**.

The delineation of Miss Emily Grierson supports A, the explanation of why the town remitted her taxes defends B. The description of the Grierson house, the nature of the small Southern town, and personalities such as Colonel Sartoris and the man-servant Tobe validate C, and the inability of the deputation to convince Miss Emily to remit her taxes bolsters D. The passage does not support choice E.

Explication of Free-Response Question One: From Herman Melville's "I and My Chimney"

The first free-response question in Sample Examination Two is based upon a somewhat whimsical short-story by Herman Melville called "I and My Chimney" The story is based upon a real chimney in Melville's residence (Arrowhead) in Pittsfield, Massachusetts, where Melville wrote his literary classic, *Moby Dick*. The prompt asked students to "discuss how the author uses literary techniques to convey the speaker's singular relationship with his chimney."

From the passage's first sentence the intimacy between speaker and chimney is apparent, the speaker personifying the chimney and referring to the pair of them as "two gray-headed old smokers [who] reside in the country" (line 1). The speaker employs a pun, suggesting that they are two "old settlers," especially his chimney which he says "settles more and more every day" (line 2). The speaker, however, does not see the relationship with his chimney as that of equals, but indicates that the chimney, because of its impressive size, takes precedence over him in the eyes of others. The speaker describes his chimney as "a huge, corpulent old Harry VIII of a chimney" (lines 6-7), his allusion to a famed English monarch endowing it with a regal bearing. Employing a simile to convey its prodigious height, the speaker says his chimney is "like Lord Rosse's monster telescope, swung vertical to hit the meridian moon" (line 8) and claims it "is the first object to greet the approaching traveler's eye" (lines 8-9). Such is its prominence that it precedes the speaker in welcoming each new season, and the speaker observes how "The snow is on its head ere on my hat; and every spring, as in a hollow beech tree, the first swallows build their nests in it" (lines 10-11).

Seen from inside, the chimney dwarfs the speaker even more dramatically, and he somberly notes that when he welcomes his guests he stands "not so much before, as, strictly speaking, behind [his] chimney, which is, indeed, the true host" (lines 14-15). Calling his chimney the "grand seignior here—the one great domineering object, not more of the landscape, than of the house [. . .]" (lines 17-18), the speaker notes how his house seems to have been built around the chimney, "leaving but the odd holes and corners to [him] [. . . .]" (lines 20-21). In fact, the chimney's girth is so pronounced that the speaker indicates the width of his residence nearly doubles its height to accommodate "the magnitude of its main content [. . . .]" (line 24).

In the closing paragraph the speaker alludes to the pyramid of Cheops to suggest the mythical proportion and ancient grandeur of his chimney. Lines 29-31—"From the exact middle of the mansion it soars from the cellar, right up through each successive floor, till, four feet square, it breaks water from the ridgepole of the roof, like an anvil-headed whale, through the crest of a billow"—the speaker offers a bit of an "inside joke" by comparing the emergence of the chimney from his mansion's roof to a whale's breaking the surface of the ocean, Melville having penned the great whale-tale of all time in *Moby Dick*. His concluding sentence, however, suggests that most people feel it looks like some defunct observation post of the heavens that has been walled up.

Successful responses to the passage will note the speaker's consciousness of his chimney's greater prominence, his humble willingness to concede his inferiority (in both physical stature and people's interest), and the variety of literary techniques (simile, personification, and allusion being perhaps the most prominent) that the author uses to convey the singular relationship between the speaker and his chimney. As the speaker concisely sums up in lines 15-16, "In the presence of my betters, I hope I know my place [. . .]."

This question has been reprinted for your convenience.

<u>Question One</u>

(Suggested time—40 minutes. This question counts as one-third of the total essay section score.)

Read the following passage carefully. Then, in a well-organized essay, discuss how the author uses literary techniques to convey the speaker's singular relationship with his chimney. In your essay, you may wish to consider such things as diction, figurative language, syntax and tone.

I and my chimney, two gray-headed old smokers, reside in the country. We are, I may say, old settlers here; particularly my old chimney, which settles more and more every day.

Though I always say, *I and my chimney*, as Cardinal Wolsey[1] used to say, *I and my King*, yet this egotistic way of speaking wherein I take precedence of my chimney, is hardly borne out (5) by the facts; in everything, except the above phrase, my chimney taking precedence over me.

Within thirty feet of the turf-sided road, my chimney—a huge, corpulent old Harry VIII of a chimney—rises full in front of me and all my possessions. Standing well up a hillside, my chimney, like Lord Rosse's[2] monster telescope, swung vertical to hit the meridian moon, is the first object to greet the approaching traveler's eye, nor is it the last which the sun salutes. My (10) chimney, too, is before me in receiving the first-fruits of the seasons. The snow is on its head ere on my hat; and every spring, as in a hollow beech tree, the first swallows build their nests in it.

But it is within doors that the pre-eminence of my chimney is most manifest. When in the rear room, set apart from that object, I stand to receive my guests (who, by the way, call more, I suspect, to see my chimney than me), I then stand, not so much before, as, strictly speaking, (15) behind my chimney, which is, indeed, the true host. Not that I demur. In the presence of my betters, I hope I know my place [. . . .].

My chimney is grand seignior here—the one great domineering object, not more of the landscape, than of the house; all the rest of which house, in each architectural arrangement, as may shortly appear, is, in the most marked manner, accommodated, not to my wants, but to my (20) chimney's, which, among other things, has the centre of the house to himself, leaving but the odd holes and corners to me [. . . .].

Most houses here, are but one and a half stories high; few exceed two. That in which I and my chimney dwell, is in width nearly twice its height, from sill to eaves—which accounts for the magnitude of its main content [. . .].

(25) The frame of the old house is of wood—which but the more sets forth the solidity of the chimney, which is of brick. And as the great wrought nails, binding the clapboards, are unknown in these degenerative days, so are the huge bricks in the chimney walls. The architect of the chimney must have had the pyramid of Cheops before him; for, after that famous structure, it seems modeled [. . .] From the exact middle of the mansion it soars from the cellar, right up through (30) each successive floor, till, four feet square, it breaks water from the ridgepole of the roof, like an anvil-headed whale, through the crest of a billow. Most people, though, liken it, in that part, to a razeed[3] observatory, masoned up [. . . .].

---

[1] influential churchman made Lord Chancellor by Henry VIII in 1515

[2] designer and builder of the 19th century's largest telescope

[3] razed; torn down

Scoring Rubric for Free-Response Question One: Herman Melville's "I and My Chimney"

8-9   These papers not only convey their authors' keen understanding of the intimate relationship between the speaker and his chimney, but also persuasively show how the author uses literary techniques to convey that relationship. Well-conceived, well-developed, and well-organized, these papers are marked by frequent and accurate references to the text, by an admirable ability to synthesize thought, and by a mature control over the elements of composition. Though not perfect, they clearly indicate the students' ability to read prose skillfully and to show how the literary elements of the passage support the poem's theme.

6-7   These essays exhibit a solid understanding of the relationship between the speaker and his chimney, but are less adept at responding to the question. This may be due to inconsistencies in textual understanding, to a lesser ability to comprehend the depth of the relationship between the speaker and his chimney, and/or to a lesser ability to show how the author's literary techniques convey that relationship. Though these essays reflect their writers' abilities to convey their points clearly, they feature less fluency, development or cogency than 9-8 papers.

5   These papers respond to the question on the Melville passage in superficial, formulaic, inconsistent or insufficiently supported ways. They may rely primarily on paraphrase, but may still convey an implicit understanding of the passage and the task. The papers are generally written in a satisfactory manner, with occasional errors in composition or mechanics that do not impede the reader's understanding. Nevertheless, these essays lack the organization, persuasiveness and development of upper-half papers.

3-4   These lower-half essays generally suggest an incomplete or overly simplistic understanding of the passage or task, an inability to perceive either the intimate relationship between the speaker and his chimney or how the author's literary techniques convey that relationship. Their arguments are often characterized by a misreading of the text, a failure to provide adequate support, or insufficient control over the elements of composition. In some instances they may consist entirely of paraphrase and/or feature acute problems in organization, clarity, fluency or development.

1-2   These essays compound the shortcomings of 3-4 papers. They often contain many serious and distracting errors in grammar or mechanics that preclude any successful response to the prompt. Though these essays may attempt to discuss the relationship between the speaker and his chimney, they are severely limited by deficiencies in organization, clarity, fluency or development.

0   Papers scored a zero make no more than a passing reference to the task.

—   Papers given this score offer a blank or totally off-topic response.

Sample Student Essay One

The narrator of this passage succeeds in establishing a relationship with his chimney. In describing to the reader the personality and history of the chimney, the reverent and historical tone of the passage, the personification of the chimney and usage of simile, and industrial diction convey the friendship, respect and awesome structure for which the speaker credits his chimney.

One can presume that the narrator is an elderly country man, having lived in one house for a long time. The speaker compares himself and his chimney: they are both, comically, "old gray-headed smokers" and "old settlers." The narrator has a tone of respect for his chimney, and refers to it in comparison to history, characteristic of an aged man looking upon an ancient structure. The chimney is a greater confidant than Wolsey was to Henry VIII. It is analogous to the original telescope of Lord Rosse, not only in its shape but importance to the course of history. The chimney is classical, according to the narrator, inspired by the pyramid of Cheops. The chimney is the master of all it can see, as the narrator dubs it "seignior." The old man venerates the chimney, admitting his secondary place to its magnitude and glory. The reverence the man has for his chimney is made evident by his dignified tone, yet his friendship with the chimney is also established by the author's use of personification.

The chimney is not just reminiscent of great people and objects past, but in fact is a being with a story onto itself, as believed by the narrator. The chimney is a dominating but hospitable presence in the home of the narrator. It is the welcoming presence in the house; it is the first to greet the sun and moon; travelers recognize it first; and nature makes its home there with snow and birds' nests. The chimney takes up its space in the house, and all the rooms arrange themselves around it, instead of around the living master. The narrator uses personification to describe it like an important house guest, whose needs must be attended. The chimney has not just human qualities but also those of the animal kingdom. The narrator uses simile to describe the appearance of the chimney before the sky like that of a "whale, through the crest of a billow." The chimney "soars" and "rises" and "dwells" as a man of great stature or height would, representing the narrator's familiar rapport with his chimney,

While the chimney may be personified and given life, the narrator also chooses to use technical and architectural diction to remind the reader that it is truly an object magnificently made. The narrator has developed knowledge of his chimney's personality, but also pays homage to the design and construction. He describes how the brickwork of the chimney makes it stick out from the rest of the house. Particularly of interest to him is the antiquity of the large bricks. He describes the minor details of the house to compare them to the intricacies of the building of his magnificent chimney. He also employs a simile, telling the reader that most people liken his chimney to a "razed observatory, masoned up." In doing this, he provides a physical description of his main character.

The narrator of the passage portrays to the reader the physical and emotional importance of his chimney. The chimney is a respected figure, and old friend, and a piece of marvelous masonry. The narrator achieves this portrait using personification, historical and reverential tone, and technical diction.

You Rate It!

1. How thorough a job did the student do in establishing the "singular relationship" between the speaker and his chimney?

_____

_____

_____

_____

2. What literary techniques did the student identify that illustrated how the author conveyed the relationship between the speaker and his chimney? How convincing were these?

_____

_____

_____

_____

3. How well-organized and fluent was the student's paper? Was the student's overall argument a persuasive one?

_____

_____

_____

_____

4. On a 0-9 scale, how would you rate this response? Explain why.

_____

_____

_____

_____

Sample Student Essay Two

The closeness of a relationship, some may claim, can often manifest itself in the outward appearance of two individuals. Perhaps two married people will develop similar features after many years spent together, or maybe a dog owner takes on certain superficial characteristics of their beloved canine. Conversely, the speaker in this passage likens himself to his inanimate chimney, displaying the tantamount relationship he seems to have with the object through the use of personification. However, as the passage progresses, the narrator's pervasive feelings of insecurity and incompetence due to his old age become clear through the author's use of diction to denote the superiority of the chimney, as well as allusion to important historical figures and a rambling sentence structure to show both the narrator's self-loathing and the domineering nature of the chimney.

At the commencement of the passage, the speaker immediately establishes his singular relationship with the chimney, as well as his aged appearance, when he personifies the entity, stating, "I and my chimney, two gray-headed old smokers, reside in the country". The narrator further shows this seemingly equivalent relationship when he later says, "The snow is on its head, ere on my hat," a statement which leads the reader to believe that speaker sees himself as being "on par" with the nature of the chimney. This notion, though, is most flagrantly refuted by the author's employment of diction. For example, the chimney is referred to as a "grand seignior," and is described as being both "corpulent" and "domineering" in its presence From this, it is understood that the speaker views himself as subservient, not equal, to his chimney.

The repetition of the phrase "my chimney" over the course of the passage also reflects the narrator's dislike of himself, as this literary technique deflects attention off the "deteriorated" protagonist. In addition to this, the author alters the syntax of the narration to a more rambling style towards the close of the passage, most noticeably in the fifth paragraph, perhaps to further reveal the narrator's insecurities and nervousness around his "master," the chimney. The author writes "as may shortly appear, is, in the most marked manner, accommodated, not to my wants, but to the chimney's, which, among other things, has the centre of the house to himself." The speaker's perception that the chimney is superior to his degenerated, elderly self is revealed through the author's frequent employment of allusion. For example, the speaker compares his chimney to an "old Henry VIII", as well as "Lord Rosse's monster telescope," and likens the massive design of the structure to the "pyramid of Cheops" and "an anvil-headed whale." By showing that the chimney is exceptional enough to even be compared to such impressive and important figures, the speaker clearly expresses his struggle with feelings of ineptitude in his state of progressive aging. The speaker even goes as far as to imply that friends come to his house for the sole purpose of observing the impressive chimney, humbly observing that the chimney "is, indeed, the true host," and later likening himself to a flimsy piece of wood and the omnipotent chimney to a solid piece of brick. Thus, the narrator's insecurities, and even loneliness, due to his old age are expressed throughout the passage by the author's use of various literary devices, most notably diction and allusion, to show the inanimate chimney's dominance of his deteriorated counterpart.

You Rate It!

1. How thorough a job did the student do in establishing the "singular relationship" between the speaker and his chimney?

_____

_____

_____

_____

2. What literary techniques did the student identify that illustrated how the author conveyed the relationship between the speaker and his chimney? How convincing were these?

_____

_____

_____

_____

3. How well-organized and fluent was the student's paper? Was the student's overall argument a persuasive one?

_____

_____

_____

_____

4. On a 0-9 scale, how would you rate this response? Explain why.

_____

_____

_____

_____

Sample Student Essay Three

Relationships are the center-piece of normal human activity. For those living in most normal social conditions, the closest relationships are created between a person and the ones they care about. Therefore, many deduce that all relationships created in solitude or near-solitude between a person and an object must be shallow and bland when in truth, they can be deeper and richer than many relationships between two humans. This is shown clearly in the author's singular relationship with his chimney. His use of tone and diction clearly prove the deepness in the singular relationship he has with his chimney.

The tone of the passage is one of the most defining devices the author uses to establish the singular relationship. Throughout the passage, the tone personifies the chimney and gives it characteristics that nearly parallel the author's. In this manner one gets the sense that the chimney and the author are part of each other, one and the same. The most obvious example of this comes in the first two sentences, when the author describes himself and the chimney as "two grey-headed old smokers" who "reside in the country" and are "old settlers." While making obvious parallels and puns, the most important part of this opening is how it establishes the tone that will follow through the passage. The tone that is set translates to the reader that the roots of the author's life and the roots of the existence of the chimney are intertwined. They are part of each other, and it has been this way for as far back as one can remember. This tone is strongly perpetuated in the third paragraph. The author relates back to the singular relationship when he comments that his guests "call more, I suspect, to see my chimney than me." This shows the close bond between the author and his chimney. The fact that he considers his chimney to be the "bait" that causes others to visit him seems to relate to the tone, insisting that the author and chimney have a very singular relationship.

The diction used in this passage helps to greatly reinforce the idea of the singular relationship between the author and his chimney. Each word in the passage seems to be chosen quite carefully, and this is explained by the author's desire to translate the nature of his relationship with the chimney. One can find an example of this use of diction to describe the chimney in the second paragraph. The author's description infers that the chimney was truly built just for him and is therefore a part of him. The words used to describe the chimney throughout the seasons (how "snow is on its head ere on my hat", and how "every spring, as in a hollow beech tree, the first swallows build their nests in it") translate the relationship. One gets the feeling that throughout the year the author and his chimney have a parallel, singular relationship.

In hindsight, there seems to be no hindrance to the author's special, singular relationship with his chimney. The idea that a unique bond can be built between a person and an object over an extended period of time in near-solitude is clearly proven. By analyzing the tone and diction of the passage, one is able to see how the original, singular relationship between the author and his chimney was created, solidified, and is constantly perpetuated.

You Rate It!

1. How thorough a job did the student do in establishing the "singular relationship" between the speaker and his chimney?

_____

_____

_____

_____

2. What literary techniques did the student identify that illustrated how the author conveyed the relationship between the speaker and his chimney? How convincing were these?

_____

_____

_____

_____

3. How well-organized and fluent was the student's paper? Was the student's overall argument a persuasive one?

_____

_____

_____

_____

4. On a 0-9 scale, how would you rate this response? Explain why.

_____

_____

_____

_____

Author's Response to Sample Student Essays on Herman Melville's "I and My Chimney"

Sample Student Essay One:

This essay does a solid job in establishing the nature of the relationship between the speaker and his chimney. Though the phrase "historical tone of the passage" may be a bit clumsy, the writer's second paragraph clarifies his point, that the author magnifies the chimney's importance by comparing it to a prestigious 16th century churchman, to the prominent telescope of an astronomer, and to the pyramid of a pharaoh. The student notes how "The chimney is not just reminiscent of great people and objects past, but in fact is a being with a story onto itself" and how "The narrator uses personification to describe it like an important house guest, whose needs must be attended." Other than the mention of personification and simile, the essay is a little light on literary techniques, but the paper's strength in establishing the nature of the relationship—"The old man venerates the chimney, admitting his secondary place to its magnitude and glory"—compensates for this. The writing, while featuring an occasional rough phrasing, is generally clear, well-organized and fluent.

Author's Score: 7

Sample Student Essay Two

The opening two sentences of the second sample paper offered tremendous promise that the essay ultimately failed to deliver. The nicely crafted thesis—"The closeness of a relationship, some may claim, can often manifest itself in the outward appearance of two individuals"—was derailed a bit by the student's off-target claim that the speaker is suffering from "pervasive feelings of insecurity and incompetence due to his old age." Though not a fatal flaw, this minor misreading pervades the paper, the student later referring to the speaker as "struggl[ing] with feelings of ineptitude in his state of progressive aging" and referring to him as "the 'deteriorated' protagonist." Though this reading suggests the student did not catch the tongue-in-cheek nature of the passage, the essay is not without merit. The writer does a good job in recognizing not only the personification but the pervasive use of allusion, and in noting that "The speaker even goes as far as to imply that friends come to his house for the sole purpose of staring at the impressive chimney, humbly observing that the chimney 'is, indeed, the true host,' and later likening himself to a flimsy piece of wood and the omnipotent chimney to a solid piece of brick." Though insisting that the speaker's emphasis on the magnificence of his chimney is intended to reveal "the narrator's insecurities, and even loneliness, due to his old age," the essay has enough accurate observation to sneak into the upper-half of the scoring rubric.

Author's Score: 6

Sample Student Essay Three:

The third and final student sample is a prototypical fence-straddler. The writer's thesis, that "all relationships created in solitude or near-solitude between a person and an object [. . .] can be deeper and richer than many relationships between two humans," is quite reasonable and insightful, and the student understands that the speaker and his chimney share an intimate relationship that goes back a long way. However, the student's control of literary techniques such as tone and diction (or at least the expression of these) is sorely lacking, and the paper is hurt by shaky phrases such as "Throughout the passage, the tone personifies the chimney" and "This tone is strongly perpetuated in the third paragraph." The writer seems unable to verbalize what the tone is, and though he refers to diction, he really does not examine any examples of it successfully. The rubric's descriptors of "superficial" and "insufficiently supported" reflect this paper well.

Author's Score: 5

Explication of Free-Response Question Two: The Influence of William Butler Yeats' poem "The Wild Swans at Coole" upon John Updike's "The Great Scarf of Birds"

Ever since John Updike's poem appeared on the AP English Literature & Composition Exam and I recognized its clear Yeatsian influence, I have been wanting to develop this question. Told that the poems they were to consider had been "written some seventy years apart by an Irishman and an American" and that their content "suggest[s] that the former poem inspired or influenced the latter," students were asked to read Yeats' acknowledged masterpiece "The Wild Swans at Coole" in tandem with Updike's "The Great Scarf of Birds," and to "discuss how the two authors use a similar scene to provoke a strikingly different response." They were further required to illustrate these different responses through a consideration of literary elements such as as diction, theme, choice of detail, figurative language or tone.

In Yeats' poem the setting is the twilight of an autumn day, with a beautiful image of fifty-nine swans setting peacefully on a lake that pristinely mirrors the sky above it. The speaker, who reveals in the second stanza of the poem that this is the nineteenth autumn in which he has observed this glorious spectacle, recalls how he saw them "All suddenly mount / And scatter wheeling in great broken rings / Upon their clamorous wings" (lines 10-12). The third stanza, however, introduces the fact that though the spectacle of the swans has remained the same, the speaker himself has changed. Now his "heart is sore" (line 14) and he admits "All's changed since I, hearing at twilight, / The first time on this shore / The bell-beat of their wings above my head, / Trod with a lighter tread" (lines 15-18). The diction here suggests that the speaker is unhappy, preoccupied with concerns (perhaps romantic ones) that trouble him and weigh upon his mind. Unlike him, the swans' "hearts have not grown old" (line 22), and as they paddle together or rise in formation, "Passion or conquest [. . .] / Attend upon them still" (lines 23-24). Though the closing image is a beautiful and tranquil one, the speaker seems troubled by the knowledge that he will "awake some day / To find they have flown away" (lines 29-30).

In contrast, Updike's poem is set on a golf course. The speaker is not alone but with a golfing companion, though the season (fall) is the same. Here the speaker's description is more imagistic, and the opening lines of the poem employ simile to describe both the abundance of ripe apples and the colorful fall foliage, though the leaf-bereft elms are metaphorically described as "swaying vases full of sky" (line 8). Overhead squadrons of honking geese stream south, seemingly prescient of the approaching winter. It is the second stanza of the poem, however, in which the Yeatsian influence first comes into clear focus. Comparing the sight to something "out of the Bible / or science fiction" (lines 14-15), the speaker describes a flock of starlings whose tight formation makes them appear "a cloud of dots / like iron filings which a magnet / underneath the paper undulates" (lines 16-18). Unlike the spectacle of the fifty-nine swans, the mystery of the flock of starlings diminishes as they fly closer, and the speaker observes how "Come nearer, it became less marvelous / more legible, and merely huge" (lines 25-26). Having returned their focus to the match, the golfers do not make much of the sight until the speaker remarks in lines 29-32, how "Later, as Lot's wife must have done, / in a pause of walking, not thinking / of calling down a consequence / I lazily looked around." The Biblical allusion to Lot's wife, who, though forbidden, turned to look back at the destruction of Sodom and Gomorrah and was turned into a pillar of salt, suggests that the speaker's decision to return his eyes to the flock is of some consequence. Over a rise in the fairway he sees a sight similar to the speaker in the Yeats' poem, the flock of starlings spread out like a drying inkstain on the "gradual rise of green" (line 38). So striking is the sight that the speaker reflects "I had thought nothing in nature could be so broad but grass" (line 39). And just as the speaker in the Yeats' poem saw the swans in unison take flight, the speaker in the Updike poem observes in lines 41-47 how

> [. . .] one bird
> prompted by accident or will to lead,
> ceased resting; and, lifting in a casual billow,
> the flock ascended as a lady's scarf,
> transparent, of gray, might be twitched
> by one corner, drawn upward and then,
> decided against, negligently tossed toward a chair [. . .].

Unlike the turbulent "bell-beat" of the swans' wings, the ascent of the starlings is virtually noiseless, and the comparison to the gray lady's scarf captures this expertly. The concluding lines of the poem—"Long had it been since my heart / had been lifted as it was by the lifting of that great scarf"—suggest that the speaker found the moment to be an emotionally uplifting and joyous one, a feeling he suggests he had not experienced for some time.

Students responding to the prompt successfully will undoubtedly explore such things as the age of the speakers and how their individual perspectives affect their reaction to the sight of the birds; the simplicity of the imagery in the Yeats' poem as opposed to the abundance of figurative language in the Updike poem; the potential symbolic import of the birds' colors; the relative importance and impact of each setting; the stanzaic structure of each piece; even perhaps the era in which each poem was written. In doing so, they should have an abundance of possibility with which to develop their arguments about how the Yeats' poem influenced the Updike one.

This question has been reprinted for your convenience.

<u>Question Two</u>

(Suggested time—40 minutes. This question counts as one-third of the total essay section score.)

The impact of one author or literary work upon another may be unconscious or deliberate. The following two poems, written some seventy years apart by an Irishman and an American, strongly suggest that the former poem inspired or influenced the latter. Read each poem carefully. Then, in a well-organized essay, discuss how the two authors use a similar scene to provoke a strikingly different response. In your essay, you may wish to consider such things as diction, theme, choice of detail, figurative language and tone.

The Wild Swans at Coole

The trees are in their autumn beauty,
The woodland paths are dry,
Under the October twilight the water
Mirrors a still sky;
(5)   Upon the brimming water among the stones
Are nine-and-fifty swans.

The nineteenth autumn has come upon me
Since I first made my count;
I saw, before I had well finished,
(10)   All suddenly mount
And scatter wheeling in great broken rings
Upon their clamorous wings.

I have looked upon these brilliant creatures,
And now my heart is sore.
(15)   All's changed since I, hearing at twilight,
The first time on this shore
The bell-beat of their wings above my head,
Trod with a lighter tread.

Unwearied still, lover by lover,
(20)   They paddle in the cold
Companionable streams or climb the air;
Their hearts have not grown old;
Passion or conquest, wander where they will,
Attend upon them still.

(25)   But now they drift on the still water,
Mysterious, beautiful;
Among what rushes will they build,
By what lake's edge or pool
Delight men's eyes when I awake some day
(30)   To find they have flown away?

—William Butler Yeats (1916, 1919)

The Great Scarf of Birds

Playing golf on Cape Ann in October,
I saw something to remember.
Ripe apples were caught like red fish in the nets
of their branches. The maples
(5) were colored like apples
part orange and red, part green.
The elms, already transparent trees,
seemed swaying vases full of sky. The sky
was dramatic with great straggling V's
(10) of geese streaming south, mare's-tails above
      them.
Their trumpeting made us look up and around.
The course sloped into salt marshes,
and this seemed to cause the abundance of birds.

As if out of the Bible
(15) or science fiction,
a cloud appeared, a cloud of dots
like iron filings which a magnet
underneath the paper undulates.
It dartingly darkened in spots,
(20) paled, pulsed, compressed, distended, yet
held an identity firm: a flock
of starlings, as much one thing as a rock.
One will moved above the trees
the liquid and hesitant drift.

(25) Come nearer, it became less marvelous,
more legible, and merely huge.
"I never saw so many birds!" my friend exclaimed.
We returned our eyes to the game.
Later, as Lot's wife must have done,
(30) in a pause of walking, not thinking
of calling down a consequence
I lazily looked around.

The rise of the fairway above us was tinted,
So evenly tinted I might not have noticed
(35) But that at the rim of the delicate shadow
The starlings were thicker and outlined the flock
As an inkstain in drying pronounces its edges.
The gradual rise of green was vastly covered:
I had thought nothing in nature could be so broad
      but grass.

(40) And as
I watched, one bird,
prompted by accident or will to lead,
ceased resting; and, lifting in a casual billow,
the flock ascended as a lady's scarf,
(45) transparent, of gray, might be twitched
by one corner, drawn upward and then,
decided against, negligently tossed toward a chair:
the southward cloud withdrew into the air.

Long had it been since my heart
(50) had been lifted as it was by the lifting of that
      great scarf.

—John Updike (1989)

Scoring Rubric for Free-Response Question Two: William Butler Yeats' poem "The Wild Swans at Coole" and John Updike's "The Great Scarf of Birds"

8-9   These papers not only convey their authors' keen understanding of the ways in which the Yeats' poem influences the Updike poem, but also persuasively show how the two authors use a similar scene to convey a strikingly different response. They also convincingly illustrate how the literary elements of each poem effect this. Well-conceived, well-developed, and well-organized, these papers are marked by frequent and accurate references to the text, by an admirable ability to synthesize thought, and by a mature control over the elements of composition. Though not perfect, they clearly indicate the students' ability to read poetry skillfully and to show how the literary elements of the poem support the poem's theme.

6-7   These essays exhibit a solid understanding of the ways in which the Yeats' poem influences the Updike poem, but are less adept at responding to the question. This may be due to inconsistencies in textual understanding, to a lesser ability to show how the two authors use a similar scene to convey a strikingly different response, and/or to a lesser ability to illustrate how the literary elements of each poem effect this. Though these essays reflect their writers' abilities to convey their points clearly, they feature less fluency, development or cogency than 9-8 papers.

5   These papers respond to the question on the Yeats and Updike poems in superficial, formulaic, inconsistent or insufficiently supported ways. They may rely primarily on paraphrase, but may still convey an implicit understanding of the poems and the task. The papers are generally written in a satisfactory manner, with occasional errors in composition or mechanics that do not impede the reader's understanding. Nevertheless, these essays lack the organization, persuasiveness and development of upper-half papers.

3-4   These lower-half essays generally suggest an incomplete or overly simplistic understanding of the passage or task, an inability to perceive how the two poets use a similar scene to convey a strikingly different response, and/or a lesser ability to illustrate how the literary elements of each poem effect this. Their arguments are often characterized by a misreading of the text, a failure to provide adequate support, or insufficient control over the elements of composition. In some instances they may consist entirely of paraphrase and/or feature acute problems in organization, clarity, fluency or development.

1-2   These essays compound the shortcomings of 3-4 papers. They often contain many serious and distracting errors in grammar or mechanics that preclude any successful response to the prompt. Though these essays may attempt to show how the two poets use a similar scene to convey a different response, they are severely limited by deficiencies in organization, clarity, fluency or development.

0   Papers scored a zero make no more than a passing reference to the task.

—   Papers given this score offer a blank or totally off-topic response.

Sample Student Essay One

W.B Yeats and John Updike describe their own experiences with birds in nature. It is evident that Updike was influenced by his Irish predecessor's style and subject matter, yet he creates a very different tone for his interaction of bird and man. Updike conveys the extraordinary situation in a nostalgic tone, recalling the remarkable event, while Yeats describes his scene with fearful anticipation of loss. Yeats uses romantic diction and Updike sets his scenario with modern diction. The choice of language and detail give the reader greater insight into the thoughts of the two poets: Yeats, the forlorn, and Updike, the inspired.

Yeats and Updike both begin their poems with a description of setting, Yeats' autumn is still, dry and quiet, a time in which he is a solitary visitor. Updike's speaker is separated from nature by modern barriers—his time with nature is playing golf—but seems to understand the connection between elements of nature. Whereas Yeats uses simplistic phrases to tell the reader that he is in a beautiful place, Updike chooses to go into great detail about how all of nature fits together: the trees match the color of the apples in their branches; the trees are full of sky; and the sky is full of geese. Yeats is an observer, almost a voyeur. He loves the sight of the "brilliant creatures," and does not want to lose his spectacle to "other men's eyes." Both are impressed with the motion and sound of the swans, Yeats using elaborate diction to describe the noise of their wings and their rapid movement, Updike employing simile and personification, a more modern tone in his simplistic vocabulary and technological comparisons ("iron filings which a magnet underneath undulates").

The use of language by the two poets helps the reader begin to understand the tones and themes of the poems. Both share a similarity in theme—that man's experience with nature can provoke personal feelings and contemplation. About what and how the two speakers contemplate are very different. The reader can feel the sadness in the young speaker of Yeats' poem. At only 19, the man has already experienced loss and a hardening of heart ("All's changed since I [. . .] trod with a lighter tread"). The reader can guess that the man's lover has left him, stripping him of dignity and immobilizing him with fear. The anxiety about the departure of the swans for some other man's lake is likely symbolic of his lover's departure. The speaker admires the swans for their unwearied action as their quotidian behaviors are indefatigable despite the troubles of love. Yeats' title—"The Wild Swans at Coole"—gives evidence to the overall tone of the poem. The uncontrollable nature of the swans tears at the young speaker who was unable to tame his own swan. The speaker looks upon the swans with fearful anticipation of when they too will leave him.

The speaker of Updike's poem had a much different thought pattern in reaction to the birds. The speaker tells the reader a story of the past, evidenced by the quote "long has it been since my heart had been lifted as it was the lifting of that great scarf." The tone of Updike's poem is initially awesome, a man impressed by the immensity of the birds, but ultimately becomes nostalgic. The speaker focused on the ability of one bird to lead so many others into flight, perhaps a statement of his own desire to effect change. The moment was also special for Updike's speaker because it showed a rare occasion of man interacting with the natural, simple world. The miracles of God are far more impressive than a round of golf. But the speaker also tells the reader that he has not had such a revelation since that moment, leaving the reader acquainted with yet another disappointed and sad speaker.

Updike and Yeats use different literary techniques and styles to represent a similar occurrence. Updike invokes an inspirational moment in the past with a hint of wistfulness, while Yeats laments his loss and manifests his depression in the viewing of the swans. The difference in time period, personality of speaker, and intended theme are conveyed by a combination of diction and appropriate tone.

You Rate It!

1. How thorough a job did the student do in establishing how the Yeats' poem influenced the Updike one? In describing how the two authors used a similar scene to provoke a strikingly different response?

_____

_____

_____

_____

2. What literary techniques did the student employ to illustrate the differences between the respective speaker's reaction to each spectacle? How effective were these?

_____

_____

_____

_____

3. How well-organized and fluent was the student's paper? Was the student's overall argument a persuasive one?

_____

_____

_____

_____

4. On a 0-9 scale, how would you rate this response? Explain why.

_____

_____

_____

_____

Sample Student Essay Two

Poetry is timeless, using familiar scenes to evoke emotions in all generations and eras of people. Nonetheless, a similar scene can be used in multiple ways and towards a different end, as is the case with "The Wild Swans at Coole" by William Butler Yeats and "The Great Scarf of Birds" by John Updike. Though "The Wild Swans at Coole," is written seventy years earlier than "The Great Scarf of Birds," and both have different tones, details, and themes, they still use the same scene to evoke emotion.

The tone of "The Swan at Coole" is strikingly different than the tone of "The Great Scarf of Birds." First, the poems' structures are utilized in creating tone and mood. "The Wild Swans at Coole" is written in couplet fashion with rhyme. This more traditional style of poetry gives the words a lyrical quality and consistency. On the other hand, "The Great Scarf of Birds" is free form, allowing the author to emphasize what he desires. This makes the poem seem more like prose as its colloquial tone tells a story. Although both are written in first person, "The Wild Swans at Coole" is more descriptive and observant of the scene, while "The Great Scarf of Birds" describes more personally the speaker's relation to the action surrounding him. The speaker in the latter is impressed by the magnitude of the scene, the "great scarf," while the speaker in "The Wild Swans at Coole" is awestricken by the creatures themselves. In turn, "The Wild Swans at Coole" seems more unearthly, in that the speaker has reached a magical level of intimacy with these birds, while "The Great Scarf of Birds" shows the majesty of the scene through the humanity of the speaker.

The two poems also utilize strikingly different details in conveying similar scenes. "The Wild Swans at Coole" uses sensory details to describe a gentle, unearthly scene; the swans "climb the air" and "the water / Mirrors a still sky" under the twilight. The scene in "The Great Scarf of Birds," on the other hand, is described using more realistic details used in uncommon fashions; for example, fish, a common proponent of everyday life, are compared to ripe apples, an unusual pairing. The birds in the first poem are said to "wander where they will," which gives the birds an independence from all other forces, while the birds in the second poem are compared to a great scarf; a singular, mindless object. While the speaker in "The Wild Swans at Coole" respects the birds, the speaker in "The Great Scarf of Birds" is merely impressed by them.

The overall themes of the two poems are distinct and reflect the other differences in tone and choice of detail. After marveling at the swans, the speaker in "The Wild Swans at Coole" concludes by asking "By what lake's edge or pool / [will they] Delight men's eyes when I awake some day / To find they have flown away?" (27-29). This speaker laments their possible departure as they have become a part of his world by the lake. In "The Great Scarf of Birds," on the other hand, the speaker is uplifted by the departure of the birds and in awe of how spectacular the scene is. This outlook is more optimistic than the other. While the speaker enjoys what he has at each moment in "The Great Scarf of Birds," the speaker in "The Wild Swans at Coole" thinks instead of how he might lose what he has.

Although birds in both "The Wild Swans at Coole" and "The Great Scarf of Birds" are brilliant and awe-inspiring, the authors of each manipulate this differently. The tone, choice of detail, and theme in each poem is distinct and in contrast to that of the other literary work. These two poems illustrate each individual author's ability to utilize literary elements towards their own purpose.

You Rate It!

1. How thorough a job did the student do in establishing how the Yeats' poem influenced the Updike one? In describing how the two authors used a similar scene to provoke a strikingly different response?

_____

_____

_____

_____

2. What literary techniques did the student employ to illustrate the differences between the respective speaker's reaction to each spectacle? How effective were these?

_____

_____

_____

_____

3. How well-organized and fluent was the student's paper? Was the student's overall argument a persuasive one?

_____

_____

_____

_____

4. On a 0-9 scale, how would you rate this response? Explain why.

_____

_____

_____

_____

Sample Student Essay Three

In reading John Updike's "The Great Scarf of Birds" it is obvious that his poem was influenced by an earlier poem, William Butler Yeats' "The Wild Swans at Coole". From their differences in figurative language, tone, and imagery, the authors are able to create different reactions though using a similar scene.

The figurative language utilized by both Yeats and Updike evokes similar scenes in the reader's mind. Yeats describes the "trees [. . .] in their autumn beauty," which suggests vast numbers of trees all sporting their colorful seasonal leaves. Updike's writing provokes the same setting by saying that "[t]he maples/ were colored like apples / part orange and red part green." Both poets depict their scenes as calm and serene, with still, beautifully silent birds. Yeats' swans drift, paddle softly on still water, and "trod with a lighter tread." Paralleling these examples, Updike's geese are slow moving, and lackadaisical. He describes the geese in his story resting, straggling, and lifting casually in a "liquid and hesitant drift."

The writers use completely different tones in order to send two differing messages to the reader. Yeats uses a saddened, aching tone to depict his connection of the swans for his reader, while Updike's tone is more hopeful and expecting. Since the swans in Yeats' poem symbolize his very soul, which is still young at the time the poem was written, he states that the swans' "hearts have not grown old." As the swans paddle "lover by lover," Yeats begins to pine for his own love as well. He fears the day when he will wake "[t]o find they have flown away" because that would mean that his love, or ability to love, has left as well. This shows his aching tone and demonstrates the heartache in his life. Updike's poem, on the other hand, evokes a very different feeling in the reader. His hopeful tone exemplifies the speaker's desires and dreams. It is evident that Updike uses the birds as a symbol for his spirits. Unlike Yeats, Updike notes nostalgically that it has been a long time since his spirits "had been lifted" by that great scarf of birds. The more hopeful tone, that there is happiness in his future, contrasts with the bleaker, aching tone of Yeats' work.

The differing imagery of the natural world in the two poems creates two different reactions. Updike's poem is slightly more imposing when it describes the enormous flock of birds that flies overhead and lands nearby. This image of these birds, though intimidating, also evokes a feeling of comfort that was obviously also felt by the speaker. The birds in flight represent his reaching out toward his dreams, and the "vastly covered," "broad" carpet of birds is tantamount to the magnitude of his wishes and hopes for life. The swans are less imposing, and in this case, they travel in "broken rings," pair by pair instead of in large groups. Yeats describes the dry, biting cold of the afternoon, which exemplifies his doubts and nervousness about the future.

From the similar figurative language in both Yeats' "The Wild Swans at Coole" and Updike's "The Great Scarf of Birds," it is obvious that the former influenced the latter. However, through use of both imagery and tone, the two authors are able to evoke completely different reactions from the reader.

You Rate It!

1. How thorough a job did the student do in establishing how the Yeats' poem influenced the Updike one? In describing how the two authors used a similar scene to provoke a strikingly different response?

_____

_____

_____

_____

2. What literary techniques did the student employ to illustrate the differences between the respective speaker's reaction to each spectacle? How effective were these?

_____

_____

_____

_____

3. How well-organized and fluent was the student's paper? Was the student's overall argument a persuasive one?

_____

_____

_____

_____

4. On a 0-9 scale, how would you rate this response? Explain why.

_____

_____

_____

_____

Author's Response to Sample Student Essays on The Influence of William Butler Yeats' poem "The Wild Swans at Coole" upon John Updike's "The Great Scarf of Birds"

Sample Student Essay One:

The first sample paper is a very uneven one as far as the consistency of its understanding and its facility with literary terms. While the writer's initial observation that "Updike conveys the extraordinary situation in a nostalgic tone, recalling the remarkable event, while Yeats describes his scene with fearful anticipation of loss," is reasonably accurate, the student misreads text in some places and understandably goes a bit off-course. For example, the writer mistakenly concludes that the speaker in the Yeats' poem is nineteen years of age when it is actually the nineteenth *year* in which he has seen the spectacle of the swans. This leads to his concluding that "The reader can guess that the man's lover has left him, stripping him of dignity and immobilizing him with fear. The anxiety about the departure of the swans for some other man's lake is likely symbolic of his lover's departure." Though this misreading is not fatal—the poem may well be about lost love—it combines with the student's shaky grasp of tone and diction (just what does he mean by "modern diction?") to weaken the overall persuasiveness of the essay. The student fares better at times with the Updike poem as evidenced by observations such as "Updike chooses to go into great detail about how all of nature fits together: the trees match the color of the apples in their branches; the trees are full of sky; and the sky is full of geese" and "Updike's speaker is separated from nature by modern barriers—his time with nature is playing golf [. . .]." His observation that the speaker in the Yeats' poem is "almost a voyeur" is very well phrased. Overall, this paper has enough going for it to make it into the upper-half, but not enough to propel it further up the scoring rubric.

Author's Score: 6, rising

Sample Student Essay Two:

This competent essay delivers a workman-like response to the two poems. The author of this essay endeavors to address differences in the poem's structure, observing that "'The Wild Swans at Coole' is written in couplet fashion with rhyme. This more traditional style of poetry gives the words a lyrical quality and consistency. On the other hand, 'The Great Scarf of Birds' is free form, allowing the author to emphasize what he desires. This makes the poem seem more like prose as its colloquial tone tells a story." Noting that both poems involve an intimate first-person perspective, the writer suggests that "'The Wild Swans at Coole' is more descriptive and observant of the scene, while 'The Great Scarf of Birds' describes more personally the speaker's relation to the action surrounding him." The writer's observation that the speaker in the Yeats' poem "has reached a magical level of intimacy with these birds" is a nice one, clearer and more effectively rendered than his claim that Updike's poem "shows the majesty of the scene through the humanity of the speaker." The writer's third paragraph reference to "sensory details" in the Yeats' poem and her claim that Updike uses "more realistic details used in uncommon fashions; for example, fish, a common proponent of everyday life, are compared to ripe apples, an unusual pairing," is also quite accurate. The writer correctly concludes that the speaker in the Yeats' poem "laments [the swans'] possible departure, as they have become a part of his world by the lake" while the speaker in Updike's poem "is uplifted by the departure of the birds and in awe of how spectacular the scene is." Though some may find this student's approach a little too lock-step, her paper is marked by a solid organizational plan which she carries out from wire-to-wire. While not an exceptional upper-half paper, it is certainly a good one.

Author's Score: 7

Sample Student Essay Three:

The third student essay does just enough to make it into the upper-half but displays inconsistencies similar to the first sample essay. The writer accurately notes the similar seasonal settings and rightly observes that "Both poets depict their scenes as calm and serene, with still, beautifully silent birds." The student is guilty of a minor misreading when he applies the words "trod with a lighter tread" to the swans in lieu of the speaker, and the choice of the word "lackadaisical" to describe the swans could probably be upgraded though neither of these is particularly deleterious to the essay. The student's assessment of the tone in the Yeats' poem as sad and aching is acceptable, more so than the terms "hopeful and expecting" that he applies to the Updike poem. The student's claims that Updike's "hopeful tone exemplifies the speaker's desires and dreams" and that the "carpet of birds is tantamount to the magnitude of his wishes and hopes for life" suggests the student may be extracting a specific moral that the generality of the poem may not intend.

Author's Score: 6

Explication of Free-Response Question Three: Literary Counterparts and How They Further a Work's Purpose

The final free-response question in Sample Examination Two asked students to identify a pair of "literary counterparts," characters who function almost as a tandem in a play or a novel. In discussing these counterparts, whose mutual involvement "may range from the acute interdependence of soul-mates to the polar hostility of rivals," students were asked to show how their "intimate involvement makes an important contribution to the work as a whole."

Though the accessibility of this question was designed in part to offset the length of the two-poem comparison of question two, it is an interesting question in its own right, enabling students to respond with extremely disparate works and extremely disparate characters. Students may readily think of the symbiotic pairing of George and Lennie in Steinbeck's *Of Mice and Men*, where the former serves as an aegis for the mentally-challenged latter, helping him negotiate daily living and sustaining him daily with an almost child-like retelling of how they will someday get a farm of their own and "live off the fat of the land." Ironically, it is the physically impressive Lennie whose Herculean strength is the main reason the two of them find ready work as ranch-hands. This combination of brains and brawn sustains the core of the novel since through Lennie's labor and George's frugality they have gradually saved enough money to make buying a piece of land a plausible reality. When the other outcasts of the novel—the aged Candy, the crippled negro Crooks, and Curly's wife—hear about their plan, they readily offer their limited monies and capabilities to make this dream a reality, wanting themselves to share in such a haven. Unfortunately, Lennie's inability to understand his own strength—he is always petting things too hard, from a rabbit, to a puppy-dog, to a woman—results in the accidental murder of Curly's wife, sabatoging their plans. In the ultimate act of friendship, George shoots Lennie behind the ear rather than see him savaged by the irrational violence of a lynch mob. The relationship between George and Lennie helps carry out the rather depressing theme—that for the outcasts of society there is no haven, and the closest one can come to achieving the "American dream" is hearing it recited like a fairy-tale before a bullet violently enters one's head.

Though time and space prohibit a similarly expansive discussion of other works, there is clearly a rich field from which to choose. Students might choose to discuss any number of Shakespearean pairings—the deluded trust Othello puts in the nefarious Iago; the familial blindness of Lear and Gloucester and the awful price of their blunders; the financial "bond" but ethnic hatred between Shylock and Antonio. Students could easily discuss the intertwined fortunes of Dickens' Charles Darnay and his wastrel look-alike Sidney Carton in *A Tale of Two Cities*, or examine two seemingly interchangeable characters such as Didi and Estragon in *Waiting for Godot* or the title characters in Stoppard's *Rosencrantz and Guildenstern are Dead*. Hester and Dimmesdale, Frankenstein and the monster, the whiskey priest and the *mestizo*, Quentin and Caddy, Heathcliff and Catherine, Sue Brideshead and Jude—the literary boundaries are limitless. The real challenge of the question, however, lies not in the selection of the counterparts, but in the student's ability to illustrate how the characters make an important contribution to the work as a whole. The most successful essays will usually address this thematically, but some more sophisticated papers may elect to examine this from a structural or stylistic perspective, and readers should remain open to this possibility.

This question has been reprinted for your convenience.

<u>Question Three</u>

(Suggested time—40 minutes. This question counts as one-third of the total essay section score.)

Frequently in literature, a novel or play focuses around a pair of "counterparts," characters who seem inseparably bound by situation or by fate. This mutual involvement, which may range from the acute interdependence of soul-mates to the polar hostility of rivals, is often used to further the work's larger literary purpose. From the novels and plays you have read, choose a work that features such a pair of "counterparts." Using your knowledge of the work, clarify the nature of the characters' relationship and indicate in what way their intimate involvement makes an important contribution to the work as a whole. You may choose from the list below or use another novel or play of recognized literary merit.

Waiting for Godot	*Of Mice and Men*
Crime and Punishment	*Jude the Obscure*
The Scarlet Letter	*Julius Caesar*
Romeo and Juliet	*The Adventures of Huckleberry Finn*
Frankenstein	*J.B.*
Death in Venice	*On the Road*
Billy Budd	*Cry, the Beloved Country*
Othello	*Dr. Jekyll and Mr. Hyde*
The Mill on the Floss	*Wuthering Heights*
Les Miserables	*Amadeus*
The Sound and the Fury	*Billy Budd*
The Importance of Being Earnest	*The Power & the Glory*

Scoring Rubric for Free-Response Question Three: Literary Counterparts and How They Further a Work's Purpose

8-9   The writers of these papers not only select a singularly appropriate pair of literary counterparts, but also persuasively show how the interaction of these two characters makes an important contribution to the work as a whole. Well-conceived, well-developed, and well-organized, these papers are marked by frequent and accurate references to the text, by an admirable ability to synthesize thought, and by a mature control over the elements of composition. Though not perfect, they clearly indicate the students' ability to respond to the prompt with fluency and cogency.

6-7   The writers of these papers also select an appropriate pair of literary counterparts, but are less adept at responding to the question. This may be due to less successful articulation of the relationship between these two counterparts, or to a less successful illustration of how the interaction of these two characters makes an important contribution to the work as a whole. Though these essays reflect their writers' abilities to convey their points clearly, they feature less fluency, development or cogency than 9-8 papers.

5   These papers respond to the question on literary counterparts in superficial, formulaic, inconsistent or insufficiently supported ways. They may rely primarily on paraphrase, but may still convey an implicit understanding of the prompt's task. The papers are generally written in a satisfactory manner, with occasional errors in composition or mechanics that do not impede the reader's understanding. Nevertheless, these essays lack the organization, persuasiveness and development of upper-half papers.

3-4   These lower-half essays generally suggest an incomplete or overly simplistic understanding of the prompt's task, an inability to select an appropriate pair of literary counterparts, and/or a lesser ability to illustrate how the interaction of these two characters makes an important contribution to the work as a whole. Their arguments are often characterized by a failure to provide adequate support or insufficient control over the elements of composition. In some instances they may consist entirely of paraphrase and/or feature acute problems in organization, clarity, fluency or development.

1-2   These essays compound the shortcomings of 3-4 papers. They often contain many serious and distracting errors in grammar or mechanics that preclude any successful response to the prompt. Though these essays may attempt to show how a pair of characters functions collaboratively in a literary work, they are severely limited by deficiencies in organization, clarity, fluency or development.

0   Papers scored a zero make no more than a passing reference to the task.

—   Papers given this score offer a blank or totally off-topic response.

Sample Student Essay One

Often in a novel, the author directs the reader's attention to a bond between two characters; in fact, the novel pivots around the connection that these two people have established. The pair of "counterparts" in a work of literature not only exhibits an important relationship between the principal characters, but also provides support for the underlying themes of the book. In her critically acclaimed novel, <u>Beloved</u>, Toni Morrison creatively integrates the union of a mother (Sethe) and daughter (Beloved) into the major premise of the book. The parasitic nature of Beloved's relationship with Sethe conveys Morrison's thesis that memories have the capability of consuming one's soul unless one is ready to accept the past and continue with the future. The author clearly illustrates the gradual intent of Beloved to consume Sethe's dreams.

The nature of Beloved's relationship is impossible to clarify without examining Sethe's past. Once a slave at Sweet Home, Sethe had two young children whom she loved dearly. Sethe decided to escape this life of slavery, but did not manage to get very far from the plantation. In a moment of fear and panic, she took a handsaw and slit the throat of her beautiful baby girl, Beloved. She decided she would rather her child be dead than forced to live a terrible life of slavery. For eighteen years, Sethe lives with guilt, knowing that she has killed her own child. Morrison illustrates the protagonist's obvious vulnerability because of the crime she committed and begins to show how her past is enveloping her current life before Beloved is "reborn." Beloved's arrival is foreshadowed by the "demon baby" that haunts Sethe's house on the first page of the novel. One of the first sentences incorporates the fact that 124 (her home) is "full of baby's venom." Eighteen years after she was killed, Beloved, the embodiment of Sethe's dead child, returns to Sethe and begins to establish a relationship that will grow stronger throughout the novel. It appears that the closer Beloved gets to her mother, the more intrusive Sethe's memories are in her life. Morrison conveys her literary purpose by increasing the intensity of the mother-daughter relationship simultaneously with Sethe's gradual surrender to her past life.

Beloved's arrival gives Sethe an opportunity to apologize for her sinful "act of love." It is difficult, though, for Sethe to accept this second chance, and her memories continue to consume her. Beloved leeches onto Sethe and makes her presence known throughout the house. She constantly begs for attention and food from her mother because, after all, she is a child at heart. Sethe gives into this manipulative behavior, showing that she is letting her past life get the better of her; Beloved only becomes more parasitic as the story progresses. Beloved and Sethe's relationship reaches a point at which Sethe is at Beloved's feet and is devoted to fulfilling all of her desires. Sethe no longer interacts with her other daughter, Denver, because she is too absorbed in reliving her memories of Sweet Home. At one instance in the novel, Sethe and Beloved are in the forest. Beloved starts to massage Sethe's neck, but her grip tightens and she begins to strangle her instead. The "demon child" then convinces Sethe it was her deceased mother-in-law who tried to choke her. In Sethe's mind, Beloved can do no wrong. It is evident that at this point Sethe is not yet capable of abandoning her traumatic past, which is why her bond with her devilish daughter strengthens, becoming more similar to a relationship between a servant and master than that of a mother and daughter. Morrison makes it clear that Beloved clings to Sethe and makes her weaker, just as her memories do; that in order to escape, Sethe must break the connection between her and Beloved.

Beloved is a powerful force in this novel that is finally driven away by Sethe at the end after Sethe realizes she must let go of her past actions in order to lead the rest of her life normally. During the climax of the story, she tries to stab someone whom she believes to be an enemy in a fit of insanity. At this point, Beloved takes the form of a pregnant woman and leaves Sethe forever. This shape that Beloved takes is significant because it shows that Sethe is being given a new life, one that is free from haunting memories.

A clear parallel can be seen between the departure of Beloved and the return of Sethe to normalcy. Although Sethe may think she has lost something valuable, she has actually gained what she has been striving for: a life in which she lives in the present and not the past. This substantiates the idea that memories are powerful and often devastating forces which can destroy a person's will to live; Morrison channels this idea through the relationships of the central characters. Toni Morrison artfully uses the nature of the relationship between these two characters to show that one must confront and accept one's past actions in order to look forward to a future.

You Rate It!

1. Did the student select an appropriate pair of "literary counterparts" and clearly establish the nature of their relationship in the work in which they appear?

_____

_____

_____

_____

2. To what degree did the student demonstrate how the relationship between these two "literary counterparts" makes an important contribution to the work as a whole? Did the student's references to the text illustrate this contribution effectively?

_____

_____

_____

_____

3. How well-organized and fluent was the student's paper? Was the student's overall argument a persuasive one?

_____

_____

_____

_____

4. On a 0-9 scale, how would you rate this response? Explain why.

_____

_____

_____

_____

Sample Student Essay Two

The novella <u>Of Mice and Men</u> by John Steinbeck is a story based around the platonic relationship of two men. The men have a paradoxically interdependent and parasitic relationship that has brought them closer together than to anyone else they are associated with. John Steinbeck uses the intimacy of their relationship and their nearly identical situations as an example of false aspiration and friendship, two major themes of the book.

Both men, Lennie and George, are migrant farm workers in California during the Great Depression who have greater aspirations than the mundane cycle of ranch work that they remain trapped in. Lennie, the giant with the heart of gold, is too strong and too dumb for his own good, and as result gets tangled in some precarious situations involving rape and murder. His protector and only friend is the equally uneducated and impecunious (but more capable and naturally smart) George, who travels with Lennie from ranch to ranch to work. Both men have only each other as companions; however, George could easily survive on his own as he often informs the dependent Lennie in fits of anger. Despite the empty threats and the hard truth that Lennie is unnecessary to George and often a burden, George's good will has made the duo virtually inseparable, and their level of success and lifestyle has become intertwined. This is evidenced by George's and Lennie's plans to "live off the fat of the land" together and George's escape from Weed with Lennie after the rape allegation. The somewhat unlikely counterparts are then used by Steinbeck to examine human yearning for prosperity and friendship.

The joint aspiration of George and Lennie was to amass enough money from farm work to purchase a small farm and live through self-sustenance for the rest of their days. This dream is left unrealized by Steinbeck as a grim reminder that often things do not turn out as well as one might wish. This pessimistic view is reflective of the attitude and mood of the Great Depression. The pair constantly discuss the farm longingly, and in the climactic moment of the book when George mercifully executes Lennie, he is reciting the story about raising rabbits on the farm, Lennie's favorite story. That scene is a particularly extreme example of how the often calming and optimistic aspirations of the destitute can lead not only to the unrealization of the dream but a fate far worse. This prevalent theme is intensified by the especially tragic demise of the dream, an effect that could have only been achieved through a dream shared by more than one person.

George and Lennie are not exactly people who fit in well with the migrant worker culture. George, although he adapts well, is a cut above the rest of the men and is distrustful, Lennie, on the other hand, is mentally challenged and is unable to grasp the idea that some people are mean and cannot be trusted. By bonding the two have fulfilled their emotional need for companionship and become inseparable. Neither man would likely make friends alone nor find much in the form of female companionship. This friendship is established by Steinbeck only to force George into the tormenting situation of choosing whether to commit an act of euthanasia, or to let his best and only true friend (other than Slim) suffer at the hands of the evil Curly and whoever else might lynch or otherwise harm Lennie.

You Rate It!

1. Did the student select an appropriate pair of "literary counterparts" and clearly establish the nature of their relationship in the work in which they appear?

_____

_____

_____

_____

2. To what degree did the student demonstrate how the relationship between these two "literary counterparts" makes an important contribution to the work as a whole? Did the student's references to the text illustrate this contribution effectively?

_____

_____

_____

_____

3. How well-organized and fluent was the student's paper? Was the student's overall argument a persuasive one?

_____

_____

_____

_____

4. On a 0-9 scale, how would you rate this response? Explain why.

_____

_____

_____

_____

Sample Student Essay Three

"Did I request thee maker from my clay. To mould me man, did I solicit thee. From darkness to promote me?"

Oftentimes in literature the interactions of characters helps to illustrate the book as a whole. In the book Frankenstein *by Mary Shelley, the intricate relationship between Dr. Frankenstein and his Monster is centered upon the inevitable destruction that their "father-son" relationship causes throughout the book. The struggle between the monster and Frankenstein is illustrated beautifully, showing the Monster's desire to be loved and Frankenstein's desire to kill his own "son" whom he "molded" into man, thus creating the conflict in the book and the main themes, which include influence and love.*

The relationship between Frankenstein and his Monster is quite complex, playing upon the roles of father and son, and good and evil. At the beginning of the book Frankenstein makes inanimate objects into this living Monster. When the Monster comes to life though, he realizes the destruction it could cause and immediately rejects it and tries to destroy it. Thus, the Monster is frightened and runs away, never having the true love of a father. From this point on, the Monster struggles to have love and to find a companion, whereas Frankenstein struggles to try to find and kill the Monster. Their relationship intensifies when the Monster, angry with Frankenstein for abandoning him, begins to kill Frankenstein's family members. This strikes deep in Frankenstein and makes his drive to kill the Monster almost greater than the Monster's desire for revenge. All the Monster really wants though is to be loved and to have Frankenstein love him, so when Frankenstein continually rejects him, their relationship thickens to the extent of hatred. Eventually the two meet again on a mountaintop where the Monster requests that Frankenstein make him a female companion. Frankenstein agrees and goes off to build this companion, but before he can complete it, he realizes the destruction another one of these "Monsters" could cause and stops.   The Monster once again feels deceived and disowned and goes on a killing spree, killing Frankenstein's wife. Therefore, once again fate takes its toll, and the father and "son" continually break apart because of the other's failures. By the end of the book Frankenstein has so much built up hatred for the Monster that he chases him into the desolate Northern country, until both can no longer go further. When Frankenstein dies a little while later, the Monster goes to his side and weeps over his dead body. The monster proclaims that he is now ready to die because his creator has died and that he regrets killing all the people he killed since all he ever wanted was to be loved, thus showing the unconditional love the Monster has for his "father." Hence, the love-hate relationship between Frankenstein and the Monster draws to a close with the tie between "father and son" now stronger than ever.

Not only does the character involvement make the book interesting for the reader, but the relationship between Frankenstein and the Monster helps to illustrate the main themes, such as the role of influence. Influence occurs for the Monster throughout the entire book, especially in the beginning when he is easily impressionable. Without a "father" figure in his life, he seeks love and knowledge, as he is lonely and frightened. He eventually goes to live in a little hovel beside a family's house, and hears books being read out loud. Eventually he learns how to speak and becomes quite smart. This new-found knowledge influences him greatly but without a guiding figure such as Frankenstein, he has no person to show him how to use such knowledge. Thus he learns things he cannot handle and becomes destructive, having knowledge but not maturity. He does not understand the feelings of anger inside of him and without a "fatherly" influence he is destructive and unable to control himself..

The last and possibly one of the most important themes in the book is the inevitability of love, portrayed by Frankenstein and the Monster's relationship. Throughout the book the Monster searches for love, but every time finds that his hideousness turns people away. Unable to comprehend such animosity, he turns evil and destroys things. As the book goes on and he is continually rejected, he loses hope for love and decides to take his anger out on the person who brought him into this world, Frankenstein. This in turn causes Frankenstein to try to kill him out of vengeance even more than before, making it an endless cycle of hatred. By the end of the book though, one can sense the inevitability of the Monster and Frankenstein coming together again as they are bonded by their fates, In the end, Frankenstein dies before he gets to kill the Monster, and the Monster comes to realize the unconditional love he has for his "father" and creator, illustrating the theme of love.

The fact that two characters could be so entwined by fate yet harbor so such hatred towards each other illustrates a character relationship that is driven by desire, as all the Monster wants to do is have love and all Frankenstein wants to do is destroy the thing which has robbed him of his family through the monster's incessant killing. In a way Frankenstein is the actual monster, as it is his hate that causes the Monster to kill those he loves, thus making Frankenstein the real killer

You Rate It!

1. Did the student select an appropriate pair of "literary counterparts" and clearly establish the nature of their relationship in the work in which they appear?

_____

_____

_____

_____

2. To what degree did the student demonstrate how the relationship between these two "literary counterparts" makes an important contribution to the work as a whole? Did the student's references to the text illustrate this contribution effectively?

_____

_____

_____

_____

3. How well-organized and fluent was the student's paper? Was the student's overall argument a persuasive one?

_____

_____

_____

_____

4. On a 0-9 scale, how would you rate this response? Explain why.

_____

_____

_____

_____

Author's Response to Sample Student Essays on Literary Counterparts and How They Further a Work's Purpose

Sample Student Essay One:

This superb essay selects a novel with an intriguing pair of counterparts, a former slave Sethe and Beloved, the spirit of the child she had killed rather than see her returned to slavery. The writer clearly defines the relationship as "parasitic" and describes how "Morrison illustrates the protagonist's obvious vulnerability because of the crime she committed and begins to show how her past is enveloping her current life before Beloved is 'reborn.'" She does a very persuasive job of showing how Beloved drains Sethe and goes so far as to attempt to strangle her. The writer shows how "Sethe is not yet capable of abandoning her traumatic past, which is why her bond with her devilish daughter strengthens, becoming more similar to a relationship between a servant and master than that of a mother and daughter." The writer clearly establishes a connection to Morrison's thematic purpose when she concludes "This substantiates the idea that memories are powerful and often devastating forces which can destroy a person's will to live; Morrison channels this idea through the relationships of the central characters, artfully using the nature of the relationship between these two characters to show that one must confront and accept one's past actions in order to look forward to a future." This is an excellent example of a high-level paper, whose only real shortcoming is perhaps a failure to comprehend the intricacies of Morrison's plot for the reader who may be unfamiliar with the novel. It probably would help clarify the situation if the reader were to indicate that Sethe was pursued by Schoolteacher, the slave-owner who wanted to recapture his lost property and that the "Beloved" who appears later in the novel is somewhat of a ghost figure, a haunting reminder of both her infanticidal action and the enslavement of the past. These, however, are carping complaints for an essay written so impressively under the duress of time.

Author's Score: 9

Sample Student Essay Two:

One of the perils of grading essays is discrediting a good paper because it has the misfortune of following a great one. This student's response, while clearly not as thorough as the previous student's paper, nevertheless answers the question with a certain degree of success. As was demonstrated in the initial explication of the question, the choice of Lennie and George as literary counterparts is a good one, though the student's use of the word "parasitic" to describe their bond is a heavy-handed one. The writer clearly establishes the nature of their relationship, describing how the hulking but mild-natured Lennie "is too strong and too dumb for his own good, and as result gets tangled in some precarious situations involving rape and murder," and how the "equally uneducated and impecunious (but more capable and naturally smart)" George is always bailing him out of trouble. The student notes differences between the two characters, how "George, although he adapts well, is a cut above the rest of the men and is distrustful," and how "Lennie, on the other hand, is mentally challenged and is unable to grasp the idea that some people are mean and cannot be trusted." He also discusses their financial dream of the farm, noting that "This dream is left unrealized by Steinbeck as a grim reminder that often things do not turn out as well as one might wish. This pessimistic view is reflective of the attitude and mood of the Great Depression." This makes a connection to the overall theme of Steinbeck's novella. The conclusion, however, ends with a somewhat perplexing and narrow observation that "This friendship is established by Steinbeck only to force George into the tormenting situation of choosing whether to commit an act of euthanasia or to let his best and only true friend (other than Slim) suffer at the hands of the evil Curly and whoever else might lynch or otherwise harm Lennie." The essay also does not attempt to connect these literary counterparts to the other characters who become obsessed with this dream. All told, this is a very good response, but not a top tier one.

Author's Score: 7

Sample Student Essay Three:

The third and final student sample was also an excellent paper. The student chooses a work which she obviously knows well and thoroughly develops the love-hate bond between Frankenstein and the monster he has created. Throughout the essay the student interweaves the themes of the "father-son" relationship and the importance of "influence" (or the lack of it) upon an individual, illustrating these with copious references to the text. The student expresses how the Monster "searches for love, but every time finds that his hideousness turns people away," how "Unable to comprehend such animosity, he turns evil and destroys things." She conveys the antithetical purposes of creator and created, noting how because the Monster "is continually rejected, he loses hope for love and decides to take his anger out on the person who brought him into this world, Frankenstein" and how "This in turn causes Frankenstein to try to kill him out of vengeance even more than before, making it an endless cycle of hatred." The student offers the concluding irony that "In a way Frankenstein is the actual monster, as it is his hate that causes the Monster to kill those he loves, thus making Frankenstein the real killer." Though this paper at times teeters close to plot summary, it never descends into plot that is not complemented by analysis, and its only other foible is a measure of redundancy. These are both minimalized by the persuasiveness of the overall argument.

Author's Score: 8

Sample Examination III

Questions 1-11. Refer to the following passage.

By the door of her son's room the mother knelt upon the floor and listened for some sound from within. When she heard the boy moving about and talking in
(5) low tones a smile came to her lips. George Willard had a habit of talking aloud to himself and to hear him doing so had always given his mother a peculiar pleasure. The habit in him, she felt,
(10) strengthened the secret bond that existed between them. A thousand times she had whispered to herself of the matter. "He is groping about, trying to find himself," she thought. "He is not a dull clod, all words
(15) and smartness. Within him there is a secret something that is striving to grow. It is the thing I let be killed in myself."

In the darkness in the hallway by the door the sick woman arose and started
(20) again toward her own room. She was afraid that the door would open and the boy come upon her. When she had reached a safe distance and was about to turn a corner into a second hallway she stopped
(25) and bracing herself with her hands waited, thinking to shake off a trembling fit of weakness that had come upon her. The presence of the boy in the room had made her happy. In her bed, during the long
(30) hours alone, the little fears that had visited her had become giants. Now they were all gone. "When I get back to my room I shall sleep," she murmured.

But Elizabeth Willard was not to
(35) return to her bed and to sleep. As she stood trembling in the darkness the door of her son's room opened and the boy's father, Tom Willard, stepped out. In the light that streamed out at the door he stood with the
(40) knob in his hand and talked. What he said infuriated the woman.

Tom Willard was ambitious for his son. He had always thought of himself as a successful man, although nothing he had
(45) ever done had turned out successfully. However, when he was out of sight of the New Willard House and had no fear of coming upon his wife, he swaggered and began to dramatize himself as one of the
(50) chief men of the town. He wanted his son to succeed. He it was who had secured for the boy the position on the *Winesburg Eagle*. Now, with a ring of earnestness in his voice, he was advising concerning
(55) some course of conduct. "I tell you what, George, you've got to wake up," he said sharply. "Will Henderson has spoken to me three times concerning the matter. He says you go along for hours not hearing
(60) when you are spoken to and acting like a gawky girl. What ails you?" Tom Willard laughed good-naturedly. "Well, I guess you'll get over it," he said. "I told Will that. You're not a fool and you're not a woman.
(65) You're Tom Willard's son and you'll wake up. I'm not afraid. What you say clears things up. If being a newspaper man had put the notion of being a writer into your mind that's all right. Only I guess you'll
(70) have to wake up to do that too, eh?"

Tom Willard went briskly along the hallway and down a flight of stairs to the office. The woman in the darkness could hear him laughing and talking with a
(75) guest who was striving to wear away a dull evening by dozing in a chair by the office door. She returned to the door of her son's room. The weakness had passed from her body as by a miracle and she stepped
(80) boldly along. A thousand ideas raced through her head When she heard the scraping of a chair and the sound of a pen scratching upon paper, she again turned and went back along the hallway to her
(85) own room.

A definite determination had come into the defeated wife of the Winesburg hotel keeper. The determination was the result of long years of quiet and rather
(90) ineffectual thinking. "Now," she told herself, "I will act. There is something threatening my boy and I will ward it off [. . . .]."

1. The passage's primary focus is on

    (A) the mysterious illness of Elizabeth Willard
    (B) Elizabeth Willard's festering animosity for
        her husband, Tom
    (C) Tom Willard's misogynistic bent
    (D) George Willard's struggle with writers' block
    (E) the conflicting interests that Mr. and Mrs.
        Willard have in their son

2. All of the following are accurate descriptors of
    Elizabeth Willard's attitude towards her son
    EXCEPT

    (A) doting
    (B) possessive
    (C) solicitous
    (D) protective
    (E) pressuring

3. Elizabeth's actions outside her son's door are
    most aptly labeled

    (A) intrusive
    (B) voyeuristic
    (C) clandestine
    (D) insidious
    (E) cryptic

4. At the end of the first paragraph Elizabeth
    figuratively depicts George's burgeoning talent in
    terms usually associated with

    (A) espionage
    (B) monasticism
    (C) maternity
    (D) insomnia
    (E) lunacy

5. Elizabeth's remark in lines 16-17, "It is the thing
    I let be killed in myself," refers to which of the
    following?

    I. A fetus.
    II. Her artistic spirit.
    III. Her love for her husband.

    (A) I only
    (B) II only
    (C) I and III
    (D) II and III
    (E) I, II and III

6. Tom Willard's comments to his son reveal all of
    the following EXCEPT

    (A) a genuine eagerness for his son to succeed
    (B) an intimation that George has been slipping
        up at work
    (C) an exaggerated—and ironic—conception of
        self
    (D) a severity that is untempered by humor
    (E) a subtle but perceptible chauvinism

7. The passage implies that Tom's mild admonition
    to George to "wake up" is prompted by a desire to

    (A) eventually ease his own financial situation
        through the success of his son
    (B) urgently intercede before George gets
        himself fired
    (C) proudly inspire George to uphold the image
        that Tom has conceived of himself
    (D) sagely offer romantic advice
    (E) preemptively dispel George's fancy of a
        career as a writer

8. The passage implies that Elizabeth's "irritation"
    over her husband's comments to George is
    prompted by Tom's

    (A) desire for his son to succeed
    (B) inflated sense of self-importance
    (C) stern admonition to George to "wake up"
    (D) labeling George a "gawky girl"
    (E) exclusive claim that George is *his* son

9. The antithetical characterization of Elizabeth Willard and her husband Tom is BEST reflected by which of the following contrasts?

   (A) sickness and health
   (B) concern and indifference
   (C) reticence and bluster
   (D) gravity and humor
   (E) madness and sanity

10. The passage suggests that both Elizabeth and Tom Willard share which of the following?

   (A) a physical infirmity that limits their mobility
   (B) a penchant for surreptitious activity
   (C) a vicarious involvement in their son's future
   (D) a mutually violent antipathy for each other
   (E) a conviction that their son George is a
        dreamer

11. Which of the following contributes LEAST to the galvanizing change that Elizabeth Willard undergoes in the final two paragraphs?

   (A) a hyperbole that depicts the rapid
        calculations of her mind
   (B) a simile that suggests a dramatic change in
        her physical well-being
   (C) an interior monologue that reveals her innate
        maternal defensiveness of her son
   (D) onomatopoeic diction that suggests that her
        son has returned to his writing
   (E) a phrase that expresses her willingness to
        defy her husband and embark on an
        immediate course of action

Questions 12-25. Refer to the following poem.

The Bee Meeting

Who are these people at the bridge to meet me? They are the
      villagers—
The rector, the midwife, the sexton, the agent for the bees.
In my sleeveless summery dress I have no protection,
And they are all gloved and covered, why did nobody tell me?
(5)   They are smiling and taking out veils tacked to ancient hats.

I am nude as a chicken neck, does nobody love me?
Yes, here is the secretary of bees with her white shop smock,
Buttoning the cuffs at my wrists and the slit from my neck to
      my knees.
Now I am milkweed silk, the bees will not notice.
(10)   They will not smell my fear, my fear, my fear.

Which is the rector now, is it that man in black?
Which is the midwife, is that her blue coat?
Everybody is nodding a square black head, they are knights in
      visors,
Breastplates of cheesecloth knotted under the armpits.
(15)   Their smiles and their voices are changing. I am led through a
      beanfield.

Strips of tinfoil winking like people,
Feather dusters fanning their hands in a sea of bean flowers,
Creamy bean flowers with black eyes and leaves like bored hearts.
Is it blood clots the tendrils are dragging up that string?
(20)   No, no, it is scarlet flowers that will one day be edible.

Now they are giving me a fashionable white straw Italian hat
And a black veil that molds to my face, they are making me
      one of them.
They are leading me to the shorn grove, the circle of hives.
Is it the hawthorn that smells so sick?
(25)   The barren body of hawthorn, etherizing its children.

Is it some operation that is taking place?
It is the surgeon my neighbors are waiting for,
This apparition in a green helmet,
Shining gloves and white suit.
(30)   Is it the butcher, the grocer, the postman, someone I know?

I cannot run, I am rooted, and the gorse hurts me
With its yellow purses, its spiky armory.
I could not run without having to run forever.
The white hive is snug as a virgin,
(35)   Sealing off her brood cells, her honey, and quietly humming.

Smoke rolls and scarves in the grove.
The mind of the hive thinks this is the end of everything.
Here they come, the outriders, on their hysterical elastics.
If I stand very still, they will think I am cow-parsley,
(40)   A gullible head untouched by their animosity,

Not even nodding, a personage in a hedgerow.
The villagers open the chambers, they are hunting the queen.
Is she hiding, is she eating honey? She is very clever.
She is old, old, old, she must live another year, and she knows it.
(45)   While in their fingerjoint cells the new virgins

Dream of a duel they will win inevitably.
A curtain of wax dividing them from the bride flight,
The upflight of a murderess into a heaven that loves her.
The villagers are moving the virgins, there will be no killing.
(50)   The old queen does not show herself, is she so ungrateful?

I am exhausted, I am exhausted—
Pillar of white in a blackout of knives.
I am the magician's girl who does not flinch.
The villagers are untying their disguises, they are shaking hands.
(55)   Whose is that long white box in the grove, what have they
         accomplished, why am I cold?

—Sylvia Plath

12. The entire poem is pervaded by symbols and images related to

(A) medievalism and chivalry
(B) death and virginity
(C) sickness and medicine
(D) religion and the apocalypse
(E) mysticism and magic

13. That the visit to the hive has a potentially symbolic significance is first intimated by the

(A) diverse personages at the bridge
(B) gloved and veiled attire of the villagers
(C) exposed skin of the speaker
(D) speaker's question "why did nobody tell me?" (line 4)
(E) speaker's inordinate fear

14. All of the following mark significant contrasts between the speaker and the villagers that she meets EXCEPT

(A) her ignorance and their knowledge
(B) her paralysis and their action
(C) her insignificance and their social status
(D) her gregariousness and their solemnity
(E) her terror and their composure

15. In the course of the poem, the speaker most frequently perceives or imagines herself to be a(n)

(A) vulnerable presence
(B) unwitting pawn
(C) unattractive flower
(D) intrepid performer
(E) potential corpse

16. In stanza three the speaker figuratively abets the blurring of role and gender through

(A) simile
(B) personification
(C) metaphor
(D) hyperbole
(E) paradox

17. The simile "like bored hearts" (line 18) is intended to emphasize which aspect of the bean flowers through which the party must pass on its way to the hive?

(A) their sanguinary color
(B) their drooping tendrils
(C) their tangled mass
(D) their gossamer-like texture
(E) their edible nature

18. The speaker's fear and confusion are augmented LEAST by

(A) the anonymity of the beekeeper
(B) her perceived inability to flee
(C) the swirling smoke in the grove
(D) the onslaught of the outrider bees
(E) the sight of the long white box in the grove

19. The speaker's claim that she is a "Pillar of white in a blackout of knives / [. . .] the magician's girl who does not flinch" (lines 52-53) is primarily intended to

(A) confirm her impressive composure on the hive expedition
(B) reveal her desperate attempt to remove herself imaginatively from a terrifying situation
(C) connect the speaker's attire with the virginal description of the hive
(D) contrast her summer dress with the dark attire of the sexton and rector
(E) paint the speaker as an innocent victim

20. In the final stanza of the poem the speaker perceives the villagers as being

(A) proud of their honey-gathering efforts
(B) relieved that their chore is over
(C) concerned for her fatigue
(D) impressed by her pluck
(E) complicit in her demise

21. For the speaker the expedition to the hive primarily becomes a(n)

(A) novel and intriguing experience
(B) troublesome vision of her own death or loss of virginity
(C) tedious waste of valuable time
(D) opportunity to befriend socially prominent people
(E) exhausting physical labor

22. That the poem may symbolically depict the speaker's preoccupation with resisting seduction is supported by all of the following EXCEPT

(A) "They are smiling and taking out veils tacked to ancient hats." (line 5)
(B) "Yes, here is the secretary of bees with her white shop smock, / Buttoning the cuffs at my wrists and the slit from my neck to my knees. / Now I am milkweed silk, the bees will not notice." (lines 7-9)
(C) "Here they come, the outriders, on their hysterical elastics. / If I stand very still, they will think I am cow-parsley, / A gullible head untouched by their animosity [. . .]." (lines 38-40).
(D) "The villagers open the chambers, they are hunting the queen. / Is she hiding, is she eating honey?" (lines 42-43)
(E) "Pillar of white in a blackout of knives. / I am the magician's girl who does not flinch." (lines 52-53).

23. Ultimately, the poem implies that the speaker's greatest fear may be her fear of

(A) strangers
(B) bee stings
(C) fire
(D) the outdoors
(E) mortality

24. In the course of the poem, the speaker directly or indirectly personifies each of the following EXCEPT

(A) the bees
(B) the strips of tinfoil
(C) the hawthorn
(D) the beehive
(E) the smoke

25. Which of the following rhetorical questions is NOT definitively resolved by other information provided by the poem?

   (A) "Who are these people at the bridge to meet me?" (line 1)
   (B) "[. . .] does nobody love me?" (line 6)
   (C) "Is it blood clots the tendrils are dragging up that string?" (line 19)
   (D) "Is it some operation that is taking place?" (line 26)
   (E) "Whose is that long white box in the grove [. . .]?" (line 55)

Questions 26-33. Refer to the following passage.

In the great days of sail, the captain of a ship was a figure of awesome authority.

(5) His word was absolute law, enforced by the petty officer's knout,[1] the master-at-arms' lash, and the hangman's noose. In the British navy, which ruled the oceans from the time of the first Spanish Armada until the turn of the twentieth

(10) century, the crews were made up of the sweepings of the assizes[2] and jails and taverns—landsmen—along with seamen impressed against their wills from the merchant ships of a dozen nations. The

(15) captain remained physically aloof from these crewmen and often nearly as aloof from his officers. When the captain emerged from his cabin onto the quarterdeck, all officers retreated from the

(20) windward side to allow him private space. Except on ship's business, they dared not speak to him unless spoken to. More often than not, he dined alone. The loneliness of command was more than a cliché—it was

(25) an essential social and psychological buffer: the captain might at any time order his men and his fellow officers into catastrophic battle in which a third or more would routinely be killed or mangled [. . . .].

(30) Yet the crews rarely rose in mutiny—though on a ship of the line, the main fleet battleship, they might number three or four hundred, including men shipped as replacements awaiting the

(35) inevitable deaths of scores of their shipmates, as against a dozen officers and fifty marines. For the captain was not only the legal dictator of their daily lives, their judge and jury when they committed

(40) infractions; he also held the magical power of the sextant [. . . .].

C. S. Forester's fictional Captain Horatio Hornblower—a composite based partly on two real-life naval heroes, Lord

(45) Horatio Nelson and Lord Thomas Cochrane—performs heroic feats of navigation in nearly every adventure. In one book, he is commanded to sail from England to the west coast of Central

(50) America without coming within sight of any land or any other ships—using only sextant and compass and slate board.

Think about that—the faith, the arrogance, that requires.

(55) With his food and water all but depleted, he makes landfall exactly where he plotted it, exactly on time. As did the real captains Cochrane and Nelson, time after time.

(60) On a schooner or merchant ship, the captain might be the only man on board who knew the art and science of navigation. To lose the captain to illness or death or mutiny—or madness, an occupational

(65) hazard—was to lose their way, literally, on the vast untracked oceans of the world.

Christopher Columbus's crew came close to mutiny on his first outbound voyage, not because he was flogging

(70) them—he didn't dare—but because they lost confidence that he knew where he was going.

So the tools of navigation, especially the chronometer and sextant,

(75) took on a magical quality and were treated with the reverent care usually reserved for sacred relics: secreted in a chest in the captain's cabin inside elaborately carved and inlaid hardwood boxes, protected from

(80) salt and sea and rough handling. Even today, if you buy even a moderately priced metal sextant, it will come in a hardwood box or a bulletproof valise.

Imagine the illiterate sailor with no

(85) education in astronomy or mathematics, little sense even of the world's geography since he had probably never seen a globe, sailing along for weeks at a time with no land in sight in any direction. It must have

(90) seemed magical indeed that a man could put his eye to a strange metal contraption, scribble some queer numerical formulae on a slate, draw lines on a piece of paper, then tack his ship toward an invisible harbor,

(95) arriving there exactly as predicted. A man who could do that, a captain, must be partly divine.

---

[1] a leather whip used for flogging

[2] courts

"Philip Gerard is the author of three novels and four books of nonfiction, as well as numerous essays, short stories, and documentary scripts. He teaches in the Creative Writing Department at University of North Carolina Wilmington"

26. The climactic structure of lines 5-7 does which of the following?

    I. Organizes the naval officers by their respective rank.
    II. Links the severity of the punishment with the severity of the infraction.
    III. Suggests the absolute nature of the captain's power.

    (A) I only
    (B) III only
    (C) I and II
    (D) II and III
    (E) I, II and III

27. The word "sweepings" (line 11) implies all of the following EXCEPT

    (A) the broad canvassing that went into compiling a crew
    (B) the menial duties that crew members were expected to perform
    (C) the poor quality of the seamen recruited
    (D) the sudden and abrupt nature of naval recruitment
    (E) the clear expendability of the amalgamated crew

28. The speaker's characterization of a captain in the "great days of sail" primarily attributes his detachment to his

    (A) aloof and reflective nature
    (B) motley and foreign crew
    (C) dislike of his subordinate officers
    (D) preference for dining alone
    (E) potential for sending his crew to their demise

29. The speaker implies that the crew's faith in their captain was grounded in his ability to

    (A) navigate them safely home through peril
    (B) adjudicate shipboard disputes fairly
    (C) manage a diverse and rambunctious crew
    (D) delegate responsibility to his junior officers
    (E) lead them to victory in battle

30. The passage suggests that for a sailor at sea on a lengthy voyage the captain assumed the role of a(n)

    (A) seer
    (B) factotum
    (C) deity
    (D) sinecure
    (E) martinet

31. The speaker intends the actions of the fictional Horatio Hornblower (lines 42-57) to be viewed as

    (A) totally impossible
    (B) blatantly insubordinate
    (C) historically inaccurate
    (D) eminently plausible
    (E) grossly irresponsible

32. In describing the navigational tools employed by the captain, the speaker uses language drawn from which of the following?

    I. Medicine
    II. The military
    III. Religion
    IV. Magic

    (A) I only
    (B) IV only
    (C) I and III
    (D) III and IV
    (E) I, II, III and IV

33. Which of the following is NOT characteristic of the passage?

    (A) allusions to literary and historical sea-captains
    (B) an informal tone that is part didactic, part wondrous
    (C) a central contrast between the omniscience of a captain and the naiveté of his crew
    (D) entreaties to the reader to appreciate the mystery of navigational skill
    (E) a detailed explanation of the exact mathematical functions of a sextant

Questions 34-44. Refer to the following poem.

If By Dull Rhymes Our English Must be Chain'd

If by dull rhymes our English must be chain'd,
    And, like Andromeda,[1] the Sonnet sweet
Fetter'd, in spite of pained loveliness;
Let us find out, if we must be constrain'd,
(5)   Sandals more interwoven and complete
To fit the naked foot of poesy;
Let us inspect the lyre, and weigh the stress
Of every chord, and see what may be gain'd
    By ear industrious and attention meet:
(10) Misers of sound and syllable, no less
    Than Midas of his coinage, let us be
Jealous of dead leaves in the bay wreath crown;
So, if we may not let the Muse be free,
    She will be bound with garlands of her own.

–John Keats

_____

1 chained by her royal parents as a sacrifice to a sea monster; rescued
  from her fate by Perseus

34. Of the following, which is NOT characteristic of the poet's style?

(A) allusions to classical myth
(B) a discontented tone
(C) inversions of descriptive adjectives and nouns
(D) the personification of poetry
(E) a traditional sequence of rhymes

35. The primary concern of the speaker is the

(A) unwarranted imprisonment of English citizenry
(B) painful isolation of unrequited love
(C) restrictive conventions of the sonnet form
(D) shoddy design of musical instruments
(E) unchecked greed of powerful men

36. Which of the following LEAST complements the theme of the poem?

(A) the simile/allusion involving Andromeda
(B) the diction of confinement
(C) the personification of the Sonnet and the Muse of poetry
(D) the poet's choice of structure
(E) the bay wreath crown

37. Phrases such as "sweet / Fetter'd" (lines 2-3) and "pained loveliness" (line 3) exemplify which of the following?

(A) allusion
(B) oxymoron
(C) metonymy
(D) onomatopoeia
(E) understatement

38. The speaker uses the metaphors of the "Sandals" (line 5) and the "lyre" (line 7) to advocate all of the following EXCEPT

(A) greater intricacy of rhyme
(B) a reconsideration of the sonnet form
(C) metric variation
(D) deeper symbolic content
(E) attentiveness to the aural quality of words

39. In regard to the lyre, the phrase "Let us inspect the lyre, and weigh the stress / Of every chord" (lines 7-8) advocates that poets

    (A) measure the size of it
    (B) attend to its rhythmic emphasis
    (C) debate the skill of its player
    (D) evaluate the quality of its tuning
    (E) appreciate its impressive volume

40. The speaker's allusion to Midas is intended to do which of the following?

    I. Parallel the doleful enchainment of Andromeda.
    II. Urge poets to scrutinize the length and sound of their words.
    III. Suggest the richness of lyrical poetry.

    (A) I only
    (B) II only
    (C) I and III
    (D) II and III
    (E) I, II and III

41. By the phrase "Jealous of dead leaves in the bay wreath crown" (line 12), the speaker expresses his

    (A) scorn of inferior poets
    (B) vigilance against hackneyed diction
    (C) dislike of public acknowledgment
    (D) hatred of the monarchy
    (E) belief that great poetry is dead

42. The poem's concluding couplet may be said to do all of the following EXCEPT

    (A) add appropriate closure to the poem's central theme
    (B) provide a contrasting image to the dead bay leaves
    (C) offer a contrasting parallel to the shackled Andromeda
    (D) admit the difficulty in changing convention
    (E) appeal to the Muse for poetic inspiration

43. Perhaps the MOST bemusing irony contained in the poem involves the fact that

    (A) love can sometimes be painful
    (B) sandals can be uncomfortable
    (C) music and poetry are similar
    (D) the poet has mastered the sonnet form
    (E) the Muse elects to be bound

44. Clearly, the primary conflict of the speaker regarding poetry involves

    (A) convention vs. originality
    (B) ignorance vs. knowledge
    (C) classical form vs. contemporary form
    (D) emotion vs. reason
    (E) jealousy vs. acceptance

Questions 45-51. Refer to the following passage.

The craft of writing poetry is a monklike occupation, as is a watchmaker's, tilting tiny cogs and wheels into place. It's ironic that poets use words to convey what (5) lies beyond words. But poetry becomes more powerful where language fails. How can we express in words that are human-made emotions that aren't? How can we express all the dramas and feelings that are (10) wordless, where language has no purchase? Words are small shapes in the gorgeous chaos of the world. But they are shapes, they bring the world to focus, they corral ideas, they hone thoughts, they paint (15) watercolors of perception. Truman Capote's *In Cold Blood* chronicles the drama of two murderers who collaborated on a particularly nasty crime. A criminal psychologist, trying to explain the event, (20) observed that neither one of them would have been capable of the crime, but together they formed a third person who was able to kill. Metaphors, though more benign, work in the same way. The (25) chemical term for what happens is hypergolic: you can take two inert substances, put them together, and produce something powerfully different (table salt), even explosive (nitroglycerine). The charm (30) of language is that, though, it's human-made, it can on rare occasions capture emotions and sensations which aren't.

The best poetry is rich with observational truths. Above all, we ask the (35) poet to teach us a way of seeing and feeling, lest one spend a lifetime on this planet without noticing how green light flares up as the setting sun rolls under, the unfurling of a dogwood blossom, the gauzy (40) spread of the Milky Way on a star-loaded summer night, or the translucent green of a dragonfly's wings. The poet refuses to let things merge, lie low, succumb to habit. Instead the poet hoists events from their (45) routine, plays with them awhile, and lays them out in the sunshine for us to celebrate and savor.

When a friend and I were cycling the other day, she mentioned that reading (50) poetry frightens her.

"What if I don't get the real meaning?" she asked. "What if I read a 'ghostly galleon' and think it's referring to a ship, when it's really referring to the lost (55) innocence of America?" I was dumbfounded. Someone had taught her (and nearly everyone else) that poems work like safes—crack the code and the safe opens to reveal its treasure.

(60) "There are many ways to read a poem" I said. "After all, you really don't know what was going through the poet's mind. Suppose he was having a tempestuous affair with a neighbor, and (65) once when they were alone he told her that her hips were like a ghostly galleon. He might have then used that image in a poem he was writing because it fit well, but also as a sly flirtation with his neighbor, whose (70) hips would be secretly commemorated in verse."

"Do poets do that" she asked, slightly scandalized that noble thoughts might be tinged with the profane.

(75) "I've done it," I admitted with a grin. "I presume other poets do."

I went on to explain, as teachers of the writerly arts do, that poems dance with many veils. Read a poem briskly, and it will (80) speak to you briskly. Delve, and it will give you rich ore to contemplate. Each time you look, a new scintillation may appear, one you missed before.

The apparent subject of the poem (85) isn't always an end in itself. It may really be an opportunity, a way for the poet to reach into herself and haul up whatever nugget of the human condition distracts her at the moment, something that can't be (90) reached in any other way. It's a kind of catapult into another metaphysical country where one has longer conceptual arms. The poet reminds us that life's seductive habits of thought and sight can be broken at will. (95) We ask the poet to shepherd us telescopically and microscopically through many perspectives, to lead us like a mountain goat through the hidden, multidimensionality of almost everything [. . . .].

45. In the course of her essay, the speaker credits poets with doing all of the following EXCEPT

    (A) elevating the mundane into something more memorable and significant
    (B) helping people to see things from antithetical perspectives
    (C) fostering sensitivity to the beauteous diversity of nature
    (D) thrusting their readers onto a higher plane of thought
    (E) inspiring individuals to try their hand at creating it

46. Which of the following pairs of words BEST captures the aspects of writing poetry that the speaker's comparisons to a monk and to a watchmaker suggest?

    (A) taciturn and noisy
    (B) transcendent and materialistic
    (C) reflective and meticulous
    (D) cloistered and public
    (E) imaginative and plodding

47. In the first paragraph, which of the following contributes LEAST towards illustrating how poets "use words to convey what lies beyond words" (lines 4-5)?

    (A) the speaker's rhetorical questions
    (B) the speaker's metaphorical diction
    (C) the speaker's description of words as "small shapes in the gorgeous chaos of the world" (lines 11-12)
    (D) the speaker's allusion to a celebrated work of nonfiction
    (E) the speaker's reference to an analogous process in chemistry

48. The speaker uses the conversation she has with her friend to do all of the following EXCEPT

    (A) expose a common insecurity people have about reading poetry
    (B) imply that many teachers place a disproportionate emphasis on the analysis of a poem
    (C) argue that there are multifarious ways in which to enjoy a poem
    (D) suggest that getting "the real meaning" is crucial to the poetic experience
    (E) intimate that the literal subject of the poem may at times be a metaphorical vehicle for more profound understandings

49. In telling her friend about the art of poetry, the speaker's tone is generally

    (A) erudite
    (B) exasperated
    (C) instructive
    (D) admonishing
    (E) imperious

50. Of the following, which BEST parallels her friend's insecurity about getting "the real meaning" (lines 51-52)?

    (A) the simile of the watchmaker (lines 2-3)
    (B) the implied metaphor of the dogwood blossom (line 39)
    (C) the personification of the poem as a veil-dancer (lines 78-79)
    (D) the implied metaphor of the miner (lines 87-88)
    (E) the simile of the mountain goat (lines 97-99)

51. In light of the context in which it appears, which of the following words would NOT have figurative import?

    (A) "corral" (line 13)
    (B) "benign" (line 24)
    (C) "unfurling" (line 39)
    (D) "hoists" (line 44)
    (E) "catapult" (line 91)

Section II
Question One

(Suggested time—40 minutes. This question counts as one-third of the total essay section score.)

Read the following passage from Shakespeare's <u>Richard II</u>, in which the Queen eavesdrops on a conversation between two commoners. Then, in a well-organized essay, discuss what she learns about the present state of the king and show how the figurative language of the piece dramatizes the king's situation.

[Enter a gardener and two servants.]

Queen:	But stay, here come the gardeners.
	Let's step into the shadow of these trees.
	My wretchedness unto a row of pins,
	They'll talk of state, for everyone doth so
	Against a change. Woe is forerun with woe. *(5)*

[Queen and ladies retire.]

Gard:	Go, bind thou up yon dangling apricocks,
	Which, like unruly children, make their sire
	Stoop with oppression of their prodigal weight.
	Give some supportance to the bending twigs.
	Go thou, and like an executioner, *(10)*
	Cut off the heads of too-fast-growing sprays
	That look too lofty in our commonwealth.
	All must be even in our government.
	You thus employed, I will go root away
	The noisome weeds which without profit suck *(15)*
	The soil's fertility from wholesome flowers.
Serv:	Why should we in the compass of a pale[1]
	Keep law and form and due proportion,
	Showing, as in a model, our firm estate,
	When our sea-wallèd garden, the whole land, *(20)*
	Is full of weeds, her fairest flowers choked up,
	Her fruit tress all unpruned, her hedges ruined,
	Her knots disordered and her wholesome herbs
	Swarming with caterpillars?
Gard:	Hold thy peace. *(25)*
	He that hath suffered this disordered spring
	Hath now himself met with the fall of leaf.
	The weeds which his broad-spreading leaves did
	shelter
	That seemed in eating him to hold him up,
	Are plucked up root and all by Bolingbroke. *(30)*
	I mean the Earl of Wiltshire, Bushy, Green.
Serv:	What, are they dead?
Gard:	They are, and Bolingbroke
	Hath seized the wasteful King. Oh, what a pity is it
	That he hath not so trimmed and dressed his land *(35)*
	As we this garden! We at time of year
	Do wound the bark, the skin of our fruit trees,
	Lest, being over-proud in sap and blood,
	With too much riches it confound itself.
	Had he done so to great and growing men, *(40)*

<pre>
                 They might have lived to bear and he to taste
                 Their fruits of duty. Superfluous branches
                 We lop away, that bearing boughs may live.
                 Had he done so, himself had borne the crown
                 Which waste of vital hours hath quite thrown down.   (45)
Serv: What, think you then the King shall be deposed?
Gard: Depressed he is already, and deposed
                 Tis doubt he will be. Letters came last night
                 To a dear friend of the good Duke of York's
                 That tell black tidings.   (50)
Queen: Oh, I am pressed to death through want
                     of speaking!   [Coming forward]
                 Thou, old Adam's likeness, set to dress this garden.
                 How dares thou harsh rude tongue sound this un-
                     pleasing news?
                 What Eve, what serpent, hath suggested thee
                 To make a second fall of cursèd man?   (55)
                 Why dost thou say King Richard is deposed?
                 Darest thou, thou little better thing than earth,
                 Divine his downfall? Say where, when, and how
                 Camest thou by this ill tidings? Speak, thou
                     wretch [. . . .].
</pre>

---

[1] a palisade, or fence

Question Two

(Suggested time—40 minutes. This question counts as one-third of the total essay section score.)

Read the following passage carefully. Then, in a well-organized essay, discuss how the final paragraph of the author's essay (lines 32-39) functions in relation to the thirty-one lines that precede it. In your essay you may wish to consider such things as choice of detail, diction, figurative language and tone.

Allowing yourself to be a subject of gossip is one of the sacrifices you make, living in a small town. And the pain caused by the loose talk of ignorant people is undeniable. One couple I know, having lost their only child to a virulent pneumonia (a robust thirty-five year old, he was dead in a matter of days) had to endure rumors that he had died of suicide, AIDS, and even
(5) anthrax. But it's also true that the gossips don't know all that they think they know, and often misread things in a comical way. My husband was once told that he was having an affair with a woman he hadn't met, and I still treasure the day I was encountered by three people who said, "Have you sold your house yet?," "When's the baby due?," and "I'm sorry to hear your mother died."
(10)   I could trace the sources of the first two rumors: we'd helped a friend move into a rented house, and I'd bought baby clothes downtown when I learned that I would soon become an aunt. The third rumor was easy enough to check; I called my mother on the phone. The flip side, the saving grace, is that despite the most diligent attentions of the die-hard gossips, it is possible to have secrets.
(15)   Of course the most important things can't be hidden: birth, sickness, death, divorce. But gossip is essentially democratic. It may be the plumber and his wife who had a screaming argument in a bar, or it could be the bank president's wife who moved out and rented a room in the motel; everyone is fair game. And although there are always those who take delight in the misfortunes of others, and relish a juicy story at the expense of truth and others' feelings, this
(20) may be the exception rather than the rule. Surprisingly often, gossip is the way small-town people express solidarity.
  I recall a marriage that was on the rocks. The couple had split up, and gossip ran wild. Much sympathy was expressed for the children, and one friend of the couple said to me, "The worst thing she could do is to take him back too soon. This will take time." Those were healing
(25) words, a kind of prayer. And when the family did reunite, the town breathed a collective sigh of relief.
  My own parents' marriage was of great interest in Lemmon back in the 1930s. My mother, the town doctor's only child, eloped with another Northwestern University student; a musician, of all things. A poor preacher's kid. "This will bear watching," one matriarch said. My
(30) parents fooled her. As time went on, the watching grew dull. Now going on fifty-five years, their marriage has outlasted all the gossip [. . . .].
  Like the desert tales that monks have used for centuries as a basis for a theology and way of life, the tales of small-town gossip are often morally instructive, illustrating the ways ordinary people survive the worst that happens to them; or, conversely, the ways in which self-pity, anger,
(35) and despair can overwhelm and destroy them. Gossip is theology translated into experience. In it we hear great stories of conversion, like the drunk who turns his or her life around, as well as stories of failure. We can see that pride really does go before a fall, and that hope is essential. We watch closely those who retire, or who lose a spouse, lest they lose interest in living. When we gossip we are also praying, not only for them but for ourselves [. . . .].

Excerpt form *Dakota: A Spiritual Geography* by Kathleen Norris. Copyright © 1993 by Kathleen Norris. Reprinted by permission of Houghton Mifflin Company. All rights reserved.

Question Three

(Suggested time—40 minutes. This question counts as one-third of the total essay section score.)

Sometimes in a work of literature a character is haunted by something shameful or dishonorable, acutely remembered or buried deep within his or her consciousness. This troubling moment—which may involve something committed or endured, an action or a failure to take action—is a specter which haunts the character long after the initial event. Choose a novel or play in which a character is haunted by a shameful or dishonorable memory. Using the novel or play for support, identify the nature of the experience and show not only how the experience has negatively impacted the character over time, but also the degree to which the character has been able to resolve it. You may choose from the list below or use another novel or play of recognized literary merit.

The Bluest Eye	*Death of A Salesman*
Hamlet	*The Things They Carried*
The Scarlet Letter	*The Informer*
Bastard Out of Carolina	*Crime and Punishment*
Native Son	*Macbeth*
Frankenstein	*The Second Coming*
The Assistant	*Beloved*
Moby Dick	*Lord Jim*
The Hairy Ape	*Equus*
The Grapes of Wrath	*The Power and the Glory*
The Sound & the Fury	*A Thousand Acres*
The Crucible	*The Caine Mutiny Court Martial*
Things Fall Apart	*A Lesson Before Dying*

Sample Examination IV

Questions 1-13. Refer to the following passage.

Mr. Duffy raised his eyes from the paper and gazed out of his window on the cheerless evening landscape. The river lay quiet beside the empty distillery and from
(5) time to time a light appeared in some house on the Lucan road. What an end! The whole narrative of her death revolted him and it revolted him to think that he had ever spoken to her of what he held sacred. The
(10) threadbare phrases, the inane expressions of sympathy, the cautious words of a reporter won over to conceal the details of a commonplace vulgar death attacked his stomach. Not merely had she degraded
(15) herself; she had degraded him. He saw the squalid tract of her vice, miserable and malodorous. His soul's companion! He thought of the hobbling wretches whom he had seen carrying cans and bottles to be
(20) filled by the barman. Just God, what an end! Evidently she had been unfit to live, without any strength of purpose, an easy prey to habits, one of the wrecks on which civilization has been reared. But that she
(25) could have sunk so low! Was it possible he had deceived himself so utterly about her? He remembered her outburst of that night and interpreted it in a harsher sense than he had ever done. He had no difficulty now
(30) approving of the course he had taken.

As the light failed and his memory began to wander he thought her hand touched his. The shock which had first at-tacked his stomach was now attacking his
(35) nerves. He put on his overcoat and hat quickly and went out. The cold air met him on the threshold; it crept into the sleeves of his coat. When he came to the public-house at Chapelizod Bridge he went in and
(40) ordered a hot punch.

The proprietor served him obsequiously but did not venture to talk. There were five or six working-men in the shop discussing the value of a gentleman's
(45) estate in County Kildare. They drank at intervals from their huge pint tumblers and smoked, spitting often on the floor and sometimes dragging the sawdust over their spits with their heavy boots. Mr. Duffy sat
(50) on his stool and gazed at them, without seeing or hearing them. After a while they went out and he called for another punch. He sat a long time over it. The shop was very quiet. The proprietor sprawled on the
(55) counter reading the *Herald* and yawning. Now and again a tram was heard swishing along the lonely road outside.

As he sat there, living over his life with her and evoking alternately the two
(60) images in which he now conceived her, he realized that she was dead, that she had ceased to exist, that she had become a memory. He began to feel ill at ease. He asked himself what else could he have
(65) done. He could not have carried on a comedy of deception with her; he could not have lived with her openly. He had done what seemed to him best. How was he to blame? Now that she was gone he
(70) understood how lonely her life must have been, sitting night after night alone in that room. His life would be lonely too until he, too, died, ceased to exist, became a memory—if anyone remembered him.
(75) It was after nine o'clock when he left the shop. The night was cold and gloomy. He entered the Park by the first gate and walked along under the gaunt trees. He walked through the bleak alleys
(80) where they had walked four years before. She seemed to be near him in the darkness. At moments he seemed to feel her voice touch his ear, her hand touch his. He stood still to listen. Why had he withheld life
(85) from her? Why had he sentenced her to death? He felt his moral nature falling to pieces.

When he gained the crest of Magazine Hill he halted and looked along
(90) the river towards Dublin, the lights of which burned red and hospitably in the cold night. He looked down the slope and, at the base, in the shadow of the wall of the Park, he saw some human figures lying. Those

(95) venal and furtive lovers filled him with
despair. He gnawed the rectitude of his life;
he felt that he had been outcast from life's
feast. One human being had seemed to love
him and he had denied her life and

(100) happiness: he had sentenced her to
ignominy, a death of shame. He knew that
the prostrate creatures down by the wall
were watching him and wished him gone.
No one wanted him; he was outcast from

(105) life's feast. He turned his eyes to the grey
gleaming river, winding along towards
Dublin. Beyond the river he saw a goods
train winding out of Kingsbridge Station,
like a worm with a fiery head winding

(110) through the darkness, obstinately and
laboriously. It passed slowly out of sight;
but still he heard in his ears the laborious
drone of the engine reiterating the syllables
of her name.

(115)   He turned back the way he had
come, the rhythm of the engine pounding in
his ears. He began to doubt the reality of
what memory told him. He halted under a
tree and allowed the rhythm to die away.

(120) He could not feel her near him in the
darkness nor her voice touch his ear. He
waited for some minutes listening. He
could hear nothing: the night was perfectly
silent. He felt that he was alone.

"A Painful Case", from DUBLINERS by James Joyce, copyright 1916
by B.W. Heubsch. Definitive text Copyright © 1967 by the Estate of
James Joyce. Used by permission of Viking Penguin, a division of
Penguin Group (USA) Inc.

1. Mr. Duffy's attitude toward the woman's death is
BEST characterized as

   (A) surprise
   (B) disbelief
   (C) empathy
   (D) disdain
   (E) indifference

2. Mr. Duffy responds to the news of the woman's
death by

   (A) denying its reality
   (B) expressing remorse
   (C) seeking reasons for it
   (D) feigning unawareness
   (E) exonerating himself from blame

3. Mr. Duffy's extremely visceral reaction to the
news of the woman's death in lines 9-14 is abetted
by all of the following EXCEPT

   (A) his strong religious scruples
   (B) his distaste for suicide
   (C) his antipathy for the weakness of her
       character
   (D) his irritation at the euphemistic manner with
       which it is reported
   (E) his belief that her impetuous action has
       somehow tarnished his character

4. Which of the following words or phrases is NOT
used by Mr. Duffy to express his distaste for the
woman and her destructive action?

   (A) "vulgar" (line 13)
   (B) "squalid" (line 16)
   (C) "malodorous" (line 17)
   (D) "unfit" (line 21)
   (E) "deceived" (line 26)

5. The author most likely includes the detail of the
"hobbling wretches" (line 18) in order to

   (A) provide an instance of local color
   (B) illustrate the dire poverty of Dublin
   (C) lament the widespread alcoholism among the
       populace
   (D) imply that others worse off than the woman
       find ways to survive
   (E) question the benevolence of a divine being

6. That Mr. Duffy begins to feel "ill at ease" in line
63 is likely a manifestation of

   (A) anxiety over his own mortality
   (B) self-pity for his own loneliness
   (C) guilt over his earlier callousness
   (D) nausea over her gruesome end
   (E) empathy for her depressed state

7. Mr. Duffy is likely distressed by the prostrate creatures down by the wall (lines 92-96) because of

   (A) his inability to circumvent them
   (B) his strict sense of moral propriety
   (C) their amorous public overtures
   (D) their perception of him as an intruder
   (E) their salient reminder of his squandered relationship

8. In light of the context in which it appears, the phrase "life's feast" (line 105) most plausibly refers to which of the following?

   I. Heavenly reward.
   II. The fellowship of other humans.
   III. The intimacy of a close relationship.

   (A) I only
   (B) III only
   (C) I and III
   (D) II and III
   (E) I, II and III

9. The goods train winding out of Kingsbridge station (lines 107-114) functions as a symbol of which of the following?

   (A) the need for Mr. Duffy to put her death behind him and move on
   (B) the diminishing consciousness of the woman in Mr. Duffy's mind
   (C) the social and emotional death experienced by the protagonist
   (D) the desire of Mr. Duffy to forsake Dublin for some other place
   (E) the restorative progress of time

10. In the course of the final three paragraphs, Mr. Duffy does all of the following EXCEPT

   (A) envy the intimacy of the embracing couple
   (B) admit his painfully isolated lot
   (C) question his inexplicable lack of compassion
   (D) perceive himself as a stern, moral judge
   (E) ponder taking his own life

11. Which of the following contributes LEAST to reinforcing symbolically the emotional barrenness of Mr. Duffy?

   (A) the dankness of the night (lines 76-77)
   (B) the deserted pathways in the park (lines 79-80)
   (C) the glowing hearths of Dublin's houses (lines 90-92)
   (D) the clandestine lovers (lines 92-96)
   (E) the haunting cadence of the freight train (lines 111-114)

12. The irony of the passage's final sentence is Mr. Duffy's belief that he has

   (A) correctly traced his way out of the park
   (B) sufficiently distanced himself from the furtive park lovers
   (C) candidly admitted his acute isolation and loneliness
   (D) successfully rid himself of any subconscious guilt for the death of the woman
   (E) finally become conscious of humanity's existential predicament

13. What make Mr. Duffy such a despicable character are his

   (A) moroseness and self-pity
   (B) indolence and lack of motivation
   (C) lack of concern and flippancy
   (D) callousness and sanctimoniousness
   (E) irritation and truculence

Questions 14-27. Refer to the following poem.

The Doctor of the Heart

Take away your knowledge, Doktor.
It doesn't butter me up.

You say my heart is sick unto.[1]
You ought to have more respect.

(5)　　You with the goo on the suction cup.
You with your wires and electrodes

fastened at my ankle and wrist,
sucking up the biological breast.

You with your zigzag machine
(10)　　playing like the stock market up and down.

Give me the Phi Beta key that you always twirl
and I will make a gold crown for my molar.

I will take a slug if you please
and make myself a perfectly good appendix.

(15)　　Give me a fingernail for an eyeglass.
The world was murky all along.

I will take an iron and press out
my slipped disk until it is flat.

But take away my mother's carcinoma
(20)　　for I have only one cup of fetus tears.

Take away my father's cerebral hemorrhage
for I have only a jigger of blood in my hand.

Take away my sister's broken neck
for I have only my schoolroom ruler for a cure.

(25)　　Is there such a device for my heart?
I have only a gimmick called magic fingers.

Here is a sponge. I can squeeze it myself.
Let me dilate like a bad debt.

O heart, tobacco red heart,
(30)　　beat like a rock guitar.

I am at the ship's prow.
I am no longer the suicide

with her raft and paddle.
Herr Doktor! I'll no longer die

(35)　　to spite you, you wallowing
seasick grounded man.

　　　　　　　　　　　　　　—Anne Sexton

_____

[1] a reference to Kierkegaard's philosophical discourse, *Sickness Unto Death*

14. The poem's opening five couplets do all of the following EXCEPT

(A) allude to deviant Nazi medical experiments
(B) censure the doctor's lack of seriousness
(C) introduce one part of the poem's imperative refrain
(D) vividly depict the dehumanization of the patient
(E) establish a disdainful and accusatory tone

15. The BEST interpretation of "butter me up" (line 2) is

(A) flatter me
(B) console me
(C) impress me
(D) satisfy me
(E) concern me

16. The omission of the object of the preposition "unto" in line 3 suggests which of the following?

    (A) the doctor's admirably sensitive bedside manner
    (B) the doctor's confidence in her complete recovery
    (C) the doctor's unwillingness to disclose the gravity of her condition
    (D) the speaker's understandable reluctance to accept the potentially fatal reality of her illness
    (E) the speaker's conviction that the doctor is wrong

17. Lines 9-10 do which of the following?

    I. Compare the speaker's heart rhythms to the vagaries of the stock market.
    II. Portray the doctor as a "mad scientist."
    III. Suggest the day-to-day inconsistencies of the speaker's health.

    (A) I only
    (B) III only
    (C) I and II
    (D) I and III
    (E) I, II and III

18. The primary difference between lines 11-18 and lines 19-24 is their change in

    (A) focus
    (B) perspective
    (C) diction
    (D) structure
    (E) setting

19. The speaker's diction and self-description through the first twenty-six lines generally paint her as a(n)

    (A) unruly prisoner
    (B) impotent pawn
    (C) manic depressive
    (D) charismatic crusader
    (E) spiritual being

20. Which of the following contributes LEAST to establishing the key change in the doctor-patient relationship that occurs in the final ten lines of the poem?

    (A) the "sponge" (line 27)
    (B) the "bad debt" (line 28)
    (C) the "rock guitar" (line 30)
    (D) the "ship's prow" (line 31)
    (E) the "raft and paddle" (line 33)

21. Lines 31-33 ("I am the ship's prow [. . .] raft and paddle") and lines 34-36 ("Herr Doktor [. . .] grounded man") suggest the speaker's change from

    (A) ignorance to knowledge
    (B) dependence to agency
    (C) defiance to resignation
    (D) triumph to ignominy
    (E) sickness to convalescence

22. The tone of the speaker in lines 34-36, "Herr Doktor! I'll no longer die / to spite you, you wallowing / seasick grounded man," is most aptly characterized as

    (A) reverential
    (B) derisive
    (C) fawning
    (D) formal
    (E) querulous

23. Which of the following offer(s) the most plausible explanation for the speaker's desire to "spite" (line 35) her physician?

    I. Her jealousy of the doctor's high level of erudition.
    II. Her distaste for the demeaning and debilitating aspects of her hospitalization.
    III. Her feminist reluctance to be totally dependent upon a man for assistance.

    (A) I only
    (B) III only
    (C) I and II
    (D) II and III
    (E) I, II and III

24. Ultimately, the poem's theme involves the speaker's demand for

    (A) self-reliance
    (B) knowledge of her condition
    (C) empathy for her family
    (D) a cure for her ailment
    (E) emotional control

25. The author's style is characterized by all of the following EXCEPT

    (A) frequent use of the imperative mode
    (B) instances of self-deprecating humor
    (C) a paucity of figurative language
    (D) images of hospitalization and illness
    (E) a series of unrhymed couplets linked, at times, by enjambment

26. The most salient symbol of the doctor's medical omniscience is the

    (A) "suction cup" (line 5)
    (B) "zig-zag machine" (line 9)
    (C) "Phi Beta key" (line 11)
    (D) "jigger of blood" (line 22)
    (E) "sponge" (line 27)

27. It may be inferred from her comments that the speaker is MOST concerned with which of the following?

    (A) her painful medical procedures
    (B) the confinement of hospitalization
    (C) the lethargy of the hospital staff
    (D) her doctor's sense of self-importance
    (E) the maladies of her immediate family

Questions 28-39. Refer to the following passage.

A visit to Mrs. Manson Mingott
was always an amusing episode to the
young man. The house in itself was already
an historic document, though not, of course,
(5)   as venerable as certain other old family
houses in University Place and lower Fifth
Avenue. Those were of the purest 1830,
with a grim harmony of cabbage-rose-
garlanded carpets, rosewood consoles,
(10) round-arched fire-places with black marble
mantels, and immense glazed book-cases of
mahogany; whereas old Mrs. Mingott, who
had built her house later, had boldly cast
out the massive furniture of her prime, and
(15) mingled with the Mingott heirlooms the
frivolous upholstery of the Second Empire.[1]
It was her habit to sit in a window of her
sitting-room on the ground floor, as if
watching calmly for life and fashion to flow
(20) northward to her solitary doors. She seemed
in no hurry to have them come, for her
patience was equaled by her confidence.
She was sure that presently the hoardings,[2]
the quarries, the one-story saloons, the
(25) wooden green-houses in ragged gardens,
and the rocks from which goats surveyed
the scene, would vanish before the advance
of residences as stately as her own—perhaps
(for she was an impartial woman) even
(30) statelier; and that the cobblestones over
which the old clattering omnibuses bumped
would be replaced by smooth asphalt, such
as people reported having seen in Paris.
Meanwhile, as everyone she cared to see
(35) came to *her* (and she could fill her rooms as
easily as the Beauforts, and without adding
a single item to the *menu* of her suppers),
she did not suffer from geographic
isolation.
(40)   The immense accretion of flesh
which had ascended on her in middle life
like a flood of lava on a doomed city had
changed her from a plump active little
woman with a neatly-turned foot and ankle
(45) into something as vast and august as a
natural phenomenon. She had accepted this
submergence as philosophically as all her
other trials, and now, in extreme old age,
was rewarded by presenting to her mirror
(50) an almost unwrinkled expanse of firm pink
and white flesh, in the centre of which the
traces of a small face survived as if

awaiting excavation. A flight of smooth
double chins led down to the dizzy depths
(55) of a still-snowy bosom veiled in snowy
muslins that were held in place by a
miniature portrait of the late Mr. Mingott;
and around and below, wave after wave of
black silk surged away over the edges of a
(60) capacious armchair, with two tiny white
hands poised like gulls on the surface of the
billows.
    The burden of Mrs. Manson
Mingott's flesh had long since made it
(65) impossible for her to go up and down stairs,
and with characteristic independence she
had made her reception rooms upstairs and
established herself (in flagrant violation of
all the New York proprieties) on the ground
(70) floor of her house; so that, as you sat in her
sitting-room window with her, you caught
(through a door that was always open, and a
looped-back yellow damask portière[3]) the
unexpected vista of a bedroom with a huge
(75) low bed upholstered like a sofa, and a
toilet-table with frivolous lace flounces and
a gilt-framed mirror.
    Her visitors were startled and
fascinated by the foreignness of this
(80) arrangement, which recalled scenes in
French fiction, and architectural incentives
to immorality such as the simple American
had never dreamed of [. . . .].

---

[1] heavily ornate decorative style developed in France in the mid-
   19th century

[2] wooden fences around structures under construction

[3] heavy curtain

28. The impression of Mrs. Manson Mingott that the author wishes to convey is that of a(n)

    (A) feeble invalid
    (B) querulous crone
    (C) aloof recluse
    (D) maverick matriarch
    (E) doting mother

29. The speaker likely mentions the décor (lines 3-16) in order to do which of the following?

    I.   Illustrate the opulence of the aristocratic houses of that era.
    II. Establish the characteristic impulsiveness and unconventionality of Mrs. Manson Mingott.
    III. Contrast the "grim" interiors of traditional houses with the "frivolous" ambience of Mrs. Manson Mingott's abode.

    (A) I only
    (B) III only
    (C) I and II
    (D) II and III
    (E) I, II and III

30. The neighborhood in which Mrs. Manson Mingott currently resides is BEST represented by which of the following pairs of adjectives?

    (A) elegant and expensive
    (B) bustling and commercial
    (C) dangerous and downtrodden
    (D) rustic and emergent
    (E) remote and agrarian

31. The "confidence" alluded to in line 22 of the passage concerns Mrs. Manson Mingott's belief in the

    (A) imminent gentrification of her neighborhood
    (B) gradual rehabilitation of her health
    (C) staunch devotion of her family members
    (D) long-term security of her finances
    (E) unquestionable rectitude of her fashion choices

32. The speaker begins her second paragraph description of Mrs. Manson Mingott with an allusion to

    (A) religion
    (B) literature
    (C) science
    (D) history
    (E) philosophy

33. The "natural phenomenon" (line 46) that Mrs. Manson Mingott is said to resemble is most likely a(n)

    (A) forest
    (B) mountain
    (C) ocean
    (D) desert
    (E) iceberg

34. The passage suggests that Mrs. Manson Mingott reacted to her physical decline with

    (A) depression
    (B) stoicism
    (C) self-deprecating humor
    (D) embarrassment
    (E) vigorous activity

35. To effect the description of Mrs. Manson Mingott in lines 53-62, the author employs all of the following EXCEPT

    (A) natural imagery
    (B) implied metaphor
    (C) alliteration
    (D) understatement
    (E) simile

36. The primary intention of the final two paragraphs is to

    (A) deplore the indecorous nature of Mrs. Manson Mingott's abode
    (B) conjure an incongruous and ironic image of sensuality
    (C) satirize the mildly conservative mores of the visitors
    (D) measure the first-floor décor of Mrs. Manson Mingott's house against the reception rooms in famous novels
    (E) deride the limitation of the American imagination

37. Which of the following contributes LEAST toward imagistically establishing the formidable presence of Mrs. Manson Mingott?

    (A) "immense accretion" (line 40)
    (B) "vast and august" (line 45)
    (C) "submergence" (line 47)
    (D) "capacious" (line 60)
    (E) "burden" (line 63)

38. For which of the following questions about Mrs. Manson Mingott does the passage NOT provide an answer?

    (A) How popular was she in society?
    (B) How had she changed over the years?
    (C) What was her taste in décor?
    (D) Why did she sleep on the first floor?
    (E) What was her relation to the young man who visited her?

39. Which of the following contributes LEAST to developing the idiosyncratic character of Mrs. Manson Mingott?

    (A) the description of her physical features
    (B) the description of the neighborhood in which she resides
    (C) the description of her daily first floor vigil
    (D) the description of the miniature of her late husband
    (E) the scandalous view of her *boudoir*

Questions 40-51. Refer to the following poem.

A Prayer for My Daughter

Once more the storm is howling, and half hid
Under this cradle-hood and coverlid
My child sleeps on. There is no obstacle
But Gregory's wood and one bare hill
(5) Whereby the haystack- and roof-leveling wind,
Bred on the Atlantic, can be stayed;
And for an hour I have walked and prayed
Because of the great gloom that is in my mind.

I have walked and prayed for this young child an
     hour
(10) And heard the sea-wind scream upon the tower,
And under the arches of the bridge, and scream
In the elms above the flooded stream;
Imagining in excited reverie
That the future years had come,
(15) Dancing to a frenzied drum,
Out of the murderous innocence of the sea.

May she be granted beauty and yet not
Beauty to make a stranger's eye distraught,
Or hers, before a looking glass, for such,
(20) Being made beautiful overmuch,
Consider beauty a sufficient end,
Lose natural kindness and maybe
The heart-revealing intimacy
That chooses right, and never find a friend.

(25) Helen[1] being chosen found life flat and dull
And later had much trouble from a fool,
While that great Queen,[2] that rose out of the spray,
Being fatherless could have her way
Yet chose a bandy-legged smith for man.
(30) It's certain that fine women eat
A crazy salad with their meat
Whereby the Horn of Plenty[3] is undone.

In courtesy I'd have her chiefly learned;
Hearts are not had as a gift but hearts are earned
(35) By those that are not entirely beautiful;
Yet many, that have played the fool
For beauty's very self, has charm made wise,
And many a poor man that has roved,
Loved and thought himself beloved,
(40) From a glad kindness cannot take his eyes.

May she become a flourishing hidden tree
That all her thoughts may like the linnet[4] be,
And have no business but dispensing round
Their magnanimities of sound,
(45) Not but in merriment begin a chase,
Nor but in merriment a quarrel.
O may she live like some green laurel
Rooted in one dear perpetual place.

My mind, because the minds that I have loved,
(50) The sort of beauty that I have approved,
Prosper but little, has dried up of late,
Yet knows that to be choked with hate
May well be of all evil chances chief.
If there's no hatred in a mind
(55) Assault and battery of the wind
Can never tear the linnet from the leaf.

An intellectual hatred is the worst,
So let her think opinions are accursed.
Have I not seen the loveliest woman born
(60) Out of the mouth of Plenty's horn,
Because of her opinionated mind
Barter that horn and every good
By quiet natures understood
For an old bellows full of angry wind?

(65) Considering that, all hatred driven hence,
The soul recovers radical innocence
And learns at last that it is self-delighting,
Self-appeasing, self-affrighting,
And that its own sweet will is Heaven's will;
(70) She can, though every face should scowl
And every windy quarter howl
Or every bellows burst, be happy still.

And may her bridegroom bring her to a house
Where all's accustomed, ceremonious;
(75) For arrogance and hatred are the wares
Peddled in the thoroughfares.
How but in custom and in ceremony
Are innocence and beauty born?
Ceremony's a name for the rich horn,
(80) And custom for the spreading laurel tree.

—William Butler Yeats, 1919

---

[1] Helen, who was married to the Greek king Menelaeus, had a dal-
liance with Paris that spurred the Trojan War.

[2] Aphrodite who, despite her fabled beauty, married the lame blacksmith Hephaestus

[3] the *cornucopia*: in various versions, an endless source of food and
drink

[4] a finch or similar bird

40. The speaker perceives all of the following as the potential perils of a young woman's beauty EXCEPT

    (A) a concomitant increase in her vanity
    (B) a decrease in her charitable spirit
    (C) an abatement of her heart-felt intuition
    (D) an ironic intimidation of potential suitors
    (E) the ability to foster heartbreak

41. The poem's central conceit links which of the following?

    (A) the innocent sleep of the child and the tranquility of the sea
    (B) the turbulence of the storm and the speaker's inner turmoil
    (C) the ephemeral nature of beauty and the brevity of the seasons
    (D) the rhythm of the linnet's cry and the cadence of the child's voice
    (E) the troubled marriage of Helen and his child's prospective bond

42. All of the following are lessons that the speaker wishes to impart to his daughter EXCEPT:

    (A) Beauty alone cannot insure romantic happiness.
    (B) Charitable benevolence is a powerful and appealing virtue.
    (C) Animosity is a powerful corruption of character.
    (D) A knowledge and acceptance of self leads one to a higher plane of contentment.
    (E) Expressing one's opinions openly is always the best policy.

43. The poet augments the intensity of the opening two stanzas through all of the following EXCEPT

    (A) onomatopoeic diction
    (B) description of the storm's destructive power
    (C) a personification of the wind
    (D) irregular rhythms that parallel the force of the storm
    (E) his characterization of the overly solicitous father

44. The speaker employs features of the local landscape primarily to do which of the following?

    (A) establish the rustic nature of his native Ireland
    (B) illustrate its geographical vulnerability to the destructive ocean winds
    (C) parallel his frustrated inability to shield his daughter from the vagaries of love
    (D) identify prayerful and contemplative sites
    (E) identify specific local customs and ceremonies

45. In light of the syntax in the third stanza, the word "hers" (line 19) refers to which aspect of the speaker's daughter?

    (A) her beauty
    (B) her eyes
    (C) her mirror
    (D) her kindness
    (E) her friends

46. The speaker's choice of allusions in lines 25-32 is primarily intended to reinforce which of the following?

    (A) the seductive wiles of mythical heroes
    (B) the unquestionable importance of paternal guidance
    (C) the deleterious effect of beauty upon judgment
    (D) the constrictive nature of marriage
    (E) the foolishness of all women

47. The phrase, "Can never tear the linnet from the leaf" (line 56), is BEST paraphrased as never separating

    (A) a father from his daughter
    (B) a mind from sanity
    (C) an individual from harmony
    (D) humanity from nature
    (E) a person from his home

48. In the eighth and ninth stanzas of the poem (lines 57-72), the speaker seems most concerned with

    (A) contrasting different types of animosities
    (B) praising the virtues of a former lover
    (C) sparing his daughter the emotional turmoil that he himself experienced
    (D) suggesting that all actions are preordained
    (E) alluding to the lost bliss of Eden

49. The "spreading laurel tree" (line 80) could perhaps symbolize which of the following?

    I. A growth in individual happiness and contentment.
    II. Childbirth and family.
    III. The virtues of adhering to institutions such as custom and ceremony.

    (A) I only
    (B) III only
    (C) I and II
    (D) I and III
    (E) I, II and III

50. Which of the following figures of speech plays the LEAST significant role in conveying the speaker's fear for his daughter's future happiness?

    (A) the foreshadowing of future trouble in the guise of an ominous storm (stanzas 1 & 2)
    (B) allusions that depict the tribulations of overly beautiful women (stanza 4)
    (C) the metaphor of the cornucopia that conveys both the abundance of conjugal bliss and the ease with which it can be squandered (stanzas 4 & 8)
    (D) the conceit that compares his daughter to a laurel tree (stanzas 6, 7 & 10)
    (E) the metaphor comparing vices to items bartered in a public market (stanza 10)

51. Which of the following BEST exemplifies the literary device of metonymy?

    (A) "cradle-hood" (line 2)
    (B) "looking glass" (line 19)
    (C) "Hearts" (line 34)
    (D) "laurel" (line 47)
    (E) "innocence" (line 66)

Section II

Question One

(Suggested time—40 minutes. This question counts as one-third of the total essay section score.)

Read the following poem carefully. Then, in a well-organized essay, discuss how the style and structure of the poem further the poem's message. In your essay, you may wish to consider such things as choice of detail, syntax, tone and figurative language.

Editor Whedon

To be able to see every side of every question;
To be on every side, to be everything, to be nothing long;
To pervert truth, to ride it for a purpose,
To use great feelings and passions of the human family
(5)   For base designs, for cunning ends,
To wear a mask like the Greek actors—
Your eight-page paper—behind which you huddle,
Bawling through the megaphone of big type:
"This is I, the giant."
(10)   Thereby also living the life of a sneak-thief,
Poisoned with the anonymous words
Of your clandestine soul.
To scratch dirt over scandal for money,
And exhume it to the winds for revenge,
(15)   Or to sell papers,
Crushing reputations, or bodies, if need be,
To win at any cost, save your own life.
To glory in the demoniac power, ditching civilization,
As a paranoiac boy puts a log on the track
(20)   And derails the express train.
To be an editor, as I was.
Then to lie here close by the river over the place
Where the sewage flows from the village,
And the empty cans and garbage are dumped,
(25)   And abortions are hidden.

Question Two

(Suggested time—40 Minutes. This question counts as one-third of the total essay section score.)

Read the following passage carefully. Then, in a well-organized essay, discuss what the choice of detail and other literary elements in the passage reveal about the complex character of Madeline Stanhope.

But the two most prominent members of the family still remain to be described. The second child had been christened Madeline, and had been a great beauty. We need not say had been, for she was never more beautiful than at the time of which we write, though her person had for many years been disfigured by an accident. It is unnecessary that we should give in detail the
(5) early history of Madeline Stanhope. She had gone to Italy when about seventeen years of age, and had been allowed to make the most of her surpassing beauty in the saloons of Milan, and among the crowded villas along the shores of the Lake of Como. She had become famous for adventures in which her character was just not lost, and had destroyed the hearts of a dozen cavaliers without once being touched in her own. Blood had flowed in quarrels about her charms, and she had
(10) heard of these encounters with pleasurable excitement. It had been told of her that on one occasion she had stood by in the disguise of a page, and had seen her lover fall.

As is so often the case, she had married the very worst of those who sought her hand. Why she had chosen Paulo Neroni, a man of no birth and no property, a mere captain on the pope's guard, one who had come up to Milan either simply as an adventurer or else as a spy, a
(15) man of harsh temper and oily manners, mean in figure, swarthy in face, and so false in words as to be hourly detected, need not now be told. When the moment for so doing came, she had probably no alternative. He, at any rate, had become her husband; and after a prolonged honeymoon among the lakes, they had gone together to Rome, the papal captain having vainly endeavoured to induce his wife to remain behind him.

(20) Six months afterwards she arrived at her father's house a cripple, and a mother. She had arrived without even notice, with hardly clothes to cover her, and without one of those many ornaments which had graced her bridal *trousseau*. Her baby was in the arms of a poor girl from Milan, whom she had taken in exchange for the Roman maid who had accompanied her thus far, and who had then, as her mistress said, become homesick and had returned. It was clear that the
(25) lady had determined that there should be no witness to tell stories of her life in Rome.

She had fallen, she said, in ascending a ruin, and had fatally injured the sinews of her knee; so fatally, that when she stood she lost eight inches of her accustomed height; so fatally, that when she assayed to move, she could only drag herself painfully along, with protruded hip and extended foot in a manner less graceful than that of a hunchback. She had consequently made
(30) up her mind, once and for ever, that she would never stand, and never attempt to move herself [. . . .].

Her resolve had not been carried out without difficulty. She had still frequented the opera at Milan; she had still been seen occasionally in the saloons of the *noblesse*; she had caused herself to be carried in and out from her carriage, and in such a manner as in no wise to disturb her charms, disarrange her dress, or expose her deformities. Her sister always accompanied her
(35) and a maid, a man-servant also, and, on state occasions, two. It was impossible that her purpose could have been achieved with less: and yet, poor as she was, she had achieved her purpose. And then again the more dissolute youths of Milan frequented the Stanhope villa and surrounded her couch, not greatly to her father's satisfaction [. . . .].

Question Three

(Suggested time—40 minutes. This question counts as one-third of the total essay section score.)

Oftentimes a novel or play centers about a "radical thinker," an artist, philosopher, scientist or individual whose vision contradicts or challenges that of the norm. Through this character the author often endeavors to convey a potent message about the conflict between social mores and independent thought. Choose a novel or play in which such a "radical thinker" plays a prominent role. Then, in a well-organized essay, illustrate what statement the author of this work is making about the thoughts and/or actions of this individual in light of the social milieu in which he/she exists. You may choose from the list below or use another novel or play of recognized literary merit.

The Plague	*Amadeus*
To the Lighthouse	*The Elephant Man*
A Portrait of the Artist as a Young Man	*Jude the Obscure*
The Picture of Dorian Gray	*The Agony and the Ecstasy*
The Fountainhead	*Dr. Jekyll & Mr. Hyde*
You Can't Go Home Again	*The Awakening*
The Master Builder	*Death in Venice*
Frankenstein	*Hamlet*
The Stranger	*A Doll's House*
Crime and Punishment	*Main Street*
The Handmaid's Tale	*The Scarlet Letter*
To the Lighthouse	*Wise Blood*

Sample Examination V

Questions 1-9. Refer to the following passage.

In the following dialogue exchange from Shakespeare's Richard II, the king, after waging a military campaign in Ireland, returns to face a rebellion against his rule in England.

K.RICHARD. Barkloughly Castle call they this at
    hand?
AUMERLE. Yea, my lord. How brooks your Grace the
    air
After your late tossing on the breaking seas?
K. RICHARD. Needs must I like it well. I weep for joy
(5)   To stand upon my kingdom once again.
Dear earth, I do salute thee with my hand,
Though rebels wound thee with their horses' hoofs.
As a long-parted mother with her child
Plays fondly with her tears and smiles in meeting,
(10)   So, weeping, smiling, I greet thee, my earth,
And do thee favors with my royal hands.
Feed not thy sovereign's foe, my gentle earth,
Nor with thy sweets comfort his ravenous sense;
But let thy spiders, that suck up thy venom,
(15)   And heavy-gaited toads lie in the way,
Doing annoyance to the treacherous feet
With which usurping steps do trample thee.
Yield stinging nettles to mine enemies,
And when they from thy bosom pluck a flower,
(20)   Guard it, I pray thee, with a lurking adder,
Whose double-tongue may with a mortal touch
Throw death upon thy sovereign's enemies.
Mock not my senseless conjuration, lords.
This earth shall have a feeling and these stones
(25)   Prove armed soldiers ere her native King
Shall falter under foul rebellion's arms [. . . .].

1. The tone of the king's response to Aumerle's question suggests that he is

(A) grateful to have survived the fighting in
    Ireland
(B) delighted to return to his native land
(C) resigned to the additional problems he must
    soon confront
(D) puzzled by the strangeness of the locale
(E) physically ill from the sea crossing

2. The BEST substitution for the word "salute," as it is used in line 6, would be

(A) appeal to
(B) welcome
(C) sanctify
(D) address
(E) caress

180

3. Lines 6-26 exemplify all of the following EXCEPT

(A) apostrophe
(B) personification
(C) pathetic fallacy
(D) paradox
(E) simile

4. Lines 8-10, "As a long-parted [. . .] I greet thee, my earth," may be said to do which of the following?

I. Emphasize the king's intimate connection to his land.
II. Convey the mixed emotions the king experiences upon his return.
III. Reveal the king's infirmity of character.

(A) I only
(B) II only
(C) I and II
(D) I and III
(E) I, II and III

5. The king solicits the earth to do all of the following EXCEPT

(A) refuse his enemies sustenance
(B) impede his enemies' progress
(C) deny his enemies its natural beauty
(D) relay his enemies' position
(E) kill his enemies

6. The king's patriotic appeal to the earth is LEAST enhanced by

(A) the simile that depicts the emotional turmoil of the long-parted mother
(B) imperatives that demand the fealty of the natural world
(C) diction that depicts the covetous and traitorous iniquity of his foes
(D) physical actions that convey his empathy for the wounds inflicted on the soil by his opponent's cavalry
(E) his admonition to his attendant lords

7. King Richard's invocation of a lurking adder to "Throw death upon thy sovereign's enemies" (line 22) seems singularly appropriate due to which of the following?

I. The lethalness of the adder's venom.
II. The surreptitious concealment of the adder beneath a beautiful flower.
III. The traditional association of the adder with duplicity and betrayal.

(A) I only
(B) III only
(C) I and II
(D) II and III
(E) I, II and III

8. In line 23, the king expresses his misgivings that his retinue has begun to consider him

(A) clueless
(B) unbalanced
(C) foolhardy
(D) suicidal
(E) craven

9. King Richard's closing boast–that "This earth shall have a feeling and these stones / Prove armed soldiers ere her native King / Shall falter under foul rebellion's arms [. . .]" (lines 24-26)–is BEST labeled

(A) confident
(B) histrionic
(C) maudlin
(D) tentative
(E) despotic

Questions 10-23. Refer to the following passage.

"Even now I can see it, the dark passage lit with dim lights and Dr. Bledsoe swaying as he went before me. At the door stood the porter and the conductor, a black
(5)   man and a white man of the South, both crying. Both weeping. And he looked up as we entered, his great eyes resigned but still aflame with nobility and courage against the white of his pillow; and he looked at his
(10)   friend and smiled. Smiled warmly at his old campaigner, his loyal champion, his adjunct, that marvelous singer of the old songs who had rallied his spirit during times of distress and discouragement, who
(15)   with his singing of the old familiar melodies soothed the doubts and fears of the multitude; he who had rallied the ignorant, the fearful and suspicious, those still wrapped in the rags of slavery; him,
(20)   there, your leader, who calmed the children of the storm. And as the founder looked up at his companion, he smiled. And reaching out his hand to his friend and companion as I now stretch out my hand to you, he said,
(25)   'Come closer. Come closer.' And he moved closer, until he stood beside the berth, and the light slanting across his shoulder as he knelt beside him. And the hand reached out and gently touched him
(30)   and he said, 'Now, you must take on the burden. Lead them the rest of the way.' And oh, the cry of that train and the pain too big for tears!
"When the train reached the
(35)   summit of the mountain, he was no longer with us. And as the train dropped down the grade he had departed.
"It had become a veritable train of sorrow. Dr. Bledsoe there, sat weary in
(40)   mind and heavy of heart. What should he do? The Leader was dead and he thrown suddenly at the head of the troops like a cavalryman catapulted into the saddle of his general felled in a charge of battle—vaulted
(45)   onto the back of his fiery and half-broken charger. Ah! And that great, black, noble beast, wall-eyed with the din of battle and twitching already with its sense of loss. What command should he give? Should he
(50)   return with this burden, home, to where already the hot wires were flashing, speaking, rattling the mournful message? Should he turn and bear the fallen soldier

down the cold and alien mountain to this
(55)   valley home? Return with the dear eyes dulled, the firm hand still, the magnificent voice silent, the Leader cold? Return to the warm valley, to the green grounds he could no longer light with his mortal vision?
(60)   Should he follow his leader's vision though he had now himself departed?
"Ah, of course you know the story: How he bore the body into the strange city, and the speech he made as his Leader lay in
(65)   state, and how when the sad news spread, a day of mourning was declared for the whole municipality. Oh, and how rich and poor, black and white, weak and powerful, young and old, all came to pay their
(70)   homage—many realizing the Leader's worth and their loss only now with his passing. And how, with his mission done, Dr. Bledsoe returned, keeping his sorrowful vigil with his friend in an humble baggage
(75)   car; and how the people came to pay their respects at the stations…A slow train. A sorrowful train. And all along the line, in mountain and valley, wherever the rails found their fateful course, the people were
(80)   one in their common mourning, and like the cold steel rails, were spiked down to their sorrow. Oh, what a sad departure!
"And what an even sadder arrival. See with me, my young friends, hear with
(85)   me: The weeping and wailing of those who shared his labors. Their sweet Leader returned to them, rock-cold in the iron immobility of death. He who had left them quick, in the prime of his manhood, author
(90)   of their own fire and illumination, returned to them cold, already a bronzed statue. Oh, the *despair*, my young friends. The black despair of black people! I see them now: wandering about these grounds, where each
(95)   brick, each bird, each blade of grass was a reminder of some precious memory; and each memory a hammer stroke driving home the blunt spikes of their sorrow [. . . .]."

From INVISIBLE MAN by Ralph Ellison, copyright 1947, 1948, 1952 by Ralph Ellison. Copyright renewed 1975, 1976, 1980 by Ralph Ellison. Used by permission of Random House, Inc.

10. Lines 1-10 establish all of the following EXCEPT

    (A) the stoic but dignified comportment of the dying Leader
    (B) the broad impact of the Leader's death
    (C) the emotional instability of Dr. Bledsoe
    (D) the indelible impress of the occasion on the speaker's memory
    (E) the passage's funereal tone

11. Which of the following is NOT used in the first paragraph to establish the importance of Dr. Bledsoe?

    (A) a series of appositives that identify his diverse service to the Leader
    (B) adjectives that capture his strength in the face of adversity
    (C) verbs which recall his ability to console and inspire
    (D) the sequential use of a pronoun and adverb to single him out to the speaker's audience
    (E) a catalog of the insecure multitude that he had to overcome

12. Which of the following pairs of words BEST describes the relationship between Dr. Bledsoe and the Leader?

    (A) father—son
    (B) friend—adversary
    (C) mentor—protégé
    (D) martinet—sycophant
    (E) believer—cynic

13. The speaker symbolically parallels the demise of the Leader via changes in

    (A) the position of the train on the mountain
    (B) light and sound
    (C) the individuals who attend him
    (D) the time of day
    (E) his facial expression

14. Which of the following statements is the only accurate observation about the speaker's description of the Leader's death?

    (A) It is embellished by pathetic fallacy.
    (B) It is dramatized by a deathbed confession.
    (C) It reflects his wish to fill the void of leadership before his demise.
    (D) It is ameliorated by a tone of relief and celebration.
    (E) It offers antithetical images of defeat and defiance.

15. By "the rest of the way" (line 31), the Leader is most likely referring to

    (A) the train's intended destination
    (B) emancipation from slavery
    (C) social equality
    (D) spiritual salvation
    (E) Bledsoe's potential return to the valley

16. Words such as "catapulted" (line 43) and "vaulted" (line 44) are intended to reveal which of the following?

    I. Dr. Bledsoe's sudden and unexpected promotion.
    II. Dr. Bledsoe's long-harbored zeal to succeed the Leader.
    III. Dr. Bledsoe's lack of experience for such an important charge.

    (A) I only
    (B) III only
    (C) I and II
    (D) I and III
    (E) I, II and III

17. The description of the horse as "wall-eyed with the din of battle" (line 47) offers an example of

    (A) onomatopoeia
    (B) hyperbole
    (C) synaesthesia
    (D) metonymy
    (E) personification

18. The series of questions that Dr. Bledsoe ponders in lines 49-61 do all of the following EXCEPT

    (A) contrast the warmth of the valley with the coldness of the Leader's corpse
    (B) suggest the initial indecision experienced by Dr. Bledsoe
    (C) provide antithetical images of the dead Leader's prominent attributes
    (D) reiterate a word that connotes an admission of failure
    (E) consider the funeral arrangements for the fallen Leader

19. The transitional sentence, "Ah, of course you know the story" (line 62), may definitively be said to serve which of the following rhetorical purposes?

    (A) permitting the speaker to omit information his audience already knows
    (B) expressing the speaker's disbelief that his audience could not be familiar with the events following the Leader's passing
    (C) allowing the speaker once again to regale his audience with a familiar and beloved tale
    (D) implying the speaker's conviction that the death of the best and the brightest is an all-too-common occurrence
    (E) suggesting that the speaker is reacting to bodily movement or murmuring in his audience

20. The speaker conveys the acute emotional agony of the Leader's death MOST forcefully through his

    (A) depiction of the diverse constituencies who come out to mourn the Leader
    (B) description of the deliberate progress of the funeral train
    (C) onomatopoeic description of the mourner's sorrow
    (D) italicization of the word "*despair*" (line 92)
    (E) crucifixion-like comparison of the rail-spiking

21. The phrase "already a bronzed statue" (line 91) serves which of the following functions?

    I. It figuratively conveys the *rigor mortis* of the Leader's corpse.
    II. It implies the artistic commemoration of his impressive legacy.
    III. It suggests the ephemeralness of human existence.

    (A) I only
    (B) II only
    (C) I and II
    (D) II and III
    (E) I, II and III

22. The speaker's description of the people in the final paragraph paints them as

    (A) dolorous and directionless
    (B) serene and nostalgic
    (C) listless and apathetic
    (D) angry and vindictive
    (E) stoic and defiant

23. The speaker's address is BEST characterized as

    (A) reassuring
    (B) fomenting
    (C) elegiac
    (D) saturnine
    (E) moralizing

Questions 24-39. Refer to the following poem.

Eros Turannos[1]

She fears him, and will always ask
    What fated her to choose him;
She meets in his engaging mask
    All reasons to refuse him;
(5) But what she meets and what she fears
    Are less than are the downward years
    Drawn slowly to the foamless weirs
        Of age were she to lose him.

Between a blurred sagacity
(10)   That once had power to sound him,
And Love, that will not let him be
    The Judas that she found him,
Her pride assuages her almost,
    As if it were alone the cost,—
(15) He sees that he will not be lost,
        And waits and looks around him.

A sense of ocean and old trees
    Envelops and allures him;
Tradition, touching all he sees,
(20)   Beguiles and reassures him;
And all her doubts of what he says
Are dimmed by what she knows of days,—
Till even prejudice delays
        And fades, and she secures him.

(25) The falling leaf inaugurates
    The reign of her confusion:
The pounding wave reverberates
    The dirge of her illusion;
And home, where passion lived and died,
(30) Becomes a place where she can hide,
While all the town and harborside
        Vibrate with her seclusion.

We tell you, tapping on our brows,
    The story as it should be,—
(35) As if the story of a house
    Were told, or ever could be,—
We'll have no kindly veil between
Her visions and those we have seen,—
As if we guessed what hers have been,
(40)   Or what they are or would be.

Meanwhile we do no harm; for they
    That with a god have striven,
Not hearing much of what we say,
    Take what the god has given;
(45) Though like waves breaking it may be
Or like a changed familiar tree,
Or like a stairway to the sea
    Where down the blind are driven.

—Edwin Arlington Robinson

_____

[1] the tyrant, love

24. The speaker in the poem is revealed to be

    (A) the woman
    (B) the woman's beloved
    (C) Love
    (D) the collective village
    (E) an omniscient third-person narrator

25. The poem's subject concerns a love that is

    (A) unrequited
    (B) star-crossed
    (C) betrayed
    (D) tested
    (E) unconsummated

26. The description of the beloved in the first two stanzas (lines 1-16) paints him as all of the following EXCEPT

    (A) intimidating
    (B) maintaining a facade
    (C) adulterous
    (D) verbally abusive
    (E) arrogantly self-assured

27. The poem suggests that the primary reason for the woman's failure to leave the man is her fear of

    (A) being physically beaten
    (B) losing her youth and beauty
    (C) sullying her reputation
    (D) feeling suicidally despondent
    (E) being unable to find someone else

28. The most accurate equivalent for the phrase "sound him" in line 10 would be

   (A) announce her suspicions
   (B) measure his truthfulness
   (C) berate his lack of consideration
   (D) inquire of his whereabouts
   (E) question the depth of his feelings

29. The difference between the speaker's use of nature in the third and fourth stanzas is BEST conveyed by which of the following?

   (A) The third stanza presents images of constancy and durability, the fourth symbols of aging and turbulence.
   (B) The third stanza alludes to the setting of their first encounter, the fourth to the scene of their parting.
   (C) The third stanza presents a sense of disorientation, the fourth a sense of clarity.
   (D) The third stanza presents images of the exotic, the fourth images of the familiar.
   (E) The third stanza presents public interludes, the fourth private ones.

30. What the woman likely "knows of days" in line 22 is that they are

   (A) often interminable
   (B) frequently cluttered by trivia
   (C) occasionally monotonous
   (D) sometimes sentimental
   (E) always dwindling

31. Each of the following helps convey the woman's willingness to compromise her discontent in order to preserve her relationship EXCEPT

   (A) "blurred" (line 9)
   (B) "assuages" (line 13)
   (C) "dimmed" (line 22)
   (D) "fades" (line 24)
   (E) "reverberates" (line 27)

32. The "Tradition" that is mentioned in line 19 could possibly refer to which of the following?

   I. The man's confidence that the woman will not leave him.
   II. The long-standing culture of the seaside village that tolerates such relationships.
   III. The marriage vow itself.

   (A) I only
   (B) III only
   (C) I and III
   (D) II and III
   (E) I, II and III

33. In the poem, the woman's house becomes a place of

   (A) unbearable humiliation
   (B) ironic refuge
   (C) pleasant remembrance
   (D) invasive scrutiny
   (E) psychological revulsion

34. The word "Vibrate" (line 32) does all of the following EXCEPT

   (A) contrast the woman's desire for seclusion
   (B) intimate the disturbing effect the couple's marital woes have had upon the community
   (C) imply the speed with which gossip runs rampant
   (D) physically mirror the buzz in the village
   (E) provide an example of pathetic fallacy

35. Lines 33-36, "We tell you, tapping on our brows [. . .] were told or ever could be," imply which of the following?

   I. That the townspeople are putting a happy spin on the episode's ending.
   II. That the townspeople have an acute sense of small-town decorum.
   III. That the townspeople wish the moral to be clear even if some details aren't known.

   (A) I only
   (B) II only
   (C) I and III
   (D) II and III
   (E) I, II and III

36. The phrase "tapping on our brows" (line 33) is meant to suggest the

    (A) woman's inordinately headstrong nature
    (B) woman's incipient senility
    (C) woman's astute decision
    (D) town's befuddlement at the woman's actions
    (E) town's sapient insight

37. The phrase "kindly veil" (line 37) BEST exemplifies which of the following?

    (A) personification
    (B) oxymoron
    (C) metonymy
    (D) euphemism
    (E) understatement

38. The poem's final stanza does all of the following EXCEPT

    (A) exculpate the townspeople from any moral transgression
    (B) parody via simile the discordant change in the couple's relation
    (C) imply that the couple has been willfully or inadvertently oblivious to the town's moral commentary on their actions
    (D) suggest that the couple has accepted their unfortunate lot
    (E) allude to the Biblical banishment from Eden

39. Of the following, which can NOT be said to be characteristic of the poem?

    (A) diction that at times connotes regality, funeral and exile
    (B) an intricate and interwoven pattern of rhyme
    (C) a specific yet ambiguous setting that fosters the poem's universality
    (D) an ironic character twist in which the woman gains the upper hand in the relationship
    (E) a thematic interest in the compromises that human beings make in relationships

Questions 40-51. Refer to the following passage.

I've just come out of the sunken lane, kneed and elbowed, thumped and bramble-scratched, and the race is two-thirds over, and a voice is going like a wireless in my mind
(5) saying that when you've had enough of feeling good like the first man on earth on a frosty morning, and you've known how it is to be taken bad like the last man on earth on a summer's afternoon, then you get at last to
(10) being like the only man on earth and don't give a bogger about either good or bad, but just trot on with your slippers slapping the good dry soil that at least would never do you a bad turn. Now the words are like coming from a crystal-
(15) set that's broken down, and something's happening inside the shell-case of my guts that bothers me and I don't know why or what to blame it on, a grinding near my ticker as though a bag of rusty screws is loose inside me
(20) and I shake them up every time I trot forward. Now and again I break my rhythm to feel my left shoulder-blade by swinging a right hand across my chest as if to rub the knife away that has somehow got stuck in there. But I know
(25) it's nothing to bother about, that more likely it's caused by too much thinking that now and again I take for worry. For sometimes I'm the greatest worrier in the world I think (as you twigged I'll bet from me having got this story
(30) out) which is funny anyway because my mam don't know the meaning of the word so I don't take after her; though dad had a hard time of worry all his life up to when he filled his bedroom with hot blood and kicked the bucket
(35) that morning when nobody was in the house. I'll never forget it, straight I won't, because I was the one that found him and I often wished I'd hadn't. Back from a session on the fruit-machines in the fish-and-chip shop, jingling
(40) my three-lemon loot to a nail-dead house, as soon as I got in I knew something was wrong, stood leaning my head against the cold mirror above the mantelpiece trying not to open my eyes and see my stone-cold clock—because I
(45) knew I'd gone white as a piece of chalk since coming in as if I'd been got at by a Dracula-vampire and even my penny-pocket winnings kept quiet on purpose.
Gunthorpe nearly caught me up. Birds
(50) were singing from the briar hedge, and a couple of thrushies flew like lightning into some thorny bushes. Corn had grown high in the next field and would be cut down soon

with scythes and mowers; but I never wanted
(55) to notice much while running in case it put me off my stroke, so by the haystack I decided to leave it all behind and put on such a spurt, in spite of nails in my guts, that before long I'd left both Gunthorpe and the birds a good way
(60) off; I wasn't far now from going into that last mile and a half like a knife through margarine, but the quietness I suddenly trotted into between two pickets was like opening my eyes underwater and looking at the pebbles on a
(65) stream bottom, reminding me again of going back that morning to the house in which my old man had croaked, which is funny because I hadn't thought about it at all since it happened and even then I didn't brood much on it. I
(70) wonder why? I suppose that since I started to think on these long-distance runs I'm liable to have anything crop up and pester at my tripes and innards, and now that I see my bloody dad behind each grass-blade in my barmy runner-
(75) brain I'm not so sure I like to think and that it's such a good thing after all. I choke my phlegm and keep on running anyway and curse the Borstal-builders and their athletics—flappity-flap, slop-slop, crunchslap-crunchslap-
(80) crunchslap—who've maybe got their own back on me from the bright beginning by sliding magic-lantern slides into my head that never stood a chance before. Only if I take whatever comes like this in my runner's stride can I keep
(85) on keeping on like my old self and beat them back; and now I've thought on this far I know I'll win, in the crunch-slap end. So anyway after a bit I went upstairs one step at a time not thinking anything about how I should find dad
(90) and what I'd do when I did. But now I'm making up for it by going over the rotten life mam led him ever since I can remember, knocking-on with different men even when he was alive and fit and she not caring whether he
(95) knew it or not, and most of the time he wasn't so blind as she thought and cursed and roared and threatened to punch her tab, and I had to stand up to stop him even though I knew she deserved it. What a life for all of us [. . . .].

From THE LONELINESS OF THE LONG-DISTANCE RUNNER
by Alan Sillitoe, copyright © 1959 by Alan Sillitoe.
Used by permission of Alfred A. Knopf, a division of Random House, Inc.

40. The author's primary concern in the passage is

    (A) depicting the excitement of a long-distance race
    (B) describing the physical toll that cross-country running exacts
    (C) illustrating the beauty of the English country landscape
    (D) revealing the unpleasant subliminal memories of the speaker
    (E) deriding the overly strong emphasis placed upon winning by his school

41. In lines 3-13, "and a voice is going [. . .] a bad turn," the speaker is expressing his

    (A) regret over a failure to accomplish something
    (B) relief than an ordeal is finally over
    (C) elation at surviving a particularly arduous trial
    (D) indifference to the vicissitudes of life
    (E) frustration over the elusiveness of victory

42. The speaker uses expressions such as "wireless" (line 4) and "crystal-set" (lines 14-15) to suggest the

    (A) rush of adrenaline he feels as he is running
    (B) random thoughts entering his mind
    (C) awareness he maintains of the position of the other runners
    (D) excited buzz of the race's spectators
    (E) inner compulsion that fuels his competitive spirit

43. The author's depiction of the frenzy of a cross-country race is LEAST enhanced by which of the following?

    (A) participles that capture the arduousness of the course
    (B) similes and metaphors that convey the bodily pain endured by the speaker
    (C) a kaleidoscopic, interior monologue narration that mirrors the frenzied pace of the contest
    (D) the single declarative sentence that begins paragraph two
    (E) occasional references to the passing idyllic landscape

44. In his flashback involving the death of his father, the speaker indicates that upon first entering the house he felt

    (A) premonitory
    (B) restrained
    (C) relieved
    (D) ecstatic
    (E) exhausted

45. The irony of the speaker's discovery of his father's body (lines 36-48) is that it occurs just after he had

    (A) won money playing penny slots
    (B) returned home from work
    (C) finished having dinner
    (D) talked about having no luck
    (E) received his paycheck

46. The speaker hints that the root of his father's problems was

    (A) medical
    (B) marital
    (C) financial
    (D) psychological
    (E) spiritual

47. The transition sentence, "Gunthorpe nearly caught me up" (line 49), may be said to do all of the following EXCEPT

    (A) cause the speaker to note features of the surrounding landscape
    (B) temporarily dispel the speaker's unpleasant flashback
    (C) bring the speaker's focus back to his running
    (D) spur the speaker into a mode of panic
    (E) motivate the speaker to separate himself from his nearest rival

48. The "it" (line 57) that the speaker wishes to leave behind could plausibly refer to which of the following?

    I. The distractions of the natural setting.
    II. Gunthorpe and the other competitors.
    III. The memory of his grisly discovery.

    (A) II only
    (B) III only
    (C) I and II
    (D) II and III
    (E) I, II and III

49. In the passage the speaker employs onomatopoeia to capture the

    (A) wireless-like voice in his head
    (B) singing of the thrushes in the vegetation
    (C) sound of his shoes on the running path
    (D) the "bag of rusty screws" he imagines moving about in his chest
    (E) the gunshot that killed his father

50. Which of the following would NOT be a suitable substitution for the colloquialism listed before it?

    (A) "don't give a bogger" (lines 10-11): "haven't a care"
    (B) "as you twigged" (lines 28-29): "as you guessed"
    (C) "croaked" (line 67): "died"
    (D) "pester at my tripes and innards" (lines 72-73): "physically upset me"
    (E) "knocking-on" (line 93): "quarreling with"

51. The passage ultimately implies that the speaker's long-distance running should be viewed as which of the following?

    I. An activity that builds his self-confidence and self-esteem.
    II. A meditative and therapeutic experience.
    III. A metaphor for his coping with the obstacles and challenges of life.

    (A) I only
    (B) II only
    (C) I and III
    (D) II and III
    (E) I, II and III

Section II

Question One

(Suggested time—40 minutes. This question counts as one-third of the total essay section score.)

Read the following poems carefully. Then, in a well-organized essay, contrast the two poems, making sure to discuss what each poem reveals about its speaker's attitude towards death. In your discussion you may wish to consider such things as diction, figurative language, structure and tone.

I have a rendezvous with Death
At some disputed barricade,
When Spring comes back with rustling shade
And apple-blossoms fill the air—
(5)   I have a rendezvous with Death
When Spring brings back blue days and fair.

It may be he shall take my hand
And lead me into his dark land
And close my eyes and quench my breath—
(10) It may be I shall pass him still.
I have a rendezvous with Death
On some scarred slope of battered hill,
When Spring comes round again this year
And the first meadow-flowers appear.

(15) God knows 'twere better to be deep
Pillowed in silk and scented down,
Where love throbs out in blissful sleep,
Pulse nigh to pulse, and breath to breath,
Where hushed awakenings are dear...
(20) But I've a rendezvous with Death
At midnight in some flaming town,
When Spring trips north again this year,
And I to my pledged word am true,
I shall not fail that rendezvous.

—Alan Seeger

Because I could not stop for Death—
He kindly stopped for me—
The Carriage held but just Ourselves—
And Immortality.

(5) We slowly drove—He knew no haste,
And I had put away,
My labor and my leisure too,
For His Civility—

We passed the School where Children strove
(10) At Recess—in the Ring—
We passed the Fields of Grazing Grain—
We passed the Setting Sun—

Or rather—He passed us—
The Dews drew quivering and chill—
(15) For only Gossamer, my Gown—
My Tippet—only Tulle—

We paused before a House that seemed
A Swelling of the ground—
The Roof was scarcely visible—
(20) The Cornice—in the Ground—

Since then—'tis Centuries—and yet
Feels shorter than the Day
I first surmised the Horses' Heads
Were toward Eternity—

—Emily Dickinson

Question Two

(Suggested time—40 minutes. This question counts as one-third of the total essay section score.)

In the following excerpt from a mid-nineteenth century novel, a young girl eagerly awaits the appearance of an actress she has looked forward to seeing. Read the following passage carefully. Then, in a well-organized essay, discuss the speaker's initial impressions of the actress and how the author uses elements of language to reveal them.

She rose at nine that December night: above the horizon I saw her come. She could shine yet with pale grandeur and steady might; but that star verged already on its judgment-day. Seen near, it was a chaos—hollow, half-consumed: an orb perished or perishing—half lava, half glow.

I had heard this woman termed "plain," and I expected bony harshness and grimness—something
(5) large, angular, sallow. What I saw was the shadow of a royal Vashti[1]: a queen, fair as the day once, turned pale now like twilight, and wasted like wax in flame.

For awhile—a long while—I thought it was only a woman, though an unique woman, who moved in might and grace before this multitude. By-and-by I recognized my mistake. Behold! I found upon her something neither of woman nor of man: in each of her eyes sat a devil. These evil forces bore her
(10) through the tragedy, kept up her feeble strength—for she was but a frail creature; and as the action rose and the stir deepened, how wildly they shook her with their passions of the pit! They wrote hell on her straight, haughty brow. They tuned her voice to the note of torment. They writhed her regal face to a demoniac mask. Hate and Murder and Madness incarnate, she stood.

It was a marvellous sight: a mighty revelation.
(15) It was a spectacle low, horrible, immoral.

Swordsmen thrust through, and dying in their blood on the arena sand; bulls goring horses disembowelled, make a meeker vision for the public—a milder condiment for a people's palate—than Vashti torn by seven devils: devils which cried sore and rent the tenement they haunted, but still refused to be exorcized.
(20) Suffering had struck that stage empress; and she stood before her audience neither yielding to, nor enduring, nor in finite measure, resenting it: she stood locked in struggle, rigid in resistance. She stood, not dressed, but draped in pale antique folds, long and regular like sculpture. A background and entourage and flooring of deepest crimson threw her out, white like alabaster—like silver: rather be it said, like Death [. . . .].
(25) I have said that she does not *resent* her grief. No; the weakness of that word would make it a lie. To her, what hurts becomes immediately embodied: she looks on it as a thing that can be attacked, worried down, torn in shreds. Scarcely a substance herself, she grapples to conflict with abstractions. Before calamity she is a tigress; she rends her woes, shivers them in convulsed abhorrence. Pain, for her, has no result in good; tears water no harvest of wisdom: on sickness, on death itself, she looks with the eye of a
(30) rebel. Wicked, perhaps, she is, but also she is strong; and her strength has conquered Beauty, has overcome Grace, and bound both at her side, captives peerlessly fair, and docile as fair. Even in the uttermost frenzy of energy is each maenad movement royally, imperially, incedingly[2] upborne. Her hair, flying loose in revel or war, is still an angel's hair, and glorious under a halo. Fallen, insurgent, banished, she remembers the heaven where she rebelled. Heaven's light, following her exile, pierces its confines,
(35) and discloses their forlorn remoteness.

Place now the Cleopatra, or any other slug, before her as an obstacle, and see her cut through the pulpy mass as the scimitar of Saladin[3] clove the down cushion. Let Paul Peter Rubens[4] wake from the dead, let him rise out of his cerements, and bring into this presence all the army of his fat women; the magian[5] power or prophet-virtue gifting that slight rod of Moses, could, at one waft, release and re-
(40) mingle a sea spell-parted, whelming the heavy host with the down-rush of overthrown sea-ramparts [. . . .].

---

[1] Old Testament queen

[2] majestically

[3] legendary 12th century Muslim warrior who fought valiantly against the Crusaders

[4] 17th century Flemish painter

[5] (adj) Magi-like; royal

Question Three

(Suggested time—40 minutes. This question counts as one-third of the total essay section score.)

Near the conclusion of Arthur Miller's *Death of a Salesman*, Willy Loman's next-door neighbor, Charlie, says of the deceased protagonist,

> "…And for a salesman, there is no rock bottom to the life. He don't put a bolt to a nut, he don't tell you the law or give you medicine. He's a man way out there in the blue, riding on a smile and a shoeshine. And when they start not smiling back—that's an earthquake….".

In literature, as in life, the size of a calamity is seldom proportional to its effect upon the individual. In fact, it is often the seemingly minor or innocuous incident that rivals the traumatic one in the extent of its impact upon the fortunes or psyche of the character who experiences it. From the novels and plays you have read, choose a work in which a seemingly minor action or event has a disproportionate impact upon the character who experiences it. Then, in a well-organized essay, identify the nature of this "earthquake" and show how its effect upon the character greatly impacts the literary work as a whole.

Oliver Twist	*Deliverance*
Farenheit 451	*King Lear*
Inherit the Wind	*Native Son*
Oedipus Rex	*Billy Budd*
Tracks	*The Plague*
Huckleberry Finn	*Lancelot*
Ethan Frome	*The Jungle*
The Pearl	*Rabbit Run*
Invisible Man	*MacBeth*
The Crucible	*Les Miserables*

Sample Examination VI

Questions 1-15. Refer to the following poem.

My Great-Grandfather's Slaves

Deep in the back ways of my mind I see them
    going in the long days
    over the same fields that I have gone
    long days over.

(5) I see the sun passing and burning high
    over that land from their day
    until mine, their shadows
    having risen and consumed them.

I see them obeying and watching
(10) the bearded tall man whose voice
    and blood are mine, whose countenance
    in stone at his grave my own resembles,
    whose blindness is my brand.

I see them kneel and pray to the white God
(15) who buys their souls with heaven.

I see them approach, quiet
    in the merchandise of their flesh
    to put down their burdens
    of firewood and hemp and tobacco
(20) into the minds of my kinsmen.

I see them moving in the rooms of my history,
    the day of my birth entering
    the horizon emptied of their days,
    their purchased lives taken back
(25) into the dust of birthright.

I see them borne, shadow within shadow,
    shroud within shroud, through all nights
    from their lives to mine, long beyond
    reparation or given liberty
(30) or any straightness.

I see them go in the bonds of my blood
    through all the time of their bodies.

I have seen that freedom cannot be taken
    from one man and given to another,
(35) and cannot be taken and kept.

I know that freedom can only be given,
    and is the gift to the giver
    from the one who receives.

I am owned by the blood of all of them
(40) who ever were owned by my blood.
    We cannot be free of each other.

1. The immediacy of the speaker's impression of his great-grandfather's plantation is enhanced by all of the following EXCEPT

   (A) an imaginative re-creation of antebellum slave life
   (B) a contrast between the slave cabins and his great-grandfather's mansion
   (C) a sense of guilt and remorse for his family's slave ownership
   (D) a use of present tense verbs
   (E) an emphatic merger of the historical past with the personal present

2. The accuracy of the speaker's imaginative recollection is compromised by his

   (A) temporal distance from his great grandfather's time
   (B) gross exaggeration of the hardships of slavery
   (C) inability as a Southern white man to maintain objectivity
   (D) romanticized conception of his ancestor
   (E) overly emotional reaction to his status as a descendant of slave owners

3. The speaker's attitude towards his great-grandfather's slave ownership is BEST characterized as

   (A) oblivious and indifferent
   (B) conscience-stricken and reflective
   (C) defiant and defensive
   (D) pragmatic and accepting
   (E) jocular and dismissive

4. Lines 9-13, I see them obeying and watching [. . .] whose blindness is my brand," do which of the following?

   I. Confirm genetic similarities between the speaker and his great-grandfather.
   II. Acknowledge the speaker's inherent sense of culpability.
   III. Establish the common ideology of the speaker and his great-grandfather.

   (A) I only
   (B) III only
   (C) I and II
   (D) II and III
   (E) I, II and III

5. The word "brand" (line 13) is BEST interpreted as

   (A) type
   (B) burn
   (C) disfigurement
   (D) legacy
   (E) stigma

6. A sardonic reading of lines 14-15 might suggest which of the following?

   (A) That the nature of God is unquestionably benevolent.
   (B) That slaves were admirably pious.
   (C) That slaves were sustained through hardship by their stalwart belief in an afterlife.
   (D) That Christ's sacrifice on the cross has ensured the slaves a place in heaven.
   (E) That the deity to whom the slaves prayed was yet another facet of their enslavement.

7. The speaker's use of the word "merchandise" in line 17 is intended to

   (A) foreshadow the subsequent list of the South's various economic staples
   (B) convey the onerous nature of the things slaves traditionally carried
   (C) reveal the slaves' painful consciousness of their own status as a commodity
   (D) display the slaves' naturally subservient nature
   (E) paint a more convincing picture of slaves working in the field

8. The phrase "dust of birthright" (line 25) is primarily intended to

   (A) imply that slaves were predestined to suffer and die
   (B) allude to the creation episode in the Book of Genesis
   (C) recall the African homeland from which slaves were translated
   (D) affirm that the slaves' physical sacrifice has assured them spiritual salvation
   (E) convey the arid quality of the land

9. The primary purpose of lines 26-30, "I see them borne, shadow within shadow, / shroud within shroud, through all nights / from their lives to mine, long beyond / reparation or given liberty / or any straightness," is to

   (A) convey the high rate of mortality for those who suffered enslavement
   (B) show the deleterious effects of taxing physical labor upon the enslaved
   (C) deplore the limited financial remuneration given to slave descendants
   (D) suggest that for the speaker his great-grandfather's slaves have become a haunting presence
   (E) imply the insignificance of African-Americans in contemporary society

10. The "straightness" that the speaker mentions in line 30 most likely alludes to the

    (A) alacrity of the slaves' release
    (B) melioration of the bent posture of the field-workers
    (C) moral reformation of criminal elements among the freedmen
    (D) need for life direction among the masses of migrating slaves
    (E) attainment of full social equality

11. The speaker's final assertion—that he is "owned by the blood of all of them, / who ever were owned by my blood. / We cannot be free of each other" (lines 39-41)—suggests all of the following EXCEPT

    (A) that the physical incarceration of the slaves has been replaced by the psychological enslavement of the speaker
    (B) that the speaker perceives the irony of his new position
    (C) that the speaker feels a vicarious sense of responsibility for his great-grandfather's wrongdoing
    (D) that the speaker feels compelled to make financial reparation to the descendants of his great-grandfather's slaves
    (E) that the speaker is conscious of the generational duration of the enslavement

12. Over the final three stanzas the speaker builds toward his climactic epiphany through

    (A) increasingly descriptive diction
    (B) more frequent instances of figurative language
    (C) subtle alteration of the present tense verbs
    (D) radical changes in syntax
    (E) adaptation of a more objective perspective

13. Which of the following does NOT help to convey the expanse of time between the speaker's and his great-grandfather's existence?

    (A) the movement of the sun (lines 5-7)
    (B) the lengthening of the slaves' shadows (lines 7-8)
    (C) his great-grandfather's monument (lines 11-12)
    (D) the metaphorical depiction of the speaker's memory (line 21)
    (E) the Biblical allusion to human mortality (lines 24-25)

14. In light of the content of the poem, the phrase "the same fields that I have gone / long days over" (lines 3-4), might plausibly be interpreted as which of the following?

    I. The actual property that is the speaker's familial legacy.
    II. The reverie of pre-bellum scenes that the speaker envisions in the first thirty-two lines.
    III. The course of the speaker's life.

    (A) I only
    (B) II only
    (C) I and II
    (D) I and III
    (E) I, II and III

15. The speaker aurally acknowledges the culpability of his family line through

    (A) onomatopoeic diction
    (B) choric repetition
    (C) alliteration
    (D) assonance
    (E) masculine rhymes

Questions 16-27. Refer to the following passage.

John Bull, for all appearance, is a
plain, downright, matter-of-fact fellow,
with much less of poetry about him than
rich prose [. . . .] He excels in humor more than
(5) in wit; is jolly rather than gay; melancholy
rather than morose; can easily be moved to
a sudden tear or surprised into a broad
laugh; but he loathes sentiment and has no
turn for light pleasantry. He is a boon
(10) companion, if you allow him to have his
humor and to talk about himself; and he
will stand by a friend in a quarrel with life
and purse, however soundly he may be
cudgeled.
(15) In this last respect, to tell the truth,
he has a propensity to be somewhat too
ready. He is a busy-minded personage who
thinks not merely for himself and family,
but for all the country round, and is most
(20) generally disposed to be everybody's
champion. He is continually volunteering
his services to settle his neighbor's affairs,
and takes it in great dudgeon if they engage
in any manner of consequence without
(25) asking his advice [. . . .] He cannot hear of a
quarrel between the most distant of his
neighbors but he begins incontinently to
fumble with the head of his cudgel, and
consider whether his interest or honor does
(30) not require that he should meddle in the
broil [. . . .] Couched in his little domain, with
these filaments stretching forth in every
direction, he is like some choleric, bottle-
bellied old spider who has woven his web
(35) over a whole chamber, so that a fly cannot
buzz nor a breeze blow without startling his
repose and causing him to sally forth
wrathfully from his den.
Though really a good-hearted.
(40) good-tempered old fellow at bottom, yet he
is singularly fond of being in the midst of
contention [. . . .] yet when the battle is over
and he comes to the reconciliation he is so
much taken up with the mere shaking of
(45) hands that he is apt to let his antagonist
pocket all that they have been quarreling
about. It is not, therefore, fighting that he
ought so much to be on his guard against as
making friends [. . . .] He is like a stout ship
(50) which will weather the roughest storm
uninjured, but roll its masts overboard in
the succeeding calm.

He is a little fond of playing the
magnifico abroad, of pulling out a long
(55) purse, flinging his money bravely about at
boxing-matches, horse races, cock-fights,
and carrying a high head among 'gentleman
of fancy:' but immediately after one of
these fits of extravagance, he will be taken
(60) with violent qualms of economy; stop short
at the most trivial expenditure; talk
desperately of being ruined and brought
upon the parish [. . . .].
What is worst of all, is the effect
(65) with which these pecuniary embarrassments
and domestic feuds have had on the poor
man himself. Instead of that jolly round
corporation and smug rosy face which he
used to present, he has of late become as
(70) shriveled and shrunk as a frost-bitten apple.
His scarlet, gold-laced waistcoat, which
bellied out so bravely in those prosperous
days when he sailed before the wind, now
hangs loosely about him like a mainsail in a
(75) calm [. . . .].
Instead of strutting about as
formerly with his three-cornered hat on one
side, flourishing his cudgel, and bringing it
down every moment with a hearty thump
(80) upon the ground, looking every one sturdily
in the face, and trolling out a stave of a
catch or drinking-song, he now goes about
whistling thoughtfully to himself, with his
head drooping down, his cudgel tucked
(85) under his arm, and his hands thrust to the
bottom of his breeches pockets, which are
evidently empty.
Such is the plight of honest John
Bull at present, yet for all this the old
(90) fellow's spirit is as tall and as gallant as
ever. If you drop the least expression of
sympathy or concern, he takes fire in an
instant; swears that he is the richest and
stoutest fellow in the country; talks of
(95) laying out large sums to adorn his house or
buy another estate; and with a valiant
swagger and grasping of his cudgel longs
exceedingly to have another bout at quarter-
staff [. . . .].

16. The theme of the passage seems to involve the

    (A) importance of allegiance to friend and family
    (B) need to greet reversals of fortune with equanimity
    (C) consequences of permitting outside intervention
    (D) deleterious effects of impulsive behavior
    (E) pernicious nature of rural gossip

17. In light of the passage as a whole, the adjective that most appropriately describes John's character is

    (A) parsimonious
    (B) deceitful
    (C) supercilious
    (D) volatile
    (E) despondent

18. Which of the following BEST clarifies the speaker's claim that John Bull has "much less of poetry about him than rich prose" (lines 3-4)?

    (A) That John is outwardly happy but inwardly morose.
    (B) That John is not highbrow but colorfully idiosyncratic
    (C) That John is intellectually barren but stridently vocal.
    (D) That John is extremely wealthy but grossly profligate.
    (E) That John is generally affable but frequently surly.

19. The speaker implies that allowing John to "have his humor" (lines 10-11) might include all of the following EXCEPT

    (A) permitting him to provide assistance
    (B) allowing him to play the "big spender"
    (C) listening to his counsel
    (D) accepting his good-natured ribbing
    (E) tolerating his braggadocio

20. By the phrase "busy-minded" (line 17), the speaker most likely means

    (A) preoccupied
    (B) industrious
    (C) intrusive
    (D) reflective
    (E) addled

21. In light of the context in which it appears, the BEST equivalent for the phrase "takes it in great dudgeon" (line 23) would be

    (A) becomes offended
    (B) accepts graciously
    (C) feels honored
    (D) flatly refuses
    (E) contemplates seriously

22. The simile that closes paragraph two is intended to reinforce which of the following?

    I. John's easily-provoked contentiousness.
    II. John's constant involvement in other people's affairs.
    III. John's substantial frame and persona.

    (A) II only
    (B) III only
    (C) I and II
    (D) I and III
    (E) I, II and III

23. Which of the following contrasts is NOT employed by the author in lines 64-87 to delineate a significant change in John?

    (A) boisterousness and reserve
    (B) health and infirmity
    (C) corpulence and slenderness
    (D) prosperity and penury
    (E) conceit and humility

24. The portrait of John that culminates the passage (lines 96-99) is BEST characterized as

    (A) vindictive
    (B) remorseful
    (C) avaricious
    (D) nostalgic
    (E) delusional

25. The author employs similes to enhance each of the following EXCEPT

    (A) John's territorial and bellicose nature
    (B) John's impulsive and self-destructive generosity
    (C) John's madcap and profligate wagering
    (D) John's aging and humorless face
    (E) John's weight loss and deflated panache

26. Which of the following objects serves as a pervasive reminder of John's characteristic pugnacity?

    (A) his ever-ready cudgel
    (B) his long purse
    (C) his colorfully embroidered waistcoat
    (D) his jauntily angled three-cornered hat
    (E) his empty breeches' pocket

27. The passage subtly implies that the root of John's problems is his

    (A) facetiousness
    (B) prodigality
    (C) belligerence
    (D) fickleness
    (E) hubris

Questions 28-39. Refer to the following poem.

Mrs. Lazarus

I had grieved. I had wept for a night and a day
over my loss, ripped the cloth I was married in
from my breasts, howled, shrieked, clawed
at the burial stones till my hands bled, retched
(5)   his name over and over again, dead, dead.

Gone home. Gutted the place. Slept in a single cot,
widow, one empty glove, white femur
in the dust, half. Stuffed dark suits
into black bags, shuffled in a dead man's shoes,
(10)   noosed the double knot of a tie round my bare neck,

gaunt nun in the mirror, touching herself. I learnt
the Stations of Bereavement,[1] the icon of my face
in each bleak frame; but all those months
he was going away from me, dwindling
(15)   to the shrunk size of a snapshot, going,

going. Till his name was no longer a certain spell
for his face. The last hair on his head
floated out from a book. His scent went from the house.
The will was read. See, he was vanishing
(20)   to the small zero held by the gold of my ring.

Then he was gone. Then he was legend, language;
my arm on the arm of a schoolteacher—the shock
of a man's strength under the sleeve of his coat—
along the hedgerows. But I was faithful
(25)   for as long as it took. Until he was memory.

So I could stand that evening in the field
in a shawl of fine air, healed, able
to watch the edge of the moon occur to the sky
and a hare thump from a hedge; then notice
(30)   the village men running towards me, shouting,

behind them the women and children, barking dogs,
and I knew. I knew by the sly light
on the blacksmith's face, the shrill eyes
of the barmaid, the sudden hands bearing me
(35)   into the hot tang of the crowd parting before me.

He lived. I saw the horror on his face.
I heard his mother's crazy song. I breathed
his stench; my bridegroom in his rotting shroud,
moist and disheveled from the grave's slack chew,
(40)   croaking his cuckold name, disinherited, out of his time.

---

[1] Stations of the Cross—scenes of Christ's suffering on His way to crucifix-
ion

Mrs. Lazarus by Carol Ann Duffy

28. The poem's central allusion is derived from

    (A) history
    (B) religion
    (C) mythology
    (D) literature
    (E) science

29. The speaker's overriding dilemma involves

    (A) accepting the finality of her husband's death
    (B) choosing which personal mementoes to save and which to discard
    (C) composing herself sufficiently to perform the post-mortem legal finalities
    (D) attracting a new love interest
    (E) overcoming subliminal guilt over her decision to see another man

30. In the first five stanzas of the poem the speaker moves from

    (A) disconsolation to acceptance
    (B) animosity to forgiveness
    (C) disbelief to comprehension
    (D) anger to indifference
    (E) depression to elation

31. In lines 1-13, the speaker seems most intent upon

    (A) lamenting her prematurely widowed state
    (B) defending the duration and extent of her mourning
    (C) divesting herself of unpleasant reminders of the deceased
    (D) conveying her emotional strength in the face of personal tragedy
    (E) questioning the existence of a deity

32. The poet dramatizes the speaker's response to her husband's death through of all of the following EXCEPT

    (A) onomatopoeic verbs that convey the wrenching emotions she experienced
    (B) a gravesite image that hyperbolizes her inability to part with the deceased
    (C) symbols of celibacy and privation
    (D) a reluctance to part with cherished mementoes of her deceased husband
    (E) diction that suggests thoughts of suicide

33. The choice of verb in the phrase "retched / his name over and over again" (lines 4-5) plausibly suggests which of the following?

    I. That the speaker's emotional angst has made her physically ill.
    II. That the speaker has been rendered inarticulate by her sadness.
    III. That the speaker may have harbored a suppressed animosity for her husband.

    (A) I only
    (B) III only
    (C) I and III
    (D) II and III
    (E) I, II and III

34. The dwindling impact of the deceased's presence on the speaker's life is MOST powerfully conveyed by the

    (A) metaphor of the snapshot
    (B) solitary hair in the book
    (C) vanishing of her husband's scent
    (D) reading of the will
    (E) cipher of the wedding ring

35. In lines 21-29 the speaker experiences feelings of

    (A) relief and emancipation
    (B) loss and abandonment
    (C) foreignness and discomfort
    (D) guilt and embarrassment
    (E) gloating and defiance

36. The speaker's claim that she has been "healed" (line 27) could plausibly imply which of the following?

    I. That she has gotten over the sadness caused by the death of her husband.
    II. That she has recovered her ability to love another individual.
    III. That she has been liberated from the unhappiness of her marriage.

    (A) I only
    (B) II only
    (C) I and II
    (D) I and III
    (E) I, II and III

37. The poet achieves the nightmarish effect of the final two stanzas through her use of all of the following EXCEPT

    (A) onomatopoeic diction that indicts the speaker for her ignominious betrayal
    (B) noisome sensory images and synaesthesia
    (C) images of infernal suffering
    (D) a cruelly ironic Biblical allusion
    (E) a personification of the grave

38. The poem implies that the horror on the dead man's face is a product of his

    (A) agonizing death throes
    (B) shock at returning to the world of the living
    (C) discomfort amidst the pressing crowd
    (D) consciousness of his wife's infidelity
    (E) embarrassment at his moribund attire

39. The title of the poem, "Mrs. Lazarus," ultimately suggests the speaker's

    (A) admirable resiliency in the face of heartbreak
    (B) stalwart faith in an afterlife
    (C) irrational denial of her husband's decease
    (D) indivisible tie to her deceased spouse
    (E) firm unwillingness to forsake her married name

Questions 40-52. Refer to the following passage.

In this passage from a contemporary novel, the author imagines the reaction of Captain Ahab's wife to the news of his death.

I am still. For the first time, I know.
If I were a lighthouse whose beam could
bend to embrace the curve of the earth, I
know I would not find him. There is no use
(5)   to look out.
I feel it in my face. My mouth is
settled at the corners. Resignation. There is
no use to look out.
But I will stand here awhile. I could
(10) be wrong.
My bones are weighing me down.
Here, my fingertips feel the splintery top of
the railing, the rough grain of the wood.
Ahab is gone.
(15) But is he gone? I only know that I
can no longer wait, looking out for him.
Still I stand and face the dark.
What is this force that tilts up my
chin? Why does my gaze climb up a ladder
(20) of stars? Why do I no longer look out, but
up? Up! And there the heavens blaze and
twinkle. In this moonless night sky, the
endless stars declare ascendancy.
With my face up, I drink and drink
(25) the black goblet, the universe.
Like funeral cloves are these stars,
spiky and spicy. Like cloves in an orange,
they are the preservers of the skin and of
the black flesh of space.
(30) Oh, Starry Sky, can you hear this
moaning of the earth? Let the sea be our
voice, our loudest voice. It speaks to every
dark corner of you, Star-studded sky, as we
spin and turn through space. The sea is
(35) moaning to your blackness and to your
bright fires. Might some warmth, some
comfort, from you kiss the cheek of earth,
light if not warmth sent unerringly over
distances too great to measure.
(40) And yet when I blink, I seem to
collect configurations of stars—perhaps it
is to know them. My eyelids slide down,
followed by a smooth, lubricated lifting,
and there you are, Starry Sky, no longer out
(45) there, but through the lens of my eye
brought home into my head. Into the brains
of all and any beings who lift their faces
and open their eyes.

There is a great journey yet to be
(50) taken. Let my mind be a ship that sails from
starry point to starry point. In my brain, I
feel those close black spaces containing
nothing. I approach a pin prick of light
closer and closer till it is a conflagration of
(55) such magnitude that I am nothing. And yet
with my mind I caliper it with
contemplation.
Where is my place before this
swirling ball of star mass, edgeless and
(60) expansive, without horizon? Where is my
place, when I know that this is but one of
ten billion? Here the categories crack.
Beauty—that gilt frame—burns at its edges
and falls to ash. *Love?* It's no more than a
(65) blade of grass. Perhaps there is *music* here,
for in all that swirling perhaps harmony
fixes the giants in their turning, marches
them always outward in their fiery parade.
That I can see their glory, that is
(70) my place. That I have these moments to be
alive—and surely *they* are alive in some
other way. Perhaps it is only *being* that we
share. But something *is* shared between me
on this rooftop and them flung wide and
(75) myriad up there. What was the golden
motto embroidered on the hem of my
baby's silk dress? *We are kin to stars.*
I reach my hands toward them,
spread my fingers and see those diamonds
(80) in the black v's between my fanning
fingers. To think that I could gather them
into my hands, stuff them in my pockets, is
folly. But I can reach. It is I myself, alive
now, who reach into the night toward stars.
(85) Their light is on my hands.
Their light is in my hands. I gasp in
the crisp air of earth and know that I am
made of what makes stars! Those atoms
burning bright—I lower my hands—why,
(90) they are here within me. I am as old as they
and will continue as long as they, and after
our demise, we will all be born again, eons
from now. What atoms they have I cannot
know. I cannot call their names, but they
(95) are not strangers to me. I know them in my
being, and they know me.
Little scrap, little morsel, the stars
sing to me, *we are the same.*

40. In relation to the speaker, Ahab's wife, the most prominent feature of the passage is its use of

    (A) simple sentences to augment her solitary vigil
    (B) rhetorical questions to convey her confusion
    (C) interior monologue to expose her innermost thoughts
    (D) exclamations to emphasize her key intellectual discoveries
    (E) figurative language to depict her wonder at the expansive heavens

41. In the course of the passage, Ahab's wife compares death to a(n)

    (A) lighthouse
    (B) ladder
    (C) sea-voyage
    (D) ship
    (E) conflagration

42. The tone of the speaker, Ahab's wife, in the opening two paragraphs is BEST classified as

    (A) stoic
    (B) buoyant
    (C) embittered
    (D) apathetic
    (E) bewildered

43. Over the course of the passage, the concern of Ahab's wife switches from the loss of her husband to

    (A) a denial of his death
    (B) the specific circumstances of his demise
    (C) questions about humanity's purpose in the universe
    (D) an indictment of the universe as arbitrary and unfair
    (E) concern over her own means of survival

44. That Ahab's wife realizes her husband is dead is apparent in all of the following EXCEPT

    (A) "For the first time, I know." (line 1)
    (B) "There is no use to look out." (lines 4-5)
    (C) "My bones are weighing me down." (line 11)
    (D) "Ahab is gone." (line 14)
    (E) "Still I stand and face the dark." (line 17)

45. What seemingly bothers Ahab's wife the most is the

    (A) bleak reality of her husband's death
    (B) incertitude of her husband's passing
    (C) lack of someone with whom to share her sorrow
    (D) implacable and unresponsive nature of the universe
    (E) uncertain future that she now confronts

46. In the context in which it appears, Ahab's wife's quaffing of the "black goblet" (lines 24-25) may plausibly represent each of the following EXCEPT

    (A) her literal mesmerism by the starry universe above her
    (B) her willing acceptance of a painful reality
    (C) her search for her husband in a spiritual, not earthly, venue
    (D) her inability to reconcile the finitude of death with the infinitude of the universe
    (E) her contemplation of taking her own life

47. Which of the following figures of speech is NOT evident in lines 30-39?

    (A) apostrophe
    (B) pathetic fallacy
    (C) personification
    (D) alliteration
    (E) allusion

48. In the imaginative reverie that begins on line 42, Ahab's wife does all of the following EXCEPT

    (A) become aware of her comparative physical insignificance
    (B) query what is her role in the natural world
    (C) recognize the ephemeral nature of beauty and love
    (D) imagine her lost husband navigating a new universe
    (E) comprehend the affinity she and all humans share with other aspects of nature

49. The transition in lines 69-70 is effected by means of a(n)

    (A) conjecture
    (B) disclaimer
    (C) assertion
    (D) query
    (E) reiteration

50. The gesture made by Ahab's wife in lines 78-85 is BEST interpreted as being one of

    (A) craven surrender
    (B) desperate imploration
    (C) brazen defiance
    (D) futile challenge
    (E) intimate acceptance

51. At the passage's end, Ahab's wife is

    (A) serene and reassured
    (B) perplexed and frustrated
    (C) dolorous and disconsolate
    (D) awed and humbled
    (E) embittered and vindictive

52. Which of the following exemplifies the literary technique of metonymy?

    (A) "black flesh" (line 29)
    (B) "pin prick" (line 53)
    (C) "gilt frame" (line 63)
    (D) "fiery parade" (line 68)
    (E) "golden motto" (lines 75-76)

Section II

Question One

(Suggested time—40 minutes. This question counts as one-third of the total essay section score.)

The following is an excerpt from a popular 1960's novel, in which a nineteenth century Bostonian is imaginatively transported into a twenty-first century world. Read the passage carefully. Then, in a well-organized essay, discuss how the literary elements of the passage illustrate the protagonist's attitude towards aspects of nineteenth century life upon his return to his own era.

Making my way back again after to this peninsular city, toward three o'clock I stood on State Street, staring, as if I had never seen them before, at the banks' and brokers' offices, and other financial institutions, of which there had been in the State Street of my dream no vestige. Businessmen, confidential clerks, and errand boys were thronging in and out of the banks, for it wanted but a few
(5) minutes of the closing hour. Opposite me was the bank where I did business, and presently I crossed the street, and, going in with the crowd, stood in a recess of the wall looking on at the army of clerks handling money, and the cues of depositors at the tellers' windows. An old gentleman whom I knew, a director at the bank, passing me and observing my contemplative attitude, stopped a moment.

"Interesting sight, isn't it, Mr. West," he said. "Wonderful piece of mechanism; I find it so myself. I
(10) like sometimes to stand and look on at it just as you are doing. It's a poem, sir, a poem, that's what I call it. Did you ever think, Mr. West, that the bank is the heart of the business system? From it and to it, the endless flux and reflux, the life blood goes. It is flowing in now. It will flow out again in the morning." And pleased with his little conceit, the old man passed on, smiling.

Yesterday I should have considered the simile apt enough, but since then I had visited a world
(15) incomparably more affluent than this, in which money was unknown and without conceivable use. I had learned that it had a use in the world around me only because the work of producing the nation's livelihood, instead of being regarded as the most strictly public and common of all concerns, and as such conducted by the nation, was abandoned to the haphazard efforts of individuals. This original mistake necessitated endless exchanges to bring about any sort of general distribution of products. These
(20) exchanges money effected—how equitably, might be seen in a walk from the tenement-house districts to the Back Bay—at the cost of an army of men taken from productive labor to manage it, with constant ruinous breakdowns of its machinery, and a generally debauching influence on mankind, which had justified its description, from ancient time, as the "root of all evil."

Alas for the poor old bank director with his poem! He had mistaken the throbbing of an abscess for
(25) the beating of the heart! What he called a "wonderful piece of mechanism" was an imperfect device to remedy an unnecessary defect, the clumsy crutch of a self-made cripple.

After the banks had closed I wandered aimlessly about the business quarter for an hour or two, and later sat awhile on one of the benches of the Common, finding an interest merely in watching the throngs that passed, such as one has in studying the populace of a foreign city, so strange since yesterday had my
(30) fellow citizens and their ways become to me. For thirty years I had lived among them, and yet I seemed to have never noted before how drawn and anxious were their faces, of the rich as of the poor, the refined, acute faces of the educated as well as the dull masks of the ignorant. And well it might be so, for I saw now, as never before I had seen so plainly, that each as he walked constantly turned to catch the whispers of a specter in his ear, the specter of Uncertainty. "Do you work never so well," the specter was
(35) whispering—"rise early and toil till late, rob cunningly or serve faithfully, you shall never know security [. . . .]."

<u>Question Two</u>

(Suggested time—40 minutes. This question counts as one-third of the total essay section score.)

Read the following poem carefully. Then, in a well-organized essay, show how the structure and the literary elements of the poem reinforce the poem's meaning. In your essay you should make certain to consider the poem's title.

The Question and Answer

When the sad ruins of that face
In its own wrinkles buried lies,
And the stiff pride of all its grace,
By time undone, falls slack and dies:
(5)   Wilt thou not sigh, and wish in some vexed fit
That it were now as when I courted it?

And when thy glass shall it present
Without those smiles which once were there,
Showing, like some stale monument,
(10) A scalp departed from its hair,
At thyself frighted wilt not start and swear
That I belied thee, when I called thee fair?

Yes, yes, I know thou wilt and so
Pity the weakness of thy scorn,
(15) That now hath humbled thee to know,
Though fair it was, it is forlorn:
Love's sweets thy agèd corpse embalming not,
What marvel if thy carcass, beauty, rot?

Then shall I live, and live to be
(20) Thy envy, thou my pity; say
Whene'er thou see me, or I thee
(Being knighted from thy beauty's day),
'Tis he, and had my pride not withered me,
I had, perhaps, been still as fresh as he.

(25) Then shall I smile, and answer: 'True; thy scorn
Left thee thus wrinkled, slacked, corrupt, forlorn.'

(1641)

—Thomas Beedome

<u>Question Three</u>

(Suggested time—40 minutes. This question counts as one-third of the total essay section score.)

Many times in literature a "mysterious stranger" makes a significant contribution to the tone, resolution, or theme of a literary work. Choose a novel or play in which such a "mysterious stranger" appears. Then, in a well-organized essay, illustrate how this unusual, unexpected, or perhaps absent character aids in advancing the work's mood, resolution, or thematic message. You may choose from the list below or use another novel or play of recognized literary merit.

Bartleby the Scrivener	*To Kill A Mockingbird*
Oedipus the King	*Dracula*
The Secret Sharer	*Killing Mr. Watson*
You Can't Go Home Again	*Hamlet*
The Scarlet Letter	*Everyman*
Wise Blood	*Light in August*
King Lear	*The Great Gatsby*
Antigone	*Beloved*
Heart of Darkness	*Night*
Waiting for Godot	*The Piano Lesson*
The Turn of the Screw	*Jane Eyre*

NOTES

NOTES

NOTES

NOTES

NOTES

NOTES